ETHICS
and
COMMUNITY

Theology and Liberation Series

In the years since its emergence in Latin America, liberation theology has challenged the church to a renewal of faith lived in solidarity with the poor and oppressed. The effects of this theology have spread throughout the world, inspiring in many Christians a deeper life of faith and commitment, but for others arousing fears and concerns.

Its proponents have insisted that liberation theology is not a subtopic of theology but really a new way of doing theology. The Liberation and Theology Series is an effort to test that claim by addressing the full spectrum of Christian faith from the perspective of the poor.

Thus, volumes in the Series are devoted to such topics as God, Christ, the church, revelation, Mary, the sacraments, and so forth. But the Series will also explore topics seldom addressed by traditional theology, though vital to Christian life—aspects of politics, culture, the role of women, the status of ethnic minorities. All these are examined in the light of faith lived in a context of oppression and liberation.

The work of over one hundred theologians, pastoral agents, and social scientists from Latin America, and supported by some one hundred and forty bishops, the Liberation and Theology Series is the most ambitious and creative theological project in the history of the Americas.

Addressed to the universal church, these volumes will be essential reading for all those interested in the challenge of faith in the modern world. They will be especially welcomed by all who are committed to the cause of the poor, by those engaged in the struggle for a new society, by all those seeking to establish a more solid link between faith and politics, prayer and action.

THEOLOGY AND LIBERATION SERIES

Enrique Dussel

ETHICS
and
COMMUNITY

Translated from the Spanish by
Robert R. Barr

ORBIS BOOKS

Maryknoll, New York 10545

The Catholic Foreign Mission Society of America (Maryknoll) recruits and trains people for overseas missionary service. Through Orbis Books Maryknoll aims to foster the international dialogue that is essential to mission. The books published, however, reflect the opinions of their authors and are not meant to represent the official position of the society.

This book is a translation of *Etica Comunitaria* © 1986 by Ediciones Paulinas (Madrid) and CESEP (São Paulo). The book has also been published in Portuguese by Editora Vozes (Petrópolis, Brazil).

First published in this translation in the United States of America by Orbis Books, Maryknoll, NY 10545; published in Great Britain by Burns & Oates, Wellwood, North Farm Road, Tunbridge Wells, Kent TN2 3DR

English translation © 1988 by Orbis Books, Maryknoll, NY 10545

Manuscript Editor: William E. Jerman

ORBIS/ISBN 0-88344-619-7
0-88344-618-9 (pbk.)

Contents

Chapter 18. **Ethics of Culture and Ecology**   **194**

Chapter 19. **The Gospel and the Social Teaching of
the Church**   **205**

Introduction

In traditional theology there is a discipline called "social ethics." The present volume will take up questions handled in that discipline. But it will do so from the viewpoint of the theology of liberation.

I do not pretend, in this brief work, to furnish the reader with a full-blown *exposition* or *explanation* of these questions. I intend only to *situate* them. That is, I shall show the place they occupy in the theology of liberation.

I do not think that it would have been helpful to distract the reader with bibliographical information in the text that would be of interest only to those who will wish to study a problem in greater depth. Hence I shall not use footnotes. I do, however, append a basic bibliography.

I have divided this work into two parts. Part 1 will pose the *basic questions* of community ethics—those constituting the point of departure for an understanding of all other problems. The order of these basic questions: from the simpler and more important to the complex and more derivative.

In Part 2 I shall present ten *quaestiones disputatae* of current interest, problems that must be elucidated if Christian praxis is to be faithful to the demands of the gospel in the present hour of history. The reader must understand that these discussions represent but a small sampling of the long list of questions that I might have taken up. Indeed, it would be well for the person in charge of a study group, or participants themselves in the course of a lecture series, to suggest other problems, thereby lending further realism to the theologico-ethical reflection of this course.

The purpose of the Subject Index is to clarify the interrelationship of the various topics considered here, with a view to enhancing the usefulness of this book for church communities, preachers, and students of theology.

Before beginning each chapter, readers should reflect on a clipping from the daily newspaper, to be selected by the coordinator or the participants. Any article referring in any way to the question under consideration will do. (For an example, see the opening of chapter 3.) After all, theology is a reflection on daily, current, concretely Christian praxis. Hence the person in charge of the community, the teacher or instructor, the coordinator, or for that matter the participants of a training or study group themselves, should choose some material from the most recent issue of the morning or evening newspaper published in the particular locale, city, or region where teachers and learners meet.

I run many risks. I try to be simple and clear, but I also wish to be scientific. I try to be understandable, but I wish to be profound as well. I try to take a sound pedagogical approach, but at the same time I want to be realistic. I shall proceed, with Thomas Aquinas in his *Commentary on the Nichomachean Ethics* (see his introduction), "from the simple to the complex"—that is, "from the abstract to the concrete."

I am altogether aware that my approach is "traditional"—that I draw upon both the oldest and the most recent *tradition* of our Christian communities. I know, then, that my position will have to be prophetic—in conformity with both the gospel and the needs of the poor. That is, my approach will have to be critical and liberative.

I have no particular wish to share in the fetishizing of famous authors, distinguished theologians, great works, and classic concepts. I am, however, interested in what all of these may in fact have to contribute to the task of solving the problems faced by Christians in today's world. Ours must not be academic mumbo jumbo, but a pursuit of relevancy—a treatment of the reality of actual life experience.

The whole of community ethics is a "road under construction." I welcome criticism, both negative and positive. In successive editions of this book I shall attempt to correct the errors that this work—like all finite discourse—must inevitably contain.

If I may be forgiven the repetition: far from pretending to replace the classic theological tractates on the subject, the present treatise refers to them, and some of them are listed in the Select Bibliography at the end of the book. Some of these works, in turn, contain their own bibliographies, some of them extensive.

I have said little or nothing about the state (except generally and indirectly), racism, or the organization of popular liberation movements. These and other such topics are treated in other volumes of the Theology and Liberation Series. Although I have not treated these subjects directly, I have accorded them *their place* in a complete discourse.

PART 1

TEN FUNDAMENTAL THEMES

Chapter 1

Praxis and the Reign of God

1.1 STATE OF THE QUESTION

Our first topic constitutes the horizon of understanding for this entire work. It may appear abstract, or very simple, but it is extremely concrete and vital.

Every day we read newspaper accounts of meetings, large demonstrations, and so on—all of them face-to-face encounters, and among the widest variety of persons, groups, and classes. The encounter among persons is the most universal of phenomena, and the least noticed.

In holy scripture we read:

> They devoted themselves to the apostles' instruction and the *communal life* [or "community"—*koinonia*], to the breaking of *bread* and the prayers. A reverent fear overtook them all, for many wonders and *signs* were performed by the apostles. Those who believed lived at one [*epi to auto*], and shared all things in common [*koina*]; they would sell their property and goods, dividing everything on the basis of each one's *need*. They went to the temple area together every day, while *in their homes* they broke bread. With *exultant* and sincere hearts they took their meals *in common*, praising God and winning the approval of all the *people* [*laos*] [Acts 2:42–47].

"Acts of the Apostles" is the expression we use to translate the Greek *Praxeis Apostolon*, or deeds of the apostles. Thus we should call that biblical book the "Praxis of the Apostles." This text recalls for us that the essence of the Christian life is *community*: being together with others. This is also the essence of the reign of God: to be together with God, face-to-face with God in community.

1.2 PRAXIS AS ACT AND RELATIONSHIP

"Praxis" or "practice" means many things in our daily life. For my purposes in this work I take these terms in their strict sense: *praxis* or *practice* denotes any human act addressed to another human person; further, praxis denotes the very relationship of one person to another. Praxis is both act and relationship: "those who believed lived at one" (Acts 2:44).

In the first place, praxis is an *act* done by a person, a human subject, but addressed to another person, either directly (like a handshake, a kiss, words in a dialogue, a blow), or indirectly (through the intermediary of something: for example, sharing a piece of bread—the bread is not a person, but it is shared with *another person*). If I am sleeping, I am not present to the world. I am resting; I am not conscious. I am not engaging in any praxis. Praxis is the actual, here-and-now manner of our being in our world before another person. It is the real presence of one person to another. For Thomas Aquinas a relationship betokened the constitutive reality of each of the persons of the most holy Trinity.

In the second place, praxis is the *relationship* between two or more persons.

For example, the relationship of a father (Diagram 1, person 1) to his daughter (person 2, arrow A) is that of parenthood. The relationship of the daughter to the father (arrow B) is that of filiation, or being-a-child-of. A person *is* a father by *being-in* relationship to (by having) a daughter or son. One who *does not have* a child *is not* a father. A practical relationship between persons is called *praxis*.

We must clearly distinguish between *praxis* and *poiesis*. *Praxis* is doing (Lat., *operari*), an acting with and upon another or others.

Diagram 1

Relationship

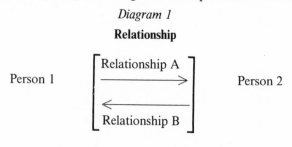

Person 1   Relationship A   Person 2

Relationship B

Poiesis means a fashioning, a making (Lat., *facere*), a producing with or in something, a working with nature. It denotes the person-nature relationship (see 18.2).

1.3 PERSON: FACE, CORPOREALITY, AND "NEIGHBOR"

The terms or poles of a *practical* relationship are persons. What is it to be a person? Strictly speaking one is a person only when one is in a relationship of praxis. A person is a person only when he or she is "before," somehow in confrontation with, another person or persons. Solitary and alone in the presence of impersonal nature, one ceases in a certain sense to be a person.

For the Hebreo-Christian tradition, the person-person relationship, the relationship of praxis, is expressed in terms like: "The Lord spoke with Moses *face to face*" (Exod. 33:11). "But never again did there arise in Israel another prophet such as Moses, with whom the Lord dealt *face to face*" (Deut. 34:10). "He spoke to him *mouth to mouth*" (Num. 12:8). Saint Paul uses the same expression: "Now we see confusedly in a mirror, but then we shall see *face to face*" (1 Cor. 13:12). "Face," in Hebrew, is *pnim*, or in Greek, *prosopon* (the conjectured idea of the Latin word *persona* [a mask] corresponds to *prosopon*). When I am face-to-face before another *in a (practical) relationship*, in the presence of praxis, that person is *someone* for me and I am *someone* for him or her. The being face-to-face of two or more is *being* a person.

The "face" indicates what appears of the other, his or her corporeality, his or her "fleshly" reality. "Flesh" in the Bible (*basar*) denotes the *whole* human being (without distinction of body and soul) who is born, who is hungry, who dies, who rises (see 3.4 and 6.3). "The word became *flesh*" (John 1.:14): not "became soul" or "became body" only, but "became a *human being*." This "face-to-face," this "person-to-person," constitutes the practical relationship of *proximity*, of nearness, between persons. The experience of the nearness of persons as persons is what constitutes *the other* as one's "neighbor" (someone "neighboring," our "near one," a "someone"), rather than as merely a thing, an instrument, a mediation.

Praxis, then, is the actualization of proximity, of the experience of being proximate, for one's neighbor. Praxis is the experience of constructing the other as person, as end of my action and not as means. We are dealing with a relationship of infinite respect.

1.4 RELATIONSHIP AS AGAPE

"Love" is one of the most discredited words in Western languages: it has so many meanings. A dictator loves his accomplices and the demon his angels. A man loves his wife—and a prostitute as well. Heroes love their native land and misers their money. But the "love" I speak of here is something very particular and precise: *agape*.

A relationship with another person can be one of selfishness; I can seek myself in the other. *Eros* was regarded by the first Christians as using another person as a medium for my own self-seeking—hedonistic or pleasurable companionship in which I make the other the means for my own enjoyment.

Philia was a love among equals. In the mind of the Greeks and Romans, we can love only our equals. A love for the poor, for the miserable, was something contemptible, and it depraved the one who pursued such a love.

For Jesus, on the other hand (Luke 11:42; John 13:35; Matt. 24:12), or Saint Paul (1 Cor. 13:1–13), real love is *agape*. It is a very special love. It is not love of oneself; it is love for the other *as other*, for the sake of that other and not for my own sake, with a respectful attitude toward the person of the other as something sacred and holy. Thus the authentic relationship among persons *as persons* is that of love, but love with respect, or agape. *That* one must love is not the point. The point is that Christian love is a very demanding kind of love. It is love for the other in view of that other's own reality, though I myself may receive nothing from that other. It is the other *as other* who is the object of this love, even were I ultimately to be required, as Christ, to lay down my life for him or her (Matt. 20:28; 25:40).

Love for the other as other is delight, beauty, goodness, and holiness. It is "gift" (the denotation of *charis* in the Greek of the New Testament, from Luke 1:30 to John 1:14): the gift of oneself, commitment, surrender, self-donation without recompense: "There is no greater love than this: to lay down one's life for one's friend" (John 15:13).

1.5 THE "WE" OF THE FACE-TO-FACE: THE COMMUNITY

The person-to-person or face-to-face relationship between two persons is an abstraction. *In the concrete*, historically, in the face-to-face of respectful love (agape)—"charity" in the authentic meaning of the word, and not in the sense that it has in the "works of charity" performed by philanthropists—Christian love is lived in the plural, in community, as a people.

When one person loves another in the love that is respectful, he or she wishes the well-being of that other. This love used to be called the "love of *bene*volence"—seeking the *good*, the *well*-being of another though it cost me my life. If the other loves me in the same way, our love is said to be *mutual*. It is this mutual love, consisting in wishing one another well, each one for the sake of the other and not for himself or herself, that is authentic "Christian love." This alone is *charity*.

The friendship of many individuals, once scattered but now joined together, once forming a "crowd" (Gk., *ochlos* or *polloi*; Heb., *rabim*) but now established in the face-to-face of unity, is what we call "community" (or in the Greek of the New Testament, *koinonia*). A "community" is so called because it holds all things in "common" (Gk., *koina*). Now let us carefully re-read the text of the Acts of the Apostles placed at the beginning of this chapter. The "crowd" has become a *community*, a "people" (Gk., *laos*; Heb., *ham*). In *community*, all individuals are persons for one another. Their relationships are "practical," and this praxis is that of the love that is charity: each serves the other for that other, in the friendship of all persons in all things. Everything is "common," then. What would an association of free persons be? It would be a community in which *individuality* is expressed in full and uncoerced communication.

The community is the real, concrete agent and mover of history. In the community we are "at home," in safety and security, "in common."

1.6 "EUCHARISTIC" COMMUNITY

Rooted and established in mutual, respectful love, grounded in the charity of its free and unfettered participants as persons, as individuals fulfilled in a life in common, the Christian community is celebration, and a celebration that takes up or assumes the totality of life.

In order to break bread together, to share bread, as we read of the first Christians in the Acts of the Apostles, there must be bread. Bread is the fruit of toil (see 11.3). It is a real, material product, something made. At the same time it is made *for another*. Therefore the relationship it incorporates is not only productive (person-to-nature) but also practical (person-to-person). The presiding relationship in the offering of bread to one's sister or brother in the community—and to God in the eu-charist (Gk., *eu-*, "good"; *charis*, "offering"; *eucharistia*: thanks-giving)—is practico-productive: *to the other* is given *the fruit* of production. This complex relationship is called "economic" (bestowing, offering, selling, buying, robbing, and so on, *something* to or from *someone*).

Sharing bread, holding all things in common, and selling one's possessions and goods all indicate the radical nature of love that is respectful of the loved person(s). The first Christians' love was not platonic—a supraemotional, immaterial love. It was a concrete, real, efficacious, bodily love. Their love was attested by *deeds* (*praxeis*), not words only. It was not only in "the prayers" that "they devoted themselves to ... the communal life." They also "took their meals in common...." Their love imbued their existence. In it their whole "bodiliness" was committed.

In the well-known text of the Didache, too, the celebration of the eucharist is a picture of very early Christians, in the small community of Jerusalem and elsewhere (as in the base communities in Latin America today), living a life that was really a life in common, without room for selfishness or deceit (recall Ananiah and Sapphira, Acts 5:1–11). This exemplary (and in this sense utopian), first, total community will always be our ideal, and our "practical" horizon.

1.7 NEED, SATISFACTION, FESTIVAL

Praxis, as action and as relationship, tends to its integral realization, which is complete happiness, joy, and gladness, the fruits of satisfaction. When the lover is with the beloved face to face, mouth to mouth (the kiss of the Song of Songs 1:2), there is festival. There is the full realization of praxis.

Because human persons are but finite participants in the life of God, they consume their vitality in the process of living. After a day's work, they are tired and hungry. What has been consumed, what has died, must be replenished. The lack to be made up—the want of nourishment, rest, clothing, and so on—is called *need*. In the very early Christian community, members received from the common store "on the basis of each one's need." Without a *theology of need*, neither the eucharist, nor community, nor justice, nor the reign of God (see 4.9) will have intelligibility.

But the negativity (*not* having something to eat: hunger) of need is a principle and an absolute *criterion* of the last judgment: "I was hungry" (Matt. 25:35). Obviously this hunger is not a random physical phenomenon, but a "historical" one—here, the fruit of sin (see 2.8, 6.5). At all events, to quiet someone's hunger, to give someone something to eat, to bestow the enjoyment of consumption, is a moment in the building of the reign of God, "Happy are you who hunger now, for you shall be *satisfied*" (Luke 6:21). "Satisfaction," as an act of *eating* and as enjoyment and joy, is negation of a negation – the removal of hunger, which is want-of – and a positive affirmation of the reign of God. As we read in the Acts of the Apostles, "They took their meals in common. . . ."

Thus the highest expression of the life of the community is a festival: "Come and celebrate with your Lord!" (Matt. 25:21). And so the Christians of the primitive community praised God in their homes, "with exultant . . . hearts," with felicity, with rejoicing.

1.8 THE REIGN OF GOD AS THE ABSOLUTE FACE-TO-FACE

Jesus came to proclaim "the good news of the kingdom" (Matt. 4:23). His messianic reign is the reign of God (Eph. 5:5). What is the essential element of the reign of Christ, of the Father, of God, of heaven?

The reign of God is total fulfillment. Some are poor now, but "the reign of God is theirs" (Matt. 5:3); those who suffer now "shall be consoled"; those who are now oppressed "shall inherit the land"; those who now hunger "will be satisfied"; those who serve now "will be served"; those who have an upright heart "shall be face to face with God"; those who struggle for peace "shall be called sons of God." As we see, in confrontation with present negatives, the reign of God is presented as the full realization of the human being as absolute, irreversible, undiminshed positivity.

But of all of the goods to be possessed by human beings in the reign, the supreme possession will be the being person-to-person before other persons, and essentially before God:

> I have given them the glory that you have given me, that of being *one* as we are one. I have joined myself with them as you are joined with me, that they may be fulfilled in oneness [John 17:22–3]. Now you are sorrowful, but when you see me again you will rejoice, and of this your *gladness* no one will deprive you. On that day you will ask me nothing [John 16:22–3].

Jesus preaches the gospel of the reign of God, the good news of the total fulfillment of humankind in the infinite gladness of God. But after Jesus is crucified and raised, he absents himself. Nevertheless, he has promised there will be an advocate, a defender of the building of the reign of God: "When the Spirit of truth comes, he will guide you in the full truth" (John 16:13).

1.9 THE REIGN BEGINS NOW IN COMMUNITY

Jesus proclaimed the reign of God. Then he was murdered. But he has left his Spirit behind, to prepare for his *second* coming. Now is the time of the church, the time of those called to complete the messianic mission of Jesus in history. But this reign will not be realized *only* in the remote future, *after* the end of history. The reign has *already* begun. Where?

The apostles questioned the risen Jesus: "Is it *now* that you will restore the kingdom of Israel?" (Acts 1:6). To be sure, they are thinking of a "political," a nationalistic, kingdom, perhaps an anti-Roman nation. Jesus responds: "You will receive a power. The Holy Spirit will come down on you" (Acts 1:8). And there the primitive Christian *community*, of which we have been speaking, was born— the community that praised God "with exultant and sincere hearts." True, the reign develops mysteriously in every man and woman of good will; but it must not be forgotten that the privileged place of its presence is the *community*.

"I shall pour out my spirit on all humankind. Their sons and daughters shall prophesy" (Acts 2:17). The community of "the consecrated" ("Christian" comes from "Christ," the "chrismated one," the one consecrated with oil, the *Messiah*, the anointed one), of believers, lived the *communal* life. This was a *communal unity*, an interpersonal face-to-face of respect and justice ("dividing everything on the basis of each one's need"), of joy, of mutual love, of such friendship that "a reverent fear overtook them all, for many wonders and *signs*"—the *miracle* of being-community—were present. In this communal unity they sought "first the reign and its justice" (Matt. 6:33), and all the rest (daily life, happiness, subsistence, security, exemplarity, holiness, and so on) was the natural fruit of that justice.

The *community* itself, community life itself, was *already* the reality of the reign: merely under way, inaugurated, still in the pangs of birth, it is true—but *reality*.

1.10 THE REIGN AS BEYOND: UTOPIA

The reign of God was proclaimed *in the past* by Jesus and is realized *in part* in every human being of good will, but in a special way in the small Christian *community* (in the interpersonal, concrete, daily face-to-face, in need satisfied, in the justice of equals, in the liberty of persons respected in the present). That reign *always* retains, as a constitutive moment, its "not yet."

The reign that is absolute *transcendence* with respect to all praxis, to all historical face-to-face, to all community, is ever a "beyond," an approach to full human realization. The reign is the sign, signal, horizon that tells us: "This is not good enough! There is still more to do!" The reign *as reality* is a something-more-to-be-practiced. The reign *as category* is the critical horizon signaling the negativity, the injustice, the selfishness of the prevailing dominant order.

Historically, the reign is a "promised land" (Exod. 3:8: a "fertile and spacious land, flowing with milk and honey") as concrete, temporal projection into the future. It is the objective of a hope *here* and *now* of a more just, happier future, where all will receive what they need. It is a future historical goal.

Transhistorically, the reign ever remains the absolute fulfillment and actualization of the human being, of temporal community, of history as final totality. It is the "above and beyond," it is *eschatological* transcendence (from the Greek *eschaton*, "last," what is to occur at the "end of days"). But we have already reached the "end of days," in the sense that Jesus has already risen and we now look forward in hope to his second coming. As *eschatological* horizon the reign of God is the absolute principle of Christian ethics, which is the measure of *all* historical undertakings—reformist and revolutionary included.

CONCLUSIONS

This first theme, "Praxis and the Reign of God," has furnished the occasion for an explanation of the *radical principle* of Christian ethics in general and of liberation and community ethics (which is the central aspect of basic theology) in particular. That radical principle will operate as the light that illumines, the horizon that criticizes, the root from which we must nourish, all our subsequent ethical discourse. This first issue, in its total simplicity, is the "font," the foundational force, the "wellspring" of all Christian ethics.

The radical principle of Christian ethics is the face-to-face of the person-to-person relationship in the concrete, real, satisfied, happy, *community*, in the gladness of being *one* with God (Saint Thomas Aquinas called God the *bonum commune*: God is our "common good" as the lover is the supreme good of the beloved and vice versa) and one with our brothers and sisters, the members (Heb., *chaberim*) of the community.

Chapter 2

Evil and Death

2.1 STATE OF THE QUESTION

As happiness, fulfillment, and holiness, the reign of God is the face-to-face of persons among themselves and with God, who also is conceived as a *community* of persons, subsuming, taking unto itself, the community of created persons. Evil, wickedness, is the interruption, the breach of this face-to-face, its nemesis. One term of the relationship absolutizes itself and negates, annihilates, "reifies" (makes a *thing* out of) the other.

Each day the media carry news of wars, murders, thefts, administrative corruption, drug addiction. We learn of the daily presence of evil. We read of the rich, the very rich—and the miserable poor. We read of powerful countries and weak ones. No one any longer believes in the Devil, the Evil One. And yet the works of the Devil are evident. We have only to open our eyes to see them for what they are.

In holy scripture we read:

> Now the serpent was the most cunning of all the animals that the Lord God had made.... The woman answered the serpent: "We may eat of the fruit of the trees in the garden; it is only about the fruit of the tree in the middle of the garden that God said, 'You shall not eat it or even touch it, lest you die.'" But the serpent said to the woman: "You certainly will not die! No, God knows well that the moment you eat of it your eyes will be opened and you will be like gods...." Then the eyes of both of them were opened, and they realized that they were naked [Gen. 3:1–7].

The subject is deeper, and more current, than we might think. The difficult thing for us to grasp is that evil begins as idolatry, fetishism, atheism; it develops in the domination of human beings by their own brothers and sisters, one person's subjugation by another. It is not the *person-person* relationship that prevails, but the *I-thing* relationship, the relationship of subject to object. Instead of two "someones," we have *one* "someone" in confrontation with "things." We have "reification."

2.2 WHAT IS WICKEDNESS, EVIL?

Evil, sin, the wickedness of the subject who commits the perverse praxis that builds the reign of the "Prince of this world" could be described in the following steps.

In the first place, the origin of evil or sin lies in a negation of the other, the other person, the other term of the person-to-person relationship. "Cain attacked his brother Abel and killed him. ... 'The blood of your brother cries to me from the ground'" (Gen. 4:8, 10). To kill, rob, humiliate, dishonor, violate, and so on, the other, Abel, is to destroy the other term of the face-to-face relationship.

Diagram 2

Domination

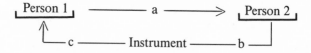

The *praxis of domination* is evil—sin (Gk., *hamartia*). It is praxis (see 1.2), but not of one person vis-à-vis another *as person*. Relationship *a* (in Diagram 2) is interrupted, and the dominator (Cain, person 1) makes (*b*) of the other (Abel, person 2) an *instrument*, a means. Person 2 is killed because he or she has been the enemy of person 1; or is robbed, used as an instrument of wealth; or is violated, used as an instrument of pleasure; and so on. Thus the status of the other person precisely as other is now reduced to that of a *thing*, a *means at the service of the dominator*. Person 2 now serves person 1 (arrow *c*). "I" am the end, the sovereign, the owner, of person 2. This is sin: the destitution of the other as person, the alienation (Lat., *alienum*, "other than oneself," sold, destroyed) of someone in some respect: reification, instrumentalization.

Offense to God is always and antecedently an act of domination committed against one's brother or sister. God is the absolute Other; hence God is offended when we dominate in some manner the other-and-neighbor, Abel; therefore does Christ take on the form of the very poorest, for what we do to our brother or sister we do to God. To dominate our neighbor is to sin against God.

2.3 IDOLATRY, FETISHISM

In negating the other, in negating God, sinners are left to themselves. They totalize themselves, asserting themselves as God, fetishizing and divinizing themselves. They fall into idolatry.

The sinner, the malefactor, is anyone who "devours my people as bread" (Ps. 14:4), who kills, who robs the other. And with the other term of the person-to-person relationship thus eliminated, the sinner—"the fool"—thinks "There is no God" (Ps. 14:1). There is no longer any "god" but "myself," says the one who has negated the other. By negating the other such persons affirm themselves sovereign over the other, for they have instrumentalized them. Thus they divinize themselves. And thus they make atheists of themselves vis-à-vis God, who is the Other par excellence, inasmuch as they have affirmed, asserted themselves to be god.

The act by which one asserts oneself as the end of other persons—as factory owners think they have a right to the factory's profit even though that profit be their workers' hunger transformed into money (see 12.10)—is idolatry. The prophets had to struggle with the idolatry of the Canaanites, and even of the Israelites. In the Adamic myth this temptation is concretized in the wish to "be like gods," to be absolute, *no longer to be in the person-to-person relationship* and at the service of the other (Ps. 115 [114]: 4–8).

This is not a reality solely of the past. For example, as we shall see below, when proprietors of capital forget that all of the value of their capital is the labor of others objectified (12.9), they forget the other term of the relationship that has occasioned their wealth: the other as a wage-earning worker. In thus forgetting others and robbing them of their work and life, they absolutize, fetishize capital, constituting it an idol to which they sacrifice their neighbor's life. These modern "gods" are the product of the "logic" of sin, of the domination of one human being over another, of the constitution by one person of another person as the mediation of the former's "own" wealth.

2.4 INDIVIDUAL OR ABSTRACT MALICE

The theologico-symbolic description of the genesis of the evil act or sin—which we might call the description of the structure of temptation in theological figures—is situated at the beginning of the biblical accounts, in the so-called Adamic myth (Gen. 2:9–3:24).

In the myth of Prometheus, human fault or sin is tragic, inevitable. The gods are unjust. Men and women are not responsible for evil, for they are not really free. In the myth of Adam, on the other hand (and "myth" here denotes a *rational* account based on *symbols*), two liberties come into confrontation: that of the tempter and that of the tempted. Nothing is "necessary" or inevitable. The tempter speaks to, "propositions," seduces the tempted who is free to say no. This is the reason for the blandishment, the "feeling out" of the intended victim, the effort at persuasion: "You will be like gods. . . ."

The Adamic myth, then, teaches that the *fall* of Adam was the fruit of his own free will. It was not a flaw decreed by the gods. The *source* of the evil is Adam's freedom. Thus the evil will be reparable, and will lay history wide open as the theater of human responsibility. Adam accepts the proposal of the tempter to constitute the other as dominator (of himself) or dominated (by himself). The tempter proposes, in essence, the following: "Dominate me," in a passive or masochistic attitude; or "Let yourself be dominated," in an aggressive or sadistic attitude. The "other"—not in his or her reality as other, but as *part* of the system—can be the tempter. We must know the discernment of "spirits."

Those who yield to temptation and fall into evil, into the praxis of the domination of the other, their neighbor, signal that they have either instrumentalized that other for their own ends or else have accepted instrumentalization by him or her. At all events, in this perspective, this sin, this fault, is not in the last analysis an individual one. It is not abstract. In concrete reality one sins only *in relation to* others.

2.5 SOCIAL OR CONCRETE SIN

True enough, speaking *abstractly* one can say that John, the individual, has sinned. But *concretely* John is Mary's father, Martha's spouse, Peter's sibling, his pupils' teacher, a citizen of his country, and so on. He is *never*—not even before God—solitary and alone: in the *concrete*, he is never *this* solitary individual. Likewise, his fault or sin is never solitary in the concrete.

An "institution" is never a structure existing in and of itself, independently of the individuals composing it. The "institution" is but the *modus quo*, the "way in which" individuals comport themselves in a stable and related manner. The *institution* of marriage is a way in which women and men *relate* as spouse-to-spouse (be this manner of *relating* monogynous or polygynous, monandrous or polyandrous, patriarchal or matriarchal, and so on). All "institutions" (from a national political state to a soccer team or a church) are stable types of *relationships* among *individuals*. (The individual is the support of the institution.)

Accordingly, if a person (or group of persons) dominates another person (or group of persons) *stably* or *historically* (as the *encomendero* dominated the Amerindian, the capitalist dominates the wage-earner, the man the woman, and so on), we may say that this praxis of domination, this defect or sin is *institutional* or social. It is a type of objective, real, *social relationship* maintained in historical groups.

From the moment an individual is *born*, he or she will never exist apart from the institutional texture that antedates and *determines* this particular individual (a *relative* determination, of course, but one that is fundamental for this particular existence). For example, someone may be born wealthy, a member of the dominant class and of a moneyed, bourgeois family. He or she is surely not responsible for *having been born there*. But just as surely, this individual *inherits* this institutional, "originary" sin. Thus, as Paul proclaims, it is possible for death to reign "even over those who had not sinned by breaking a precept as did Adam" (Rom 5:14).

2.6 INHERITED SIN

Writing against Pelagius (who held that sin is inherited "through the evil example set by Adam"), Saint Augustine proposed that sin was inherited in virtue of human conception in concupiscence. That is, an erotic bodily desire, constitutive of our material being from birth, transmitted Adam's fault. This is scarcely the only possible explanation.

For our purposes, I shall define "original sin"—without posing the question whether it is original sin in the traditional sense—as the sin that is constitutive of *our being* from its origin, from our birth. But our "being" is more than our materiality, our corporeality, despite what some have thought. Our most radical *being* is our social being, our "being" in virtue of our being human (and not merely animal). The *place* we occupy in the social texture (see 2.4) determines (although not absolutely) our *being*. And as I have indicated above, we *receive* our membership in the dominant or the dominated class (this is an observable, evident *fact*, not a judgment) from the first instant of our origin.

When the individual subjectivity of the human person achieves effective freedom (psychologically in adolescence), it *already finds* itself that of a bourgeois or a proletarian, a peasant or a petit bourgeois, a woman or a man, and so on. We are *this way* already. *Upon* this foundation we can construct our life. But we must inevitably construct it precisely *from* the original constitution we have received and inherited.

Thus historical, social sin is transmitted by institutions—by cultural, political, economic, religious, erotic, and so on, structures. In taking up our position as one of the terms of the social relationship of sin (as a proprietary or dispossessed individual—that is, as the member of such and such a family, in the particular social class in which we fall, as a citizen of such and such a country), we inherit a praxis that constitutes us relatively and "originally."

2.7 THE "POOR"

"Poor," in the biblical sense, denotes the dominated, oppressed, humiliated, instrumentalized term of the practical relationship called sin (see 2.2). The constitutive act of the "poor" in the Bible is not lacking goods, but *being dominated*, and this *by the sinner*. The poor are the correlative of sin. As the fruit of sin, their formality as "poor" constitutes the poor or oppressed, and as such, the just and holy.

The "poor" are those who, in the *relationship of domination*, are the dominated, the instrumentalized, the alienated. *Outside* this relationship they can be "rich." *Poor* and *rich*, in the Bible, in addition to being concrete persons, are dialectical *categories*: the proper content of each correlative term includes the other, just as the term "parent" includes having a "child." No one is a parent unless he or she has a child. Nor is anyone "poor" in the biblical sense unless there are "rich."

Diagram 3

Despoliation

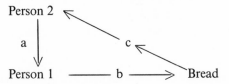

"Bread is the life of the poor; who robs him of it murders him" (Ecclus. 34:21). In Diagram 3 the person (1) who toils (*b*) produces the product of his or her hands ("Bread" symbolizes that product). Another person (2) dominates (*a*) person 1—commits sin against him or her, as in the case of the suffering Job. *Because of this domination*, and in virtue of the basic fact of sin, person 2 robs (*c*) person 1 of the fruit of his or her toil (*b*). The poverty or want suffered by the poor (person 1) is not the sheer absence of goods. No, the poverty of the poor consists in having been *despoiled* of the fruit of their labor by reason of the objective domination of sin.

Thus the alienation of the other (fruit of the praxis of the sinner) produces the poverty of the poor (fruit of sin) as robbery, or dispossession.

2.8 "DEATH"

When a human being dominates a brother or sister, the result is that described by Paul: "Sin entered the world, and by sin, *death*" (Rom. 5:12). "Death" in what sense? We immediately think of eternal death (condemnation), and correctly, to be sure. Or we think of physical death (the death that consists in the extinction of biological life). But let us consider a third type of death, the cause of the sinner's "eternal death."

It is because the poor objectify their *life* in the product of their hands (in bread, for example—see 11.3) that "he murders his neighbor who deprives him of his sustenance; who will not pay a just wage spills blood" (Ecclus. 34:22). For the Bible, "blood" is the seat of *life* (see 11.2). If I deprive a living being of its blood, I kill it. To take the "blood" of the poor is to kill them. This is the third type of death, to which I have just alluded—the death suffered by the poor as the fruit of the sin of the sinner, the "rich": "Woe to you rich, for you have had your consolation" (Luke 6:24). The "rich," the dominator, the sinner (because he or she snatches from the poor their product, because the dominator "kills" the poor in their very life) is condemned to "eternal death," to a "second death," as we hear: "Depart from me, ye cursed, into everlasting fire, prepared for the devil and *his angels*. For I was hungry and you did not feed me" (Matt. 25:41–2).

Thus the life of the poor is accumulated by the rich (see 12.6). The latter live the life of the rich in virtue of the death of the poor. The life of the sinner feeds on the blood of the poor, just as the idol lives by the death of its victims, like Moloch of old, to whom children were immolated, or the Aztec Huitzilopochtli. The fetish god was "animated" or ensouled by the blood of its victims.

"They have broken my covenant by rebelling against my law. ... With their silver and their gold they have fashioned idols for their perdition" (Hos. 8:1–4). "The Egyptians imposed heavy labor on them, and embittered their life with harsh slavery" (Exod. 1:13).

2.9 CONSCIENCE AND RESPONSIBILITY

One might think that, inasmuch as sin is inherited (as the social relationship of domination by the sinner over the poor), there would be neither personal (individual) awareness nor personal responsibility in that praxis of alienation of the other.

Each individual, as a real term of social relationships (see 1.2, 2.5), consciously assumes—in the lights and shades of his or her biography (historical, psychological, familial) and to a greater or lesser degree—the meaning of his or her "place" in the institutional structure of sin (as also of the "covenant," as we shall see later on—see 3.5, 3.6). Moses was the pharaoh's adopted son (Exod. 2:10): he belonged institutionally to the number of those who dominated the poor, those who were the sinners.

The strength, wealth, beauty, culture, and so on, of the dominant group to which one belongs is consciously known, enjoyed, and affirmed. Humiliation, weakness, cultural deprivation, serfdom, and so on, are consciously known and consented to by the despised poor. Thus it is that, day by day, dominators take on personal, individual *responsibility* for their sin of domination. After all, they daily assert the privileges and the potential (the opportunities) accruing to them in virtue of this inherited sin. And never again will dominators be able to claim innocence of that of which they have the use and enjoyment.

Too many signs furnish the rich with a *daily* indication of the distressing presence of the poor. The radical separation of one's own satisfaction in the use of wealth from the suffering of the poor in their poverty (not to see that the one is cause of the other) is a *wish not to be guilty*. "If they will not hear Moses and the prophets, neither will they listen to one returned from the dead" (Luke 16:31). Nor will they take any heed of a poor person who dies of hunger as a result of their domination. To a greater or lesser degree, one is always conscious of, and thus responsible for, one's sin—one's personal, individual lapse (in virtue of one's personal, individual constitution as one of the real terms of a social relationship).

2.10 THE "PRINCE OF THIS WORLD"

Jesus answered: "You have the devil for your father, and you seek to accomplish your father's desires—who was a murderer from the beginning" (John 8:44). "Now begins a judgment upon the world: now the Prince *of this world* will be cast out" (John 12:31). In our one, single history—our one *place* of confrontation—sin is organized as a society, as a "world," as an order.

Sin is not only not exclusively individual, sin is not only social and historical, institutional, a social relationship—sin is actually an organized, self-conscious, functioning "subject" or agent: Satan, the "power" of evil, the Evil One. The essential question here is not whether this objectification of evil in a pure, substantive, personal spirit corresponds to a literal reality—which I do not deny. What is essential here is that we understand his historical praxis, along with that of *his angels* (Matt. 25:41), who include the dominators, sinners, the "rich," and so on.

"The princes of the nations lord it over them, and the mighty oppress them" (Matt. 20:25). The praxis of sin, of domination (the constitution of oneself as the sovereign of the alienated other), is insitutionalized by way of political, ideological, religious, and economic structures. There is no such thing as a religious sin that is not a political or economic sin— and vice versa. All domination, or offense, committed against the other is *sin* against God. It is chimerical to separate sin, on the one side, from historical structures and institutions on the other. The latter are the *concrete* forms of Satan's exercise of his dominion *in this world*, through the mediation of his angels: the human beings who dominate their sisters and brothers.

The sinners, the "rich," the dominators, are the *angelos*, the "envoys" dispatched by the Prince *of this world* for the institutionalization of his reign: namely, the historical structures of sin as "*social* relationship."

CONCLUSIONS

Our second theme, "Evil and Death"—negative counterpart of the first ("Praxis and the Reign of God")—leads us to consider the *principle of sin* that constitutes the perverse, negative point of departure of a Christian ethics. That principle is an impediment to the constitution of community: it is the assertion of individuality *against* community. In authentic community, genuine individuality is fully actualized. In anticommunity, individuality is fetishized and ultimately destroys itself, by way of the death of the poor. It is this *death* that is now of interest to us.

Although it is true that sinners—"the rich" as a category and as social relationships, rich *persons*—can be saved, they cannot be saved if they remain in their sinners', rich persons', *relationship of domination*. Then they will be condemned (second death) to eternal death, deserved by reason of their responsibility (also personal and individual) exercised in the murder of the poor: because they will have caused the *death* of the poor "in this world."

Chapter 3

Prevailing Social Morality: The "Babylon Principle"

3.1 STATE OF THE QUESTION

Now we must take a further step. We must discover and identify the mechanisms of evil.

We read in a newspaper:

> The Salvadoran army shot into the crowd indiscriminately, and burned the fields of the campesinos of Morazán Department, while Radio Venceremos announced that dozens of young persons were becoming the victims of forced recruitment in the central zone of the country..... Elsewhere, following upon the violent resurgence of the so-called death squads of the extreme right, the bodies of three persons shot to death "execution-style" on San Salvador's south side were found today. ... Meanwhile Archbishop Arturo Rivera y Damas of San Salvador today asked "those responsible for the structure of oppression" in the country to have faith in the dialogue for peace [*El Día*, International Edition (Mexico City), February 18, 1985, p. 13].

We read in holy scripture:

> In her hand she held a gold cup that was filled with the abominable and sordid deeds of her lewdness. On her forehead was written a symbolic name, "*Babylon the great*, mother of harlots and all the world's abominations." I saw that the

woman was drunk with the blood of God's holy ones and the blood of those martyred for their faith in Jesus.

When I saw her I was greatly astonished. The angel said to me: "Why are you so taken aback? I will explain to you the symbolism of the woman and of the seven-headed and ten-horned beast carrying her" [Rev. 17:4–7].

Evil, sin—whether individual but subsumed in the social, or concretely and historically social—is organized or "institutionalized." The mystery revealed in the Book of Revelation is actually more current today than ever, and merits our close attention. The Dragon, the Beast, the kings and authorities at their disposal, their envoys or angels, their servants, their customs, laws, and powers, all constitute a full-fledged order, that of *this world*—as category—and its prevailing morality.

3.2 SOME NECESSARY DISTINCTIONS

I now propose to borrow a number of terms from ordinary speech and endow each of them with a narrower, more precise, meaning for purposes of our discourse.

First, for purposes of our discourse, the term "morality" (or "morals," and so on)—of Latin origin—will denote any "practical" (from "praxis") system of the prevailing, established order, the order now in place (see 3.3). By "ethics" ("ethical," and so on)—of Greek derivation—I denote the future order of liberation, the demands of justice with respect to the poor, the oppressed, and their project (historical—see 1.9; or eschatological—see 1.10) of salvation. Thus something might be "moral" without being "ethical," and vice versa. All of this will become clearer in the following pages.

Secondly, "prevailing social," "social," even "society," will have a restricted, negative meaning, and will denote the "worldly"—the condition of the individual (labor, toil, and so on) in the prevailing order of domination, of sin. "Community," on the other hand (along with "communal," and so on), will stand for the face-to-face relationship of persons standing in a relationship of justice. So "community" will denote a utopian order from whose perspective we shall be able to criticize the prevailing "social" element. This is why I have entitled this work "Ethics and Community," and not

"Prevailing Social Morality," or even "Social Morality."

Thus a praxis can be "good" in the eyes of the prevailing *morality* and "evil" for an *ethics* of liberation. Jesus was a blasphemer, a disturber of the social order, one who deserved to die, and so on— in other words, "evil"—for the order of the dominant values of the "elders, priests, and scribes," for Herod (governor of the nation), and for Pilate (representative of the occupying imperial power).

3.3 "THIS WORLD"

In the New Testament the word "world" (Gk., *kosmos*) denotes the universe, locus of our single history, humanity, a certain order. I shall use the word, however, in a sense more directly apposite to our subject matter.

"This world" is both a reality and a category. "My reign is not of *this world*. If my reign belonged to *this world*, my armies would have fought to prevent my being delivered into the hands of the Jewish authorities" (John 18:36). "*This* world," then, is a "practical" totality (a totality constituted and characterized by relationships of praxis), a system or structure of prevailing, dominant *social* actions and relationships, under the hegemony of evil. It is the reign of the Evil One. "This world" is Egypt as a *system of practices* confronting Moses. It is the monarchy of Israel confronting the prophets. It is the kingdom of Judea confronting Jesus. It is Christendom as the City of Earth. It is the feudal system confronting Saint Francis of Assisi. It is capitalism in the eyes of the oppressed of today.

"This world" has the Devil, Satan, or the Dragon as its principle and authority—"the Prince of *this world*" (John 12:31; 14:30). The Dragon (the Devil: Luke 4:5–6) has given its power to the Beast (Rev. 17:12), and thus "the entire world is in the power of the Evil One" (1 John 5:19). "The spirit of the world" is opposed to the "Spirit of God" (1 Cor. 2:12). Hence "whatever there is in the world—base appetites, insatiable eyes, the arrogance of money—none of it comes from the Father. It comes from the world" (1 John 2:16).

The "world" is closed in upon itself. It is self-totalizing, self-fetishizing. The "world" in this sense is identical with "the sin of the world" (John 1:29). The world hates Jesus (John 15:18) because he discloses "the perversity of its machinations" (John 7:7).

3.4 THE "FLESH"

In like manner, "flesh" (Heb., *basar*) can have the biblical meaning of muscles, the body, the entire human being. Or it can mean, as for Epicurus, the place where the appetites emerge.

I shall use the word in a stronger sense. The "flesh," like the "world," is an order, a level. "Flesh" denotes the order of the natural, the human. "Of flesh is born flesh" (John 3:6). Hence "the flesh is weak" (Matt. 26:41). The "flesh" is the seat of the appetites or desires of pride, idolatry, and domination over another as instrument. "Let them not foster the desires of the flesh" (Rom. 13:14).

Thus understood, the "flesh" is the order of sin: "When we were subject to the flesh, to the passions of sin, that the law arouses, it was activating our members in the practices of death" (Rom. 7:5). The flesh is the subjective aspect, the aspect of the passions, the region of the human being where the imperium of the world is exercised. Saint Paul explained that he was subject "by the flesh to the law of sin" (Rom. 7:25). The world has its structure, its laws, its customs, the point of departure from which "it judges according to the flesh" (John 8:15). As "flesh," we are members of the world in its capacity as subject or agent of sin (Rom. 8:13ff.; Gal. 4:23). A struggle is being waged between the "flesh" and the "Spirit," between human or carnal knowledge and the madness of God (1 Cor. 2:6–14).

In the totality of the *systems of practices* of the world, as objective and social reality, the "carnal" subject or agent desires the permanency of order, which, however, attempts to legitimate itself by appealing to the "gods" as its foundation. The "flesh" is idolatrized in the "kingdom of *this world*," and promulgates its own law, its own morality, its own goodness.

3.5 THE "BABYLON PRINCIPLE"

Original Hebreo-Christian theology possessed a category to express the structural *totality* of the practices of sin. This totality assumed a distinct concrete physiognomy at each historical moment, while retaining an analogous essence.

At the time of Moses, the world—the system according to the dictates of the flesh—was Egypt. And God said, "I have beheld the oppression of my people in Egypt. I have heard their cries against their oppressors. I have fixed on their sufferings" (Exod. 3:7). "*In Egypt*" is a category. The Monarchy, which was founded on idolatry, came to represent the same category. God addressed the prophet Samuel: "As they dealt with me from the day I led them forth from Egypt, abandoning me to serve other gods, thus they treat you" (1 Sam. 8:8). The new order, the system of the practices of the kings, will make of the people an oppressed mass. "You shall be slaves! Then will you cry out against the kings they have chosen for themselves, but God will not answer you" (1 Sam. 8:18).

Later the people was to have yet another experience of suffering and oppression: the Babylonion captivity: "All this land will lie desolate, and the neighboring nations will be subject to the king of Babylon" (Jer. 25:11). "Babylon" signifies the order of oppression, that of the Devil. "All, great and small, rich and poor, slave and free, he made that they mark them on the right hand or the forehead" (Rev. 13:17).

This system is closed in upon itself. It has replaced the universal human project with its own particular historical project. Its laws become natural, its virtues perfect, and the blood of those who offer any resistance—the blood of the prophets and heroes—is spilled by the system as if it were the blood of the wicked, the totally subversive.

3.6 THE SYSTEM OF MORAL PRACTICES

Essential to an ethics of liberation is a clear understanding of the starting point of the praxis of liberation. This starting point is sin, the world as a system of sin, the flesh as idolatrous desire, and a system that nevertheless is "moral," having its own morality and a justified, tranquil conscience.

Any system of prevailing, dominant practices (from Egypt or Babylon to Rome, the several Christendoms, or capitalist society) determines its established practices to be good. Its project (its end, its *telos*, its *beatitudo*, as the Latin theologians termed it) is confused with the "perfect human good" as such. Thus the norms that demand the execution of this project are "natural law." The prohibition, "Thou shalt not steal the private property of thy neighbor," for example, has been part of capitalism's "natural law" since the eighteenth century. The virtues of the project are now obligatory as the highest virtues of all. Somehow the habit of amassing wealth fails to remind anyone of the usury or avarice of feudalism.

Thus arises a "prevailing" *moral system* (regardless of its origin, regardless of the fact that it owes its subsistence to an "original," institutional sin of domination at all levels—see, e.g., 12.3). The persons who comply with this system, in its practices, its norms, its values, its "virtues," its laws, are good, just, and meritorious persons, and they win the praise of their peers.

Now a total inversion has been achieved. Domination and sin have been transformed into the very foundation of reality. Perverse praxis is now goodness and justice. Ideology, operating as a cloak over the reality of domination, now legitimates the praxis of the flesh and of the world as if it were the praxis of the very reign of God.

3.7 MORALITY OF PRAXIS

The "practical" universe within the moral system of the prevailing order is inverted. Accordingly, it is this system itself that determines the good or evil of an act.

The classic definition of morality was expressed in terms of relationship to a norm or law. Kant demanded the moral law be loved. For Thomas Aquinas it was the relations of an act to the moral law that determined its morality. The problem, obviously, is that once the system of the world has asserted itself as the foundation or law, morality will depend precisely on the actualization of the system. An act will be *morally* good if it is "adequated to," if it complies with, the ends of the prevailing system. If I pay taxes, the minimum wage, and so on, as required by law, I shall be a "just" person, a "good" person. The law itself may be unjust. The taxes may be insufficient, the wages may be starvation wages. But all of that lies *outside* any possible moral consideration.

Correlatively, *immorality* will be constituted by the sheer non-realization of the prevailing norm. The thief whose thievery is a vice is now less wicked than the prophet who criticizes the system in its totality. Barabbas and Jesus are both "evil" for the Jewish and Roman morality of their time. Juan del Valle, bishop of Popayán, was regarded by the *encomenderos* of sixteenth-century Latin America as "the *worst* bishop in the Indies" because he defended the Indians.

And so it comes about that, in their respect and love for the law of the prevailing system—its norms, its ends, its values—dominators, though they are sinners, are nevertheless seen to be just and good. The "Prince of *this world*" is now the judge of good and evil. Morality itself has been inverted. The "wisdom of the world" has become norm and law.

3.8 "MORAL" CONSCIENCE

To complete the circle, the "world" forms or educates the "moral" conscience of its members according to criteria of the flesh.

Classically, "*moral* conscience" was that faculty of the practical intelligence that applies moral principles to concrete cases. A principle states: "You shall not steal." But in this concrete case I desire to appropriate goods regarded by the system of prevailing practical moral principles as belonging to someone else. In this case my conscience commands me: "Do not do so, for by doing so you would constitute yourself liable to the penalty determined for those who 'steal' something." Whereupon, if I "steal" nonetheless, my conscience will recriminate me, accuse me, give me subjective culpability, by reason of this *morally* evil act.

If my *moral* conscience has been formed within a framework of the principles of the system, it will recriminate me if I fail to comply with the laws of the system. But it will be unable to tell me that the system *as a totality* is perverse (for conscience *applies* principles, and does not establish them). Thus the theft of property that is the private possession of someone else is a moral offense, and conscience indicates it to me. But my own private property, which may well constitute, in its origin, the (objectified) *dispossession of others of their labor* (see 11.6)—although that dispossession may have occurred imperceptibly as far as my own consciousness, my own conscience, is concerned—presents itself as legitimate and good. All other persons, "Hands off!"

Here I am being *blind* to the fact that private property denied to the workers whose labor has produced it is unjustified accumulation, taking over the capital of the fruits of their labor, previously stolen from them *without* my being conscious of the theft.

In this fashion, "moral" conscience, formed in the moral principles of the dominant system, creates a peaceful, remorseless conscience vis-à-vis a practice that the system approves but that may originally have been perverse (a praxis of domination).

3.9 THE POOR "BY NATURE"

In the order of the world—the order according to the flesh, the system of the practices of sin, of dominators, of the "rich"—the "poor" (see 2.7), like the slaves discussed by Aristotle or the conquered natives discussed by Ginés de Sepúlveda, are such "by nature" (Gk., *phusei*). They are "poor" not only factually and from birth, but by the eternal design of the gods (or God).

For the Greeks some beings manifest themselves, "by nature," as others as human beings: some as free, others as slaves. No one is guilty of the poverty of the poor. No crime on the part of any human liberty is the creative font of this injustice. The "poor" are poor by natural inclination, by reason of the evil disposition of their body or their soul, by reason of their vagrancy, or want of virtue, or simply their ill luck (as dictated by fate or divine providence). A theology of resignation justifies the fact that some are poor by exclaiming, "It is the will of God!"

Another theology, as pernicious as the first, simply proposes love and reconciliation between "rich" (dominating sinners—see 2.8) and "poor" (those oppressed and murdered by sin)—without requiring the objective conditions necessary for *forgiveness*. Forgiveness requires a clear, antecedent awareness of guilt on the part of the sinner, the "rich" person, together with just reparation (repentance and restitution), as Ripalda's fine catechism put it. Without a real, objective, shared, historical equality between the two persons— which means that the "rich" can no longer be rich nor the "poor" poor—there can be no reconciliation.

To assert that the poverty of the poor (which means their death) stems naturally from the will of God, or to pretend to a reconciliation that would take place without an *antecedent* hatred of the world and praxis of justice, are propositions of a theology of domination.

3.10 THE "CROSS" AS EFFECT OF REPRESSION BY SIN

Not only do the poor keep dying by keeping an idol alive through the sacrifice of their lifeblood—whether the fetish be a European Christian state or a Western Christian civilization—the prophets and heroes, too, are murdered.

Babylon is "drunk on the blood of the consecrated," the prophet wrote. "The bodies of three persons shot to death 'execution-style' ... were found today," says the newspaper quoted at the beginning of this chapter. All who risk their lives to rescue the lost lives of the poor, the lives squandered every day in acts of worship of the idol, suffer repression and risk murder. What the system (the world, the flesh) fears more than anything else are "teachers" who threaten to arouse the masses and lead them toward liberation from the oppression (economic, political, ideological, religious, and so on) of sin.

"The high priests and the doctors of the law entered into a conspiracy, as they were afraid. ... They sought how they might murder him" (Mark 11:18). When the system of the moral and social practices of domination realizes that the prophet is denouncing its wickedness, its injustice (thus destroying the *consent* of the oppressed masses, calling into question the ideological hegemony or domination that justifies sin), it must physically eliminate the critic, the dissident, the martyr—the one bearing witness to the future reign of justice.

The hour of the ultimate repression practiced by any system (see 9.8), the moment when that system's daily oppression makes a quantum leap to a new and still more perverse form of institutional violence—at the hands of armies, the police, or paramilitary groups such as the Latin American "death squads"—foretells the "hour of the manifestation of glory" (John 17:1).

CONCLUSIONS

We have taken a further step. The negation of the *community* by sin, wickedness, and the death of the poor, has become a *society*, in which relationships among individuals enjoy institutionalization due to a *principle* of wickedness, of injustice: the reign of *this world*, Babylon. Sin, the domination of one human being by another, not only is not exclusively individual—its "socialness" has taken on historical, concrete form. Sin has a transcendent principle (the Evil One, the Dragon), a principle immanent in history (the Beast—at the time of the prophet of Revelation, the Roman empire), its kings at its disposal, and its angels to fulfill its commands. They are the "rich," all those who are sinners and dominators in their being subjects or agents of sin and of the praxis that instrumentalizes neighbors as "things."

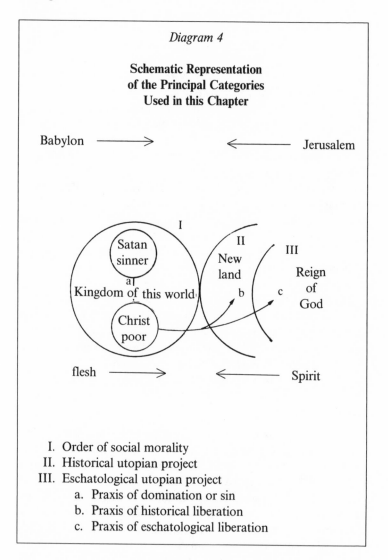

Diagram 4

**Schematic Representation
of the Principal Categories
Used in this Chapter**

   I. Order of social morality
  II. Historical utopian project
 III. Eschatological utopian project
   a. Praxis of domination or sin
   b. Praxis of historical liberation
   c. Praxis of eschatological liberation

Chapter 4

Goodness and Life

4.1 STATE OF THE QUESTION

It is time to take a new step in our reflection. Evil, which produces death (see 2.8), destroys the communal face-to-face of love. The praxis of domination inaugurates a "moral" order that legitimates sin: Babylon. Now we must see how, out of the reign of *this world*, the good, goodness, holiness, the gift of the other, emerges.

Every day the newspapers carry news of courageous and valiant acts. A child rescues a companion swept away by a river. A union is founded for the defense of its members. A liberation movement is organized somewhere in Africa or Asia. A popular party wins an election. A country declares or attains its independence. The papers are full of accounts of praxes of goodness, of holiness.

We read in holy scripture:

> Dry bones, hear the word of the Lord! . . . I will put sinews upon you, make flesh grow over you, cover you with skin, and put spirit in you so that you may come to life. . . . O my people, I will open your graves and have you rise from them, and bring you back to the land of Israel. . . . I will put my spirit in you that you may live, and I will settle you upon your land; thus you shall know that I am the Lord. I have promised, and I will do it, says the Lord [Ezek. 37:4–14].

Our task is to see how God brings forth goodness—holiness—among men and women in "social" relationships that institutionalize sin. God cannot accomplish an irruption into history by forcing the human will. That will is free. At the same time, human beings, be they ever so meritorious or heroic, cannot coerce the self-bestowal of the other person. They cannot force that other to open and to establish the face-to-face. The mutual face-to-face presupposes the free self-proposal of both parties as absolute gratuity.

4.2 ETHICAL CONSCIENCE AND THE VOICE OF THE POOR

The inversion of the reign of evil begins with the breach with that reign effectuated by those who can hear the voice *of the other*. Why did the Samaritan, rather than the priest or the Levite, take pity on the victim of the roadside ambush? How did it come about that the Samaritan, "seeing him, was moved to compassion" (Luke 10:33)?

The "practical" system of domination, Babylon, is the system wielded by all those who have denied the other term of the face-to-face relationship, all who have constituted themselves that other's sovereign. Accordingly, the obliteration of the reign of evil will commence with someone's reconstitution of the face-to-face relationship with the other. This is what the Samaritan did. He *constituted* the half-dead victim *a person*. The victim had been beaten, robbed, and thrown into a ditch. This was a dangerous place to be (and perhaps this is why the priest and the Levite, in their selfishness, avoided any delay hereabouts, such as would have been entailed in any attempt to rescue the victim themselves). And yet the Samaritan pulled him up on to the road and bestowed on him the dignity of personhood, of being served, and thus rendered him an *other*, a neighbor.

In order to *constitute* the mere "thing" that had been dropped by the side of the road "an *other*," the Samaritan obviously had to *hear the voice of the other*. That voice may cry, "I have been beaten! Help me!" Or it may cry, "I am starving! Help me!" But in all cases it is precisely the capacity to hear the voice of the other that constitutes *ethical* conscience. In the Bible the supreme sign of goodness is to have "a heart that can *listen*" (1 Kgs. 5:9—*Biblia Latinoamericana*). The Lord "awakens my ears daily that I may hear, as a disciple" (Isa. 50:4). "Keep silent, Israel, and listen!" (Deut. 27:9). In this case *conscience* is not so much the application of principles to concrete cases, but a listening, a hearing the voice calling to me from outside, from beyond the horizon of the system: the voice of the poor calling for justice, calling from deep within their absolute, sacred right, the right of the person as person.

Ethical conscience (very distinct from *moral* conscience—see 3.8) consists in knowing how to "open up" to the other and to take that other in charge (take re-sponsibility for him or her)—*for the sake of* the other, *vis-à-vis* the system.

4.3 CONVERSION

Of course, to be able to hear the voice of the other is a gift in itself. Why do some hear that voice, whereas others, with their hands over their ears, immersed in their fetishism, remain deaf to it?

It is the "other," others in their cry, in their shout, in their pain, who "pro-voke" us (call us forth), "con-voke" us (call us to them, to help them), "inter-pellate" us (call us to account, call us as witnesses before the reality of their poverty). It suddenly becomes clear to us that they have rights, and that we are guilty of their disaster and have the duty to serve them, that we carry the responsibility of their saving, their salvation, their happiness, their health, their sustenance. Awareness of our *guilt* for the catastrophe of others, our guilt for their unhappiness, upon hearing their voice, is the root and wellspring of conversion.

Conversion, *metanoia* (a changing of one's ways, one's life, motivated by repentance—Matt. 3:3–8), is a breach with Babylon, a breach with the prevailing *social* relationship in whose toils we had been snared. Hence "unless one is born *again* one cannot enjoy the reign of God" (John 3:3). This breach and this meeting with the other is a *gift*: "The Spirit breathes where it will" (John 3:8). The irruption of the Spirit that consecrates (Isa. 61:1), baptism as the gift of God that brings us into community, the grace that cannot be merited, justification by gratuity—all these things are expressions of the fact that the other comes toward us *from within that other*, in freedom and spontaneity.

Goodness, holiness, irrupts as breach, as violence, as painful change of life. Moses belonged to the pharaoh's family; Jeremiah enjoyed the privileges of the priestly families. Conversion is experienced as that soul-rending "Cursed be the day I was born!"

4.4 THE "COVENANT"

It is not the human being who takes the first step. It is God who calls first, through the poor. "Conversion" has to be seen, first, as proceeding from the other but, secondly, as taking place in community. Conversion is incorporating a historical process into a "covenant."

Now we see why the Lord said to Abram: "Leave your native land and your father's house for the land I shall show you. I shall make of you a great people. ... Abram went forth as the Lord had commanded him" (Gen. 12:1-4). The act of "departure," the act of emerging from one's *former* land, is the praxis by which the old order, the "moral" system of Babylon, is transcended. But the departure is possible only because God strikes a covenant with the one who is to depart, constituting that one the first of many, the first of a whole people (Rom. 5:15-19).

Covenant, as its daily working-out indicates, is the meeting of a plurality of wills in view of a common end, a strategic project. A covenant differs from an order or command in that the parties are partners, equal partners, "community." Covenant is the reconstitution of the "community" negated by sin. It is the reign of God, which begins in smallness, among an original few, among a small "remnant," the little community.

Breach with the "flesh," with the "world," is the unification, encounter, and solidarity of those who originate a new order of service, of justice, of mutual friendship. *Diatheke*—the word for "covenant" in the Greek of the New Testament (in Hebrew, *b'rith*)—denotes a pact ratified in blood (Luke 20:22; Amos 1:9). It is also a "pact of peace" (Ezek. 34:25), a pact for the good of the community. The covenant is *Immanuel*, "God with us," God among us, God our equal, God as the one who has kept the promise. The right, the law that God has now established, will abide unshakable, for the "covenanted" are now God's "adopted children" (Rom. 9:4).

4.5 GOODNESS AS SERVICE

Those "born anew," converted, are the "covenanted," the allies, of God. They accomplish the good deed, the good praxis, the good, the holy. In what, essentially and basically, does good, holy, ethical praxis consist?

Just as it is proper to the Prince of this world to dominate, to exercise power, so ethical praxis will consist in the exact opposite.

"This man has come not to be served, but to serve (*diakonesai*), and to give his life as a ransom for the many (*pollon*)" (Matt. 20:28). "To serve"—the attribute of the *diakonos*, the deacon—is *habodah* in Hebrew: labor, service, the activity of the *hebed*, the "worker" or "servant" of God (Isa. 53:10–12).

The service in question is addressed to the other term of the face-to-face relationship—the poor, in community. The Bible calls the potential, possible, future community—the object of the service of the one who is ethically just—the "crowd" (*hoi polloi* in Greek, "the many"; *rabim* in Hebrew). It indicates an indefinite number of poor who are not yet a "people," because they lack the service that is the task of the shepherd; they are without the leadership of the just one, the prophet, the "Servant of Yahweh." These "many," who are outside the laws of the system, who indeed live "in exteriority" even with respect to social class, are the special object of the good, the holy, human being, the person who practices justice, goodness, holiness, love of the other as other. "Personal" goodness is praxis as performed by those who struggle, even to the point of giving up their lives, for the fulfillment of the other.

If conversion is breach with the system, with the world, with the totality, then the service of the poor that emerges from that conversion will be explicit, concrete, "practical" struggle. Service to the other is the negation of domination. It is the practice that contradicts the established legality, the prevailing structures. It is the toil emerging from a liberation project that transcends the present order, which dominates the poor. If the world hates the just, they have no choice but to continue the struggle with Satan.

4.6 COMMUNAL GOODNESS

Personal goodness or holiness, however, is abstract. *In the concrete*, goodness is communal, historical, and itself institutionalized.

The reason why those who serve an other, breaking with the structure of the system of the flesh to enter into solidarity with that other, are able to do this is because the Lord has first struck a covenant with them. But to be part of a covenant is to be part of a "community." In the Bible the Lord's designation for the "covenant community" is "my people." Here we have a people (Deut. 4:34; Exod. 7:5; Luke 1:17; 1 Cor. 10:18—see below, 8.5–8.7) who can betray its God: "Call them 'not-my-people,' for you are not my people and I am not with you" (Hos. 1:9). Nevertheless—and this is the point—we have a *theological category* as well (in addition to its objective historical reality). As theological category, "people" expresses the presence in the world, in history, of holiness or goodness as community, as institution (see 2.5)—in the positive sense of this term.

Such expressions or realities as "small community," "base community," "association of free persons" all denote the institutional ambit where the person-to-person relationship, as the face-to-face of love, has been reconstituted. Thus the good is not only the good will of a person, or even the isolated, individual act of someone who is good. No, now the good is "community," as well, with all its real, empirical, sociological consistency. It is now holiness, and its members are "the holy ones of Jerusalem." It is capable of a strategy, of tactics, it can have its mysteries and its functions, it can mount a concrete resistance. As the community of holy ones it is a "*utopian* community." In other words it has "no-place" (Gk., *ou topos*) in the system. From *outside* the world, outside the flesh and the system, in virtue of its actual, concrete solidarity, it can exercise the concrete function of liberation and service to the *poor*, to the *people*, in the form of criticism of that system. It is this prophetic community that makes the "crowd" a "people," and makes the "poor" a historical subject.

4.7 INHERITANCE OF THE GOOD

If continuance in the age of evil is institutional, in virtue of inherited "social" relationships of domination, in analogous fashion the *gift* of the Lord, the gratuity of God's covenant, penetrates time thanks to the community called by God "my people," the community founded on the abiding stability of God's promise and faithful word.

There is such a thing as inherited good, too, then. Good is no more a matter of spontaneous subjectivity than evil is. "This is the heritage (Heb., *najalat*) of the servants of Yahweh; I am their justifier" (Isa. 54:17). In Hebrew, "to justify," to cause to be accepted as just, to grant amnesty to, is derived from *tsadakah*—innocence, justice, goodness, holiness. In Saint Paul, "justification" (*dikaiosune*, Rom. 1:18ff.) is a reality proceeding not from the law (Gal. 3:21)—that is, not from "social morality "—but from God:from the antecedent forgiveness and amnesty granted by the Lord and no other (Rom. 4:7).

The covenantal presence of the Lord in the community constitutes the historical institutionalization of the communal *relationship*. "Thus also the gift (grace) becomes reign (*basileusei*), by means of justification" (Rom. 5:21). The servant, the converted one, the community, can rely on God's promise: "the promise God assured to David, making him a witness before the peoples" (Isa. 55:3–4). Once the communal relationship is historicized, it can be communicated in time: "Your children will be disciples of the Lord" (Isa. 54:13). That is, we have precisely the opposite of what happens in the case of "originary" sin. Children will be born into the covenant community, where a *community* relationship is waiting to receive them.

This re-established relationship—which is not "natural" ("native," inborn), but communitarian, historical, a gift of the Spirit in the passage through the laver of purification and repentance—this new face-to-face, is an *encounter*. Human beings, justified, now address themselves, through their community praxis of service to the poor, to a God who comes to meet them, a God approaching as holiness, justification, and forgiveness.

4.8 LIFE REGAINED

As by sin death entered the world, through the encounter with God *life* is poured into the world. The theology of liberation is a theology of *life* against death.

In community, the just share bread. They produce it, divide it, and distribute it. The needy are needy no longer. Now they live.

We read: "the Spirit tends to life. . . . The Spirit is life. . . . The One who raised the Messiah will also give life to his mortal beings" (Rom. 8:6–11). "I shall strike a covenant of peace with them. . . . They shall camp in the wilderness in safety. . . . They shall know that I am their Lord when I cause them to snap the couplings of their yoke, when I deliver them from the power of their tyrants" (Ezek. 34:25–29). Today this resurrection to life, to be prolonged in resurrection at the end of the ages, is the bestowal of life for the new *community relationship* of mutual service in the friendship of the face-to-face.

Diagram 5
Life in the Spirit

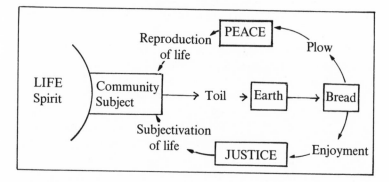

The *subject* of this resurrection to life, of this receipt of life, is the people of God in community—"flesh, risen," risen to the life of the new covenant, risen to the new system of justice that has left oppressive, death-dealing Egypt behind, abandoned that producer of the death that is the fruit of sin. If sin was domination, if it was by domination that the "rich" dispossessed the poor of their labor, so it is through the mutual service of goodness that the fruit of the toil of all means life for all. "Of their swords they shall forge plowshares; of their pikes, pruning hooks" (Isa. 2:4).

4.9 THE POOR HAVE THEIR FILL

Wealth is good. It is the gift of the creator and the work of human hands. The evil of wealth resides in its *accumulation*, which produces poverty in the other. Wealth *in itself* belongs to that of which we read: "And God saw that it was *very good*" (Gen. 1:31—see our 18.3).

The fruit of good, of holiness, is life. "Happy the poor, for theirs is the reign of God" (Matt. 5:3). Again, the reign is fulfillment. "Happy . . . because they shall receive consolation . . . shall inherit the earth . . . shall be satisfied . . . shall receive help . . . shall be face to face with God (in *community*) . . . shall be the daughters and sons of God" (Matt. 5:4–9). All these positivities, affirmations, joys, are the reign "already," for those who *have been* poor. Wealth shared today is the good that negates and defeats the poverty of yesterday.

Eating is a material, biological activity. Animals eat when they are hungry. But in history, in the human reality of social structures, to feed the hungry is not a mere material, animal, biological activity. Inasmuch as the hunger of another is the fruit of sin, of a satanic act, of evil, it constitutes a moment in the "reign of this world." Hatred of Satan, the struggle against the structure of "this world," against sin, is a *spiritual* activity—an activity inspired by the Spirit that moves the prophets and the people to build the reign of God.

The feeding of the hungry, or for that matter the very activity of eating when performed by the hungry, is a "spiritual" activity, and not merely a material one, because it is an act of service, of *diakonia*, of love, of *risk* (because it is against the system). "Happy those persecuted for struggling on behalf of justice ... for this is how they persecuted the prophets before you" (Matt. 5:10–12).

4.10 THE REIGN OF THE SERVANT

The community of the reign of God cannot be organized in the manner of a state, by way of coercive laws, with a police force to ensure the observance of these laws, and an army to rule, coerce the will of, others despotically and by force of arms (15.9). These are the instruments of death, not of life. This is the sword, not the plowshare. As Saint Augustine put it: "Cain built his city. Abel never built his."

The community of the reign grows slowly, by way of the daily, simple, patient, ethical, faithful face-to-face. Its method is not that of the politics of domination, if by politics we understand the state's technique of coercion (see 9.8).

The community of the reign is built by the servant: "Behold my servant, whom I champion. Upon him have I placed my Spirit, that he may promote justice among the nations. He shall not shout or cry aloud" (Isa. 42:1–2). Into the deepest heart of the structures of evil irrupts the reign of God. Its methodology cannot be that of the "reign of this world." It will be the unmistakable methodology of goodness, holiness, and the good. The *martyria* (Gk., "witness," martyrdom) of the utopia of justice, the praxis of service, the love of justice, alive and operative in the face-to-face relationship, moves, converts, animates, and vivifies (see chapter 9).

The reign of the servant (Matt 12:17–21; 20:28) is not a reign of coercion. It is not a society of dominators. It is not even an association of mutual assistance in the selfishness of the common good of its own members to the exclusion of all others. It is a community of service that stands open to the other. It is the people itself as servant of the future.

CONCLUSIONS

Good irrupts, bursts forth, into the heart of the structures of sin. The "good" is to hear the voice of the poor exclaiming, "I am starving!" To hear that voice is the root or *conditio sine qua non* of goodness, of holiness. To take the other in charge, to make myself responsible for that other, is conversion, whose immediate embodiment is a covenant with the Lord. The "covenanted" of the reign of God *serve*, do justice to, the oppressed. As members of that reign, they stir up in their hearts, as a legacy of grace that they have received, good among themselves, their own children, and all the sons and daughters of their Father. And so the poor have their fill. This satisfaction is their *life*, regained as the fruit of the praxis of goodness, of justice. Thus in the very midst of "this world" a new reign springs up and grows strong, the reign of the servant of Yahweh, a reign whose subjects inaugurate the community of a love that serves, a community of holiness.

Chapter 5

Community Ethics:
the "Jerusalem Principle"

5.1 STATE OF THE QUESTION

Our task in this chapter will be to make a clear distinction between "community" on the one hand, and "society" of domination on the other.

Every day the newspapers carry reports of some popular celebration: a popular carnival, a national patron saint's day or independence day, a birthday, a golden wedding anniversary. Festivals express joy, happiness, a being-together with one another.

We read in holy scripture:

Then I saw *new* heavens and a *new* earth. The former heavens and the former earth had passed away, and the sea was no longer. I also saw a *new Jerusalem, the holy city*, coming down out of heaven from God, beautiful as a bride prepared to meet her husband. I heard a loud voice from the throne cry out: "This is God's dwelling *among humans*. He shall dwell *with them* and they shall be his people and he shall be their God who is always *with them*. He shall wipe every tear from their eyes, and there shall be no more death or mourning, crying out or pain, for the *former* world has passed away" [Rev. 21:1–4].

In the theology of the prophets of Israel, as also in Jesus' theology and in that of his disciples (and the New Testament authors), we encounter a striking dialectic between the "before" of the *old* world—as being the world of sin, domination—and the "after" of the future, of the "new," of a world to be created by goodness, justice, community. What "is coming," the future as fulfillment, is proposed here and now as a praxis of a love that will embrace justice, a community relationship. Further: never is God a private good to be possessed. God's self-bestowal is *among* human beings, *with* them, as one who is *among others*, one who is in the midst of *one's own people*. Grace, salvation, the reign, is communal. At the same time it constitutes the transcendence *of* an order of evil and a trajectory *toward* the order of good. The two reigns are in a dialectical relationship.

5.2 SOME NECESSARY DISTINCTIONS

To continue in our discourse on the ethical theology of liberation, I need to set down three distinctions.

First, two categories, or interpretive instruments, make up the main focus of the whole ethical discourse of the prophets, of Jesus, and of the martyrs. In a basic sense, the category of *totality* ("this world," the order of the flesh, which can be represented as Babylon when it closes in upon itself) stands for the prevailing system as point of departure—for Moses, Egypt; for the Book of Revelation, Babylon—in a word, the prevailing *"moral" order* (see 3.6).

In a still more basic sense, by *exteriority* I understand that which is not given or established under the dominion of the "Prince of this world." I mean the other, the poor, the people as the social bloc of the oppressed, the Spirit (God, as the absolutely Other, never became *part* of a system of sin). "Exteriority" indicates the absolute *transcendence* of the reign of God.

Secondly, the *prevailing project*, the common good of the order of domination (that of Pilate or Herod, that of the Beast—the Roman state that functions in the name of the Dragon, Satan), is the end and objective of social praxis, the morality that justifies the death of the poor. By *liberation project*, on the other hand, I understand the utopian (in a positive sense) end and objective, the object of hope (here we have the "hope principle"), a goal at once historical (a more just, though not perfect, temporal system) and eschatological (see 1.9 and 1.10).

Accordingly, and in the third place, the Bible never tires of showing us the dialectic between the two "lands": "leave your native *land* for the *land* that I shall show you" (Gen. 12:1). "I have come down to deliver them from the Egyptians, to take them out of *this land* to lead them to a land fertile and spacious, a *land flowing with milk and honey*" (Exod. 3:8). "The dead shall hear the voice of the Son of God, and hearing it shall have life" (John 5:25). The first land is a land of death. The second is a land of life, to be entered by "resurrection" (our 4.8). "One must be born *anew*" (John 3:7).

5.3 FROM "MORALITY" TO "ETHICS"

From start to finish, the Sermon on the Mount (Matt. 5:1–8:1) is one great lesson in theology. It is an instruction on the difference between "morality" (the prevailing morality, taught, commanded by dominators) and "ethics" (see 3.2).

Human beings who have been converted to life, who have been raised up by the Spirit and rendered capable of hearing the voice of the poor as the word of God, who are the *allies* of the God of service, soon realize that the entire "moral" order (the norms and praxis of dominators) is against them. Therefore they will have to strip off its mask. "You have been taught that the ancients were commanded. . . . You have been taught that it was commanded, 'eye for eye, tooth for tooth'" (Matt. 5:21–38). Over against these "moral" (unjust, dominating, hypocritical) precepts, Jesus poses "ethical" exigencies: "Then *I* say to you. . . . For I tell you: Do not stand against the one who offends you. . . . Be completely good, as your Father in heaven is good" (Matt. 5:22–48).

To many, Jesus' ethical demands have seemed paradoxical. Are these "obligations" not impossible to understand or fulfill? If "paradoxical" (Gk., *para*, "alongside of, beyond"; *doxa*, "opinion, decree") be taken to mean something opposed to the prevailing moral opinion, then Jesus' teaching is indeed paradoxical. It flies in the face of the whole morality of domination. It contradicts prevailing morality, in the name of the absolute, transcendent, critical horizon of all morality: the "ethical." And in what does the ethical consist? The ethical consists in praxis. It consists in praxis as activity directed toward, and relationship to (1.2), the other as other, as person, as sacred, as absolute. The ethical is not governed by moral norms—by what the system proclaims to be good (3.7). The ethical is governed by what the poor require, by the needs of the oppressed by the struggle with the domination, the structures, and the relationships established by the Prince of "this world" (2.10).

Thus the ethical transcends the moral. Moral systems are relative. Latin American history has witnessed the Aztec, the colonial, and the capitalistic morality. Each of these systems has sought to legitimate the praxis of domination as good, each in its own way. Ethics, by contrast, is one, and absolute—valid in every situation and every age.

5.4 THE POOR IN SPIRIT

One of the decisive aspects of any ethics (and any ethics that is not an ethics of liberation will be a mere "morality") is its interpretation of Matthew 3:5: "Blessed are the poor *to pneumati*"—which can be translated "in spirit," "spiritually," "by choice," and so on. In other words, the crucial modifier can be an open door to the evacuation, the inversion, the annihilation of the ethics of the gospel and its transformation into a morality of domination. Now the rich, too, may be poor, and blessed—and keep their riches! All they need do is become poor "in intention."

"Spirit" and "spiritual" can mean a great number of things in the New Testament. But it always translates the Hebrew *ruah*, which can have our familiar psychological meaning (as later on, as well, for the Stoics), or that of bodily force, or breath, or wind. Its strongest meaning is: the presence or manifestation of the *power* of God (Ezek. 1:12). Thus *pneuma* becomes God's own creative might, the power that launched the prophets. Spirit is the immanent essence of God (Isa. 31:3). It is set over against the flesh, as God (*El*) is set over against the human being (*adam*). But a human being may be possessed by the Spirit (Hos. 9:7; 1 Sam. 10:6). The "living" (or "natural," as we would say today) human being is the opposite of the "spiritual" human being (*soma pneumatikon*: 1 Cor. 15:44–6). "Flesh" is merely alive (*psychikos*). One born anew receives the Spirit, and becomes spiritual (*pneumatikos*—1 Cor. 2:13–15).

The moral order of the dominant system is a totality of carnal practices. It is a moral order "according to the law." This is the old order. The ethical order—the praxis of liberation that builds the reign of God—is the system of "spiritual" practices "according to (*kata*) the Spirit" of God. This is the new order, the new human being.

Just so, the poor according to the flesh are, merely, those lacking in goods, as an empirical, natural, bodily datum. In the order according to the flesh, in the moral system of domination, the poor are in their death, in their poverty, which is the fruit of sin. Precisely as so situated, the poor, like the innocent Job in his suffering, are not sinners. But the poor "according to the Spirit" (and these may be wealthy, like Moses, or poor, like Jesus of Nazareth, who belonged to the *'am ha'aretz*, the "people of the earth") are those the Spirit converts, moves, consecrates, launches into the world as prophets to evangelize the poor (Isa. 61:1; Luke 4:18). They are poor for the reign, for the sake of the reign (Matt. 6:19–34).

5.5 THE JERUSALEM PRINCIPLE

In the theology of the prophets, as in that of Jesus, in dialectical opposition to the categories of totality, world, flesh, Egypt, or Babylon, we find a series of correlative categories. To the world, the reign of God is opposed; to the flesh, the Spirit; to Egypt, the land of promise; to Babylon, the new Jerusalem. Or, abstractly: in dialectical opposition to the prevailing order of the established system stand exteriority and transcendence.

Confronted with the persecution and murder of Christians in the first century of our era, which took place at the hands of the imperialism of that age ("suffered under Pontius Pilate"), today other Christian-murdering empires carry on the Roman empire's tradition of sin. The author of the Book of Revelation has formulated an explicit political theology. Christians are murdered because they are "witnesses" ("martyrs") of the "heavenly Jerusalem," the "*new* Jerusalem"—called "new" lest it be confused with the "old" Jerusalem, the empirical one, the one that killed Jesus and was destroyed for its infidelity. The *new* City of God—and future Christendoms will be the "earthly city" of Cain, still claiming to be the City of God—is utopian. It comes from the future, and is built of the blood of the heroes, the saints, and the martyrs.

Why does the empire, yesterday as today, murder the heroes and martyrs? For the simple reason that, in proclaiming the new order—a future system of justice and satisfaction for the starving poor—they destroy consent. They shatter hegemony. They undermine the foundation of the prevailing morality: they obliterate its justification. The "new Jerusalem" is the project of liberation, the new homeland, the new land "where milk and honey flow."

The hope of the new Jerusalem is the "Jerusalem principle." It is a utopian Christianity that believes in the reign of God, hates the Prince of "this world" and his reign, and inaugurates a praxis of liberation where all will receive "on the basis of each one's need." But in order for Jerusalem to exist, obviously Babylon must be destroyed, and the poor, the heroes, the saints, and the martyrs rejoice at its fall: "Alleluia! Triumph, glory, and power to God! ... He has condemned the great prostitute ... and has lost count of the blood of her slaves" (Rev. 19:1–2).

5.6 UTOPIAN PRACTICES

Saint Paul spoke of "madness" (1 Cor 1:18–2:16): that which is absurd for the prevailing morality. For the dominant, present rationality, which dictates the true and the false (as does Karl Popper in his *The Open Society and Its Enemies*), the construction of the new Jerusalem is the absolute evil (because it calls in question the current system in its totality). Builders of the new Jerusalem are, for conservative groups, "prophets of hate," radical critics of the absurd, and the new Jerusalem is, for conservatives, the "utopia" that, wishing to improve the current state of affairs, destroys all.

The poor set out on their journey. They pass *beyond* Egypt's frontier, they transcend the horizon of the system, they cross the barrier of death. Now there is nothing to follow, no one to heed, but the Lord. They have now embarked on the *nothing*-of-the-system, the non-being of the prevailing morality. They are on the road to the "wilderness." (Heb., *bamidbar*, "in the wilderness," is a theological category.) The "wilderness" (Matt. 3:3; 4:1) is exteriority, the expanse over which domination no longer has sovereignty. As a people, the Israelites have escaped the reach of the *power* of sin: "The Israelites marched from Ramses to Sukkoth" (Exod. 12:37). "The Lord walked before them" (Exod. 13:21).

Praxis, as an action and a relationship of the members of the community, of a people that has transcended the morality of sin (as Nicaragua, after its 1979 revolution, became a "new land"—an earthly one, it is true, but nevertheless a historical "new land"), is utopian, meaningless, absurd, mad, subversive, destructive, *danger-*

ous for the system left behind, left in the past: "But they cried out the more: Crucify him!" (Matt. 27:23). His physical elimination was necessary, for it had thrown the "realism" of the dominant classes (the "elders, priests, and scribes," who, to their own advantage, acquiesced in Herod's inauthenticity and the Roman occupation) into a state of crisis.

The practices of the liberators, those complying with *ethical* demands, *have no meaning* for the system: "They ridiculed them" (Acts 17:32). The system just laughs. The Israelites, however, who have moved out into the wilderness, know that God is *with them*, Emmanu-el.

5.7 THE NEW ETHICAL CODE

There are no highways in the wilderness. One makes one's own way. The morality of Egypt, of the flesh, has been left behind, it is true. It has been left "in the past." But new demands arise, and these operate as a compass for the Israelites in their journey toward the promised land, the "new Jerusalem."

The emigrants traveling through the wilderness toward the future had no norms or requirements to guide them in blazing this *new* trail. The law of Egypt was no longer. But there was as yet no new law. They were a people without a law, without a new legality. "It is not good what you do" (Exod. 18:18), counsels the old father-in-law. But the *new* law will not be a "moral" code (and indeed, to the extent that it is "moralized" it becomes the old law all over again, and will have to be renewed once more). In fact, the seeming negatives, the prohibitions ("you shall *not* have other gods ... you shall *not* take the name of the Lord ... you shall *not* kill. You shall *not* commit adultery. You shall *not* steal"—Exod. 20:3–17) are implicitly positive injunctions. As negations of negations, they are basically affirmative. "You shall not make idols for yourself": to make idols for oneself is to deny God; to deny the idol is to assert God. "You shall not steal": to steal is to say no to the good of another; not to steal is to respect one's neighbor.

On the other hand, these *ethical* norms ("ethical" because they were not those of the dominators of a *moral* order, but of poor desert bedouins) could be transformed into a *moral* code:

Woe to you scribes and Pharisees, you frauds! You shut the doors of the kingdom of God in men's faces. ... You pay tithes on mint and herbs and seeds while neglecting the weightier matters of the law, justice and mercy and good faith... until retribution overtakes you for all the blood of the just ones shed on earth" [Matt. 23:13–35].

Over against this *morality* of domination, with its thousand precepts but not one jot of justice for the poor, Jesus establishes a new code, with new, ethical demands: "Blessed the poor, for theirs is the reign of heaven" (Luke 6:20 ff.). The Beatitudes are the *ethical* code par excellence. Jesus curses the *morality* of the dominators, the satisfied rich, those who laugh in "this world," the world "according to the flesh," and proclaims that the goodness, the absolute holiness of service to the poor, to the hungry, to all who suffer, are building up the reign of God.

5.8 THE POOR AS AGENTS OF THE REIGN OF GOD

The poor as the subject of poverty are the victims of evil, of sin. Their poverty is death, the fruit of domination and pillage on the part of the rich. But as the poor grow in awareness, they hear the voice of the other, the other poor among the people, and they are transformed into subjects, agents, of the reign—its primary builders, its principal protagonists.

Under the domination of the *moral* order of "this world," the poor frequently accept the structure of domination in a spirit of passivity. In this condition, that of passive domination, they are merely part of the "crowd." They belong to "the many," the masses, who have introjected the norms of the flesh. It was on them that Jesus of Nazareth "took pity" (Matt. 14:14).

It is precisely the sign of Jesus' messiahship that, when he is present, "the poor have the gospel preached to them" (Luke 7:22; Matt. 11:5). We do not read that the poor are to be "saved." Not being sinners, they are already saved, at least in their formality as term of the concrete relationship in which they are poor. (They can be sinners, or "rich," in another relationship, if they dominate "others.") The order of "salvation" is a function of "good will," of receiving "sufficient grace" to be saved. The order of "evangelization," of hearing the preaching of the gospel, is on another level. The poor are evangelized or receive the "good news" in which they are "happy," "blessed" by God, and so on, because they are poor. Thus they come to awareness that they are the *subject*, the agent, of the reign of God, but only insofar as they are active participants in its construction—only to the extent that they understand, with Job, that their poverty and suffering are the fruit, not of *their* sin, but of the sin of domination. "The dead rise" (Luke 7:22): the passive objects of the domination of sin, the poor, have become the active subjects of the reign.

In the system of "this world," the subject or agent is the Dragon (Satan), who has given his power to the Beast (the dominating state, the order of sin) and to its angels. The poor are the *nothing*, the non-being, of "this world." And it is in virtue of their not having been stained in "this world" that they are "subjects" of the reign of God.

5.9 "ETHICITY" OF THE PRAXIS OF LIBERATION

Thus if there is a *morality* (see 3.7) of the praxis of the prevailing system, there is an "ethicity" of the praxis of liberation. In the dominant system, an act is *morally* good when it complies with prevailing norms. An act will be *ethically* good in situations of greater difficulty, and principally when it is in conformity with the conscience of the agents of liberation themselves. Heroes and great critics of domination often throw out the baby with the bathwater. They discard *ethics* because they have discovered the inhumanity of the prevailing *morality*. Legitimacy and respect must be restored to the heroes and martyrs, and to ethics.

In their journey through the wilderness, the Israelites, a people without a law (or with the *new* law of absolute demands, not always mediated) frequently wonder: Are we doing the right thing? Is this the correct way to act? Is God with us? In other words they mistrust the holiness or *goodness* of an act because it is inconsistent with the morality that they have always been taught. They will suffer the ongoing temptation to change their minds and "return to Egypt" (Exod. 13:17). And behold the moment of uncertainty: What ought I to do? (Luke 18:18). In the absence of prevailing, established, dominant criteria, only the authority of the prophet is valid (Luke 20:2)—a confidence and trust that the right manner of action will appear in the need to serve the poor, the other.

Even in the moment of praxis "without a prevailing law," however, there are clear and absolute principles, norms that will be valid everywhere and always. The first of these is: "Free the poor," as an imperative of practical reason.

In *any* system of domination, of sin, there are those who are, by definition, dominated—the poor. The discovery of these poor here and now, in the concrete, belongs to the ethical conscience, to an ethical awareness. All praxis directed to the liberation of the poor is basically good. There are conditions that will limit the goodness of this praxis and even render it unjust. But the "liberation of the poor," and not compliance with *moral* norms (as with the praxis of the Pharisees), is the practical principle of the *ethicity* of praxis (Matt. 12:1–8).

5.10 THE NEW JERUSALEM

Jerusalem is the symbol of the reign of God that is beyond history. But it is also a metaphor for the new order beyond the prevailing system of domination. The new Jerusalem is historical, then, as well. In the historical new Jerusalem, the journey through the wilderness, and the tenuous occupation of the promised land by the people of God, are at an end (see 1.9, 1.10, 4.9).

The death of Moses is another symbol of this transition from one historical era to another. "Go! Cross the Jordan, with this whole people, on the way to the land that I shall give you" (Josh. 1:2). Similarly, "the dispossessed of their land will go up from Babylon to Jerusalem" (Ezra 1:11). In Jerusalem, the promised land, the new order, "the people went to eat and drink, send portions, and organize a great festival" (Neh. 8:12). Now in its land, the people had to organize a new life. First, like Nicaragua, besieged from the North by the Contras and the soldiers of the Empire, they had to build a wall that would protect them. "Let us rebuild the walls of Jerusalem," they said (Neh. 2:17). Now that the new order prevailed, "those who had returned to Jerusalem from captivity began the work of building the temple" (Ezra 3:8). God was with the liberated people. There were no poor. All lived in justice, in community, in the covenant, and all their needs were satisfied.

The heavenly Jerusalem, which will come only at the end of days, once and for all, as the bride of the Lamb that was slain, will no longer be able to fall into sin. But the earthly Jerusalem can do so. It can close in upon itself idolatrously, and let the promises fall into oblivion. In this case the land of promise would be transformed dialectically into a new Egypt: "Jerusalem, Jerusalem, who kill the prophets and stone those sent to you!" (Matt. 23:37). "They came to Jerusalem. He entered the temple and began to cast out the buyers and sellers. . . . 'You have made it a robbers' cave'" (Mark 11:15–17). The task will have to be begun again and again, until the end of time.

CONCLUSIONS

Community ethics, which is distinguished from the prevailing moral order as Jerusalem from Babylon, is the ethics in force during the time of passage from the former land to the land of promise. Morality is not ethics. The builders of the new order are the prophets, the poor, in accordance with the demands of the Spirit. Thus they build the utopian city, the *new* Jerusalem, the future, a more just order. The praxis of those delivered from the hand of the pharaoh into the wilderness is "madness" for "this world." It is absurd, it is senseless. All along the course of their journey from slavery to the future, the Israelites have a *new*, ethical code. It does not consist in the norms of a dominant morality. Its demands are those of an ethics of the liberation of the poor. Under this ethics, the poor are evangelized. They receive the "good news" of their hope: they are transformed into the "subject" of the active construction of the reign of God. The "ethicity" of the goodness or holiness of their praxis no longer depends on the old law. Theirs is the very praxis of the prophet, of a pilgrim people, whose norm is a living norm, the new law. Yet the new earthly Jerusalem—not the eschatological one, which will gleam with a glory that will never fade—can still be totalized. It can still constitute itself an old Egypt, by way of a breach with the covenant. And once more a mere moral order will prevail.

Chapter 6

Sensibility, Justice, and Sacramentality

6.1 STATE OF THE QUESTION

I have now treated the five basic problems of community ethics. We are in possession of a foundation upon which to erect all our subsequent discourse. In view of the importance of these five topics, however, I should like to go back over some of them. They all involve some aspect of corporality ("bodiliness"—see 1.3), satisfaction (in general terms—1.7), death (2.8), the flesh (3.4), or the satisfaction of the poor in particular (4.9). That is, they all deal in some way with *sensibility*.

We read stories in the newspaper every day about the cruel starvation of so many of our brothers and sisters in Ethiopia and the Sudan; we read of the human rights violations documented by Amnesty International; we read of the stifling heat of the desert or the cold of other regions; we read of the poverty of the beggars in Paris and London, of the poverty of the peripheral countries, the dominated classes, and so on.

We read in holy scripture:

Come! You have my Father's blessing! Inherit the kingdom prepared for you from the creation of the world. For I was hungry and you gave me food, I was thirsty and you gave me drink. I was a stranger and you welcomed me, naked and you clothed me. I was ill and you comforted me, in prison and you came to visit me [Matt. 25:34–6].

Let us return to this theme. After all, this is the prime criterion of Christian ethics, of the ethics of liberation. This is the absolute criterion of the goodness or evil of actions, of praxis. Bodiliness, the "flesh," is what *feels*, suffers, sorrows, enjoys. If the flesh had no dignity, then we might renounce it. But as we see, it has a central place in Christian ethics.

6.2 HELLENISM, GNOSTICISM, AND MANICHEISM

In the early Christian centuries, there were three currents of thought or mentality that disparaged corporality, the flesh, and sensibility, as evil.

First of all, the Indo-European mentality, and Greek thought in particular, spurned the "body" as the origin of evil. This was the prevailing attitude from the pre-Socratics onward, but it reached its zenith in Plato and Plotinus. "Matter is the original sin," said Plotinus, inasmuch as, it seemed to him, matter limited, determined, partialized the "soul" of the universe as "my" soul, inclining it by its desires to petty, selfish, low things.

Secondly, Hindu and Buddhist thought took a similar tack, preaching a morals of "liberation from the body" that would leave one free to pursue the contemplation of divine things—a goal that only an aristocracy could reasonably aspire to.

Thirdly, somewhat later, the Gnostics (including the Docetists) came on the Christian scene. For the Gnostics, the body was the result of the sin of one of the "eons" (the eternal substances in the complex structure of beliefs of these early heretics)—namely, Sophia, wisdom. The body was evil. Jesus must have only seemed to have a body, then, as otherwise the Word would have taken on evil. Irenaeus of Lyons valiantly combated the Gnostics.

The Manicheans, disciples of a third-century A.D. Zoroastrian called Mani, held matter to be an external principle along with God, and the origin of the evil that imprisoned the soul in its body. "Cursed be those who formed my body and enchained my soul," runs an ancient Manichean text.

6.3 DIGNITY OF THE "FLESH"

As we have seen, "flesh" stands for the human, natural order—whatever is not Spirit (see 3.4). However, "flesh" has a positive meaning, as well, in Hebreo-Christian thought. "The Word became flesh" (John 1:14), the evangelist tells us—not "body."

Hebrew and Christian thought asserts the *unity* of the human being. We are not composed of two distinct substances, "body" and "soul." Earliest Christian thought refers to the entire human being as "flesh." (If the word "body"—*soma*, in Greek—sometimes appears instead, it too means "flesh," the whole human being, body and soul, and is used only because the Greek version of the Old Testament known as the Septuagint often translated the Hebrew *basar*, "flesh," as *soma*, "body.") The "flesh" is the whole human being, then, the human order of things, the history and society of human beings. The "soul" (Heb., *nefesh*) is simply the "life" of the flesh, and not a spiritual substance—which latter, with its co-principle, the body, would constitute the human being for the dualists, such as the Indo-Europeans. The "person," the flesh, the "face," is an indivisible "someone." A body-soul dualism is unacceptable to the deepest and most central thinking of the prophetic tradition.

For the Greeks and other Indo-Europeans, the "soul" was divine, uncreated, eternal, immortal, incorruptible. Hence the apologists would insist that "only God is increate and incorruptible. . . . For this cause souls die and are punished" (Justin, *Dialogue with Trypho*, 5). With the dying of the "flesh," human beings die utterly.

The "flesh," the "flesh" of the other, his or her "face" (*persona*— see 1.3), is the only sacred thing in creation. It is second only to God in worth and dignity. Hence everything bound up in any way with "flesh" (sexuality, sensibility, pleasure, and so on) is good, worthy, and positive, not to be rejected. Only sin in the flesh, which occurs when the flesh idolatrously totalizes itself, is to be rejected (3.4, 2.3).

6.4 SENSIBILITY: THE "SKIN"

I now address the central moment in our reflection—a point that, in the moral systems of domination, frequently passes unnoticed. But it is the very springboard of the discourse of the ethics of liberation.

By "sensibility" ("sensitivity") here I do not mean only the sensible cognitive faculty, the "senses"—sight, hearing, and so on—as a means of the constitution of the "sense" or meaning of what appears in the world (referring to the intuitive moment). No, here I wish to stress *sensing* itself—the actual sensation of pain, hunger, cold, and so on, or indeed of pleasure, satisfaction, empirical happiness. Our subjectivity is wounded in deepest, most secret, intimacy when something wounds our "skin"–when our corporality is assaulted in its constitution by some trauma. By "sensibility," then, I mean the resonance of, the impact on, our capacity for "contentment," for suffering, for joy or sorrow in reaction to some stimulus irrupting from the world around us.

Every living being, even the unicellular (such as the amoeba), has an outer frontier that unifies its living structure and separates it from its "medium," from that which is "outside": a membrane. In the human being, this membrane, which may have any of a very wide variety of structures, is called the "skin" (here taken to include, interiorly, the various mucous membranes, or, externally, the cornea of the eye, the eardrum, the taste buds, and so on). Through this "skin" we "feel" what comes from without—often enough either as pleasure, enjoyment, or satisfaction, or as pain, disgust, or the suffering of a traumatism.

Life seeks to protect itself from danger. Life exults in the presence of its fulfillment, and a degree of this fulfillment is to be had in "sensibility," which acts as a red or green light signaling its own fulfillment or nonfulfillment.

6.5 INJUSTICE AND SENSIBILITY

Hedonists—or for that matter the Stoics, the Epicureans, even Buddhists—habitually pronounced for or against "pleasure." I am not speaking of pleasure here. I am speaking of "sensibility." And the "sensibility" of which I speak is that of *others*. What is under consideration here is *their* hunger, thirst, homelessness, cold, illness—the "negatives of sensibility" that sin produces.

Sin is domination over the other. Its fruit is the poverty of that other. Poverty is a broad concept, and denotes the negative side of the sensibility of the other: his or her hunger, thirst, homelessness, cold, and the like—anything constituting the other's poverty under its formality of the result of sin (which has dispossessed that other of his or her food, drink, home, clothing, health, and so on). If the "flesh" is something positive, something worthy and good, then hunger, thirst, homelessness, cold, and so on, will be evil. And their evil is not only physical, but ethical, political, communal, as well.

These things are evil as the fruit of sin, of injustice.

The suffering of the starving (who, after all, starve only because they have been robbed) or of the tortured (as Jesus among the Roman soldiers or hanging from the cross as his requital for having committed himself to the evangelization of the poor) is experienced in the "skin," in the mucous lining of the stomach or in the muscles of one's members. The "flesh" cries out, suffers, undergoes pain. Thus "sensibility" serves notice, in the just who suffer oppression (as it did with Job),of the reality of sin—the sin of the other subjectivity, the other pole of the relationship, as dominator, robber, torturer. Sin, the praxis of dominators (and their satisfaction, because it is by virtue of their sin that their sensibility now enjoys the good of another), appears as pain (in the sensible subjectivity of the oppressed).

Thus the pain of the flesh, in its sensibility, constitutes the "last judgment" of any human praxis. Jesus' expression, "I was hungry and you ...," capsulizes the sensitization in the oppressed of the *sense* of the praxis of the dominator and the just, respectively.

6.6 ASCETICAL MORALITY, CORPOREAL ETHICS

All moralities of domination (see 3.2) are ascetical. Their end and aim is "liberation from the body." The body is of no value. That is, the body of the *other* is of no value. A morality of domination may be defined as insensibility to the sensibility or pain of another. All ethics of liberation is corporeal: it is affirmation of the flesh, of sensibility; it is sensitivity to the pain of another (when that pain is the result of the sin of domination).

The ascetical morality of domination begins with the enunciation that the "spiritual"—not Spirit, but the mental, the immaterial, the "good intention," and so on—the soul, is sacred, and "virtuous"; the material, the bodily, the sexual, the sensible, however, is of no value whatever, but "vicious." Accordingly, nothing transpiring on this negative level—the realm of the body—is of any importance: daily manual labor, torture at the hands of a Latin American dictator or CIA trainee, and so on. Nothing is of any worth except in the light of eternal values, or from the perspective of the "spiritual" and cultural virtues of the soul. This is the morality of domination.

The ethics of liberation is "fleshly"—if by "flesh" we understand the *whole* human being in his or her indivisible unity. Thus there is no such thing as a human "material body"; there is only "flesh." Nor is there such a thing as an incorporeal soul; there is only "flesh." "The Word became flesh"—neither body nor soul separately.

We need only restore the human "composite" to its authentic unity, its concrete oneness, and behold, our neighbor's pain becomes a sign. Now this pain glows like a red light. We see that something has gone wrong. Suddenly this pain is a sign of sin—or at least of the urgent imperative that we go to the aid of this neighbor of ours, as did the Samaritan. Sensitivity (or com-miseration, com-passion— the capacity to suffer with another) to the pain of another becomes the very criterion of praxis. The criterion is a "corporeal" one: "I was hungry. ..." The commitment it calls for, however, is "spiritual": it is the Spirit that moves me to the service of my neighbor (see 4.5, 5.4).

6.7 EATING AND FOOD, RESIDING AND HABITATION, DRESSING AND CLOTHES

Sensibility reaps enjoyment from its satisfaction, from its act of consumption, from its use or possession of the products of the labor needed to produce them (see 1.7). This is the very life cycle intended by God. But between need and satisfaction a whole history takes place—the history of sin as the holocaust of life and the theft of the product of labor.

"I was hungry and you gave me *to eat*." Eating is an act of consumption, of destruction—for example, of bread. It is the moment when "the other" (the product) becomes my flesh. The flesh, revived, restored, revitalized, having incorporated that which it lacked in the moment of negativity, enjoys, is satisfied, because it *really* revives. Having declared its own death, in the form of hunger, now sensibility signals the reproduction of its life in the form of enjoyment, satisfaction.

At the same time, the enjoyment, the joy, of eating, dwelling, being clothed (against the cold, for example) never materializes in the absence of the thing, the object of production, that will negate the correlative need. But that thing, that object, that product is the fruit of toil, and is distributed under the auspices of social institutions. In capitalism the object of consumption is possessed in return for a payment of money (11.8). Persons may be hungry; if they have no money, they stay hungry. My impecuniousness does nothing for my sensibility (my hunger). I must simply endure the ethical injustice. And prevailing social morality can find no one to blame.

Food, housing, clothing are objects of consumption. But they are signs of goodness, as well, when they are the product of the service, the justice, the praxis, of liberation (James 2:15; our 17.4). They are signs of the "grace" of the other: they are sensible, material signs for sensibility. That is, they are the bestowal, the gift of the hero and the prophet. They are the "milk and honey" of the land of promise. "I am the bread of life" (John 6:48).

6.8 CULTURAL POVERTY

It is not only in their coporality or fleshliness, their sensibility, their deprivation of material consumer goods, that the poor suffer. They suffer as well in their lack of other goods. Life asserts itself through our natural organs, such as our eyes, our hands, or the body parts that allow us to move in space. Living beings are equipped with natural instruments or organs to perform the vital functions of sight, manipulation, locomotion, and so on.

Human beings, however, have learned to extend these natural organs, by means of artificial, historical, cultural organs. These organs consist in those objects of production *by means of which* natural activities are extended or otherwise enhanced. In the activity of eating, the knife extends the teeth, the fork the hands. The hammer hits harder than does a fist. These products are "cultural instruments"—the extension of our own bodiliness.

Not only have the poor been deprived of their bread, their housing, their vesture—their consumer goods—they have been robbed of their productive goods as well, the tools they need to reproduce their life. They have no land of their own. They have no labor of their own initiative. They have only their suffering *skin* and their marketable labor. Today we might hear not only, "I was hungry," but "I was out of work and you did not help me, I was landless and you exploited me, I had no tools," and so on.

The lack of culture (18.6) as instrumental totality, of technology as the extension of corporality, is likewise the cause of pain, suffering, and inequality. The totality of culture is "flesh," and the poor suffer its want.

6.9 IT IS THE FLESH THAT RISES

The English translation of the Apostles' Creed says: "I believe in the resurrection of the *body*." This is not a true translation of the Latin Apostles' Creed: "I believe in the resurrection of the flesh." Nor is it the formulation of the Nicene Creed: "We look for the resurrection of the *dead*." Is the meaning of all these enunciations identical?

In original Hebreo-Christian teaching, it is "the flesh" that rises, "the dead" that rise. "Flesh" and "the dead" in that teaching stand for the *whole* human being. Thus the more primitive formulations indicate that it is the *whole* human being who has died, and the *whole* human being who will rise—not just the body. Socrates, the Greek sage who believed in the immortality of the soul, was joyful in the face of approaching death, as Plato tells us in his *Apologia* (of Socrates). If the body is the origin of evil, death will be the origin of happiness, and a return to life among the gods. By contrast, Jesus was seized with terror and anguish in the face of death (Luke 22:40–45). Why? Because death is the death of the *whole* human being.

For Christianity, the "flesh" is a positive thing. Its pain is something that must be defeated, its hunger something that must be quenched. Hence the reign of God preached in Christianity will be a resurrection of the flesh. For those who disparage materiality or fleshly sensibility, this is simply absurd. Thus the Greeks ridiculed Paul's talk of the "resurrection of the dead" (Acts 17:32). To what end could we possibly need a body in the company and happiness of the gods? What good is the body after death if the soul is immortal? (Of course, the Greeks, who were slaveholders, required their slaves to toil in their bodies. But these bodies were of no actual worth—for the Greeks.)

Maintenance of the doctrine of the "resurrection *of the flesh*" is essential, then. And it is essential not only as eschatological doctrine (regarding a life after death), but as historical ethical doctrine as well. In attributing to the flesh its whole dignity, this doctrine calls for the stilling of its "hunger" as the criterion of goodness and holiness.

6.10 SACRAMENTALITY

Classically, a sacrament is an "outward sign of grace." On its materiality rests its capacity to "signify." But a certain aversion to bodiliness has forgotten the sacramental corporality of ethics.

The water of baptism, the chrism of any consecretation—and most of all the eucharistic bread—speak to us once more of sensibility (see 1.6, 4.9), of sacramentality. The real is not defined as the object of thought. The real is anything constituting the object of sensibility, as Kant and Feuerbach have shown us. When I feel, touch, anything, I experience the reality of that thing (Luke 24:38–43).

If Christianity were an intimistic, individual, "spiritualistic" (in the sense of incorporeal) religion, a religion of the "good intention" alone, without objective parameters, without community—then why sacrament? A morality of domination will either deny sacrament, through a negation of bodiliness, or fetishize it (as if the sacraments worked magically and of themselves, regardless of the adequacy of one's subjective, individual disposition).

The sacramentality of the Christian life establishes the essential importance of sensibility, of the reality of the "bread," or the *fruit of toil*, when it comes to the *life* of the laborer. A prerequisite of the offering of bread to God is the objective existence of a community that has satisfied the needs of its members. Sacramentality gathers in its embrace the totality of human life—its politics, its economics, its erotics, its pedagogy, and so forth—as a sign recognizable by sensibility, a sign arising out of the satisfaction, through justice, of corporeal sensibility. Sacramentality and sensibility are partners.

CONCLUSIONS

On the present subject I have found it necessary to retrace my steps, and bring together what I had already said on a key topic frequently forgotten by satisfied dominators. My guideline has been, "I was hungry and you gave me to eat." Many heretics (such as the Gnostics, the Manicheans, the Albigensians, certain charismatics, and others) forgot the dignity of the "flesh"—as has a whole modern capitalist culture, beginning with Descartes. Sensibility, as pain or pleasure, the "skin" as the locus of cold or torture, remind us that injustice, sin, the oppression of the poor, crucify those poor in their sensibility. The morality of dominators denies the value of the body precisely in order that it may continue to dominate it and exploit it without a feeling of guilt. The ethics of liberation appreciates the "flesh," asserting its faith in its resurrection and mobilizing a praxis calculated to feed the hunger of the hungry and deliver the instruments of work to the poor. It understands that sensibility is the road to Christian sacramentality.

Chapter 7

Moral Legality and Ethical Illegality

7.1 STATE OF THE QUESTION

Let us now return to a topic already treated—the moral and the ethical (see 3.6, 3.7, 5.3, 5.7). This deserves to be reviewed at this point.

Every day we read of alleged thieves or murderers on trial. We also become aware that terrorist groups are sentenced as political prisoners; priests and nuns or lay persons who have committed themselves to the cause of the poor are jailed, sentenced, even judicially murdered. How are we to discern the legality, the lawfulness of these judicial acts?

We read in holy scripture:

> What occasion is there then for boasting? It is ruled out. By what law, the law of works? Not at all! By the law of faith. For we hold that a man is justified by faith apart from observance of the law [Rom 3:27–8].

> When we were in the flesh, the sinful passions roused by the law worked in our members and we bore fruit for death. Now we have been released from the law—for we have died to what bound us—and we serve in the new spirit, not the antiquated letter [Rom. 7:5–6].

If we apply our categories appropriately, and correctly distinguish the scope and setting of the various letters of the New Testament, then these passages from Saint Paul's Letter to the Romans, both so rightly appreciated by Luther, become consistent with the texts of the Letter of James that are so heavily emphasized by Catholics. "What good is it to anyone to say he has faith if he has not works?" (James 2:14).

7.2 SOME NECESSARY DISTINCTIONS

I shall continue my practice of making some distinctions at the beginning of a chapter. Here it will only be a matter of reviewing some distinctions I have already indicated.

"Illegal" or "unlawful" means opposed to law. An action is unlawful when it opposes a law promulgated for the purpose of the concrete application of prevailing "morality," moral norms, or social institutions (see 3.2). "Legal" or "lawful," on the other hand, denotes anything found to be in compliance with prevailing law, which has at its disposal the coercive power of such "legal" institutions as the army and the police.

The hero (see 7.6, 9.3) refuses to comply with prevailing laws. Washington opposed English laws; San Martín, Bolívar, and Hidalgo opposed Spanish laws; Comandante Borge opposed the laws of the Somoza dynasty; Jesus opposed the Herodian, Roman, and temple laws or prescriptions. Heroes, then, will be "outlaws." Their "outlawry" is a sign of their goodness, their holiness, in refusing to comply with oppressive, unjust, anti-human laws. In serving the poor, Christians frequently oppose the dominant legality. The important thing is not the law (for example, laws pertaining to the Sabbath) but human beings (the poor as persons).

However, lest we forget: what is unlawful for the prevailing legality of the dominant order is *lawful* in terms of the law of the poor, the law of a people en route to liberation. Hidalgo was proclaimed a heretic by a faculty of theology in 1811, and was excommunicated by the bishops of Mexico. His praxis, however, was *lawful*, good, proper, in terms of the *future legality* of a new homeland, the "promised land" (Mexico no longer as a Spanish colony but as an independent country).

7.3 THE LAW OF MORALITY

Philosophers and theologians have distinguished many kinds of laws. They speak of the natural law, positive law, the law of nations (*jus gentium*) or international law, divine law, and so on. They have not, however, made these distinctions in terms of the theology of the New Testament and in light of current Latin American needs, as I attempt to do in these pages.

Positive law is a norm of praxis promulgated by those who wield political power. Of course, if they exercise power, they will be the dominant, dominating classes or strata. All positive law, then, as juridical ordination, is potentially ambivalent. It can be unjust, as Thomas Aquinas himself expressly notes. Prevailing law cannot, therefore, constitute the absolute criterion of goodness, holiness, or justice.

Hence, our theologians and philosophers have held, "natural law," or what is demanded by nature—what is dictated by God as creator—will furnish a more adequate foundation for judging the rightness or wrongness of an action. But the problem remains how to determine this "natural" law concretely and positively. Frequently the prevailing order has simply been projected as "nature." Thus in bourgeois society private property has come to be regarded as a right guaranteed by "natural law," despite the contrary opinion of the church Fathers from the fourth century onward or that of Thomas Aquinas in the age of feudalism.

Jesus never appealed to a "natural law." The Greeks or Romans, the Indo-Europeans, posited law as the foundation of all things, by reason of their persuasion that the legality of the gods, of the natural cosmos, and of human polity were identical. This legal fetishism (which in reality, as we have seen, simply projected the prevailing order of a slave society as *natural*, as for example in Aristotle) was simply a tool for hegemonic domination.

7.4 PAUL AGAINST MORAL LEGALITY

For Paul, the order of law (morality) is opposed to the order of faith (ethics). Let us see how this is to be explained. We need only apply categories we have already examined.

Paul counterposes the "regime of law" to the "regime of grace" (Rom. 6:15), the order of death to the order of life, of the new spirit, of faith. The order of law (morality) has norms, a foundation, and a legality. Compliance with the law does not "save," however, for the law represents an old order, that of the first covenant. It represents the "old human being," or "Adam." No matter the extent of compliance with all its (moral) precepts, that order has no capacity to bestow the life of the Spirit.

On the other hand, "the promise depends on faith" (Rom. 4:16). Without faith there is no promise. That is, the promise will remain ineffective. What is faith? Faith is "the anticipation of what is hoped, proof of realities unseen" (Heb. 11:1). In other words, faith is an ethical tension toward the future order, toward the reign of God (both in the here and now, and beyond time). The reign to which faith aspires is the one actualized after the resurrection (both here and now, and after biological death). Hence "in dying to what had bound us, we remain *free* from the law" (Rom. 7:6). We are free of the law, liberated from the "moral" order. We have left Egypt, Babylon, the reign of "this world" behind.

For Paul, the law, sin, and death pertain to the "moral" order (see 3.6, 3.7), that of the "flesh." Faith, grace, and life constitute the ethical order, the order *beyond*, the order beyond Babylon (3.5). It is faith, not *moral* works, that saves.

7.5 ETHICAL PRAXIS AND FAITH

Paul rejects Pharisaical Judaism (as does Luther, who rightly criticizes Latin Christendom for failing to do so). Paul insists that works performed under the law (of the prevailing, dominating *moral* system) do not save. James, for his part, is dealing with another reality. (Thus he does not contradict Paul or Luther.) Faith does not save, either, nor hope, nor the currency of the promise, unless these be accompanied by an *ethical* praxis (no longer a *moral* praxis, such as has prevailed in the past, under a regime of domination) of effective service to the poor in the construction of the new order (see 4.5).

In the *moral* system of domination it was hope, it was faith in the reign, the future promised order, that saved. Now, however, *in the new order*, "what good is it to someone to say he has faith if he does not have works? ... Suppose a brother or sister has nothing to put on and is going without daily sustenance, and one of you tells him or her: God be with you, keep warm, good luck!—but without giving him or her the necessary for the body?" (James 2:14, 16). After all, "the demons, too, believe." But they cannot build the reign of God.

In the order of law, *moral* works corroborate the law. After all, they are founded on it, just as are sin and death. Only faith saved *there*. Today, by contrast, when one has died to the death of sin, when it is the *ethical* demands of service to the poor and the building of the reign that are in force, hope or faith in the reign no longer save. What saves now is the objective, "practical" (praxis) construction of that reign of God.

That is, what saves now is service to the poor. The *ethical* praxis of liberation begins with faith and hope, and actualizes them. The *moral* praxis of the law, however lawful that praxis, and however it might fulfill that (moral) law, is a praxis that stands in relation with sin and death. *Ethical* practice, by contrast, is founded on faith, and actualizes that faith.

7.6 LAWFULNESS OF THE PROPHET AND HERO

The prophets and heroes so frequently sentenced or executed are condemned or executed under the law. They are "outlaws."

The moral order is founded on "good conscience." Hence the champions and beneficiaries of that order declare: "Had we lived in the time of our fathers, we should not have been their accomplices in the murder of the prophets" (Matt. 23:30). They may as well have said, had they lived in the time of Hidalgo or Morelos, Farabundo Martí or Lumumba, they would not have murdered them. But they do as much today in Central America: they murder the Sandinistas and Farabundistas:

> Behold for this I shall send you prophets, sages, and lawyers: some you will kill and crucify, others you will scourge in your synagogues and pursue them from town to town. And so upon you will fall all the blood shed on earth, from the blood of the just Abel to the blood of Zachary [Matt. 23:34–5].

Or the blood of Bishop Enrique Angelelli in Argentina or Archbishop Oscar Romero in El Salvador.

The prophet and the hero, still together and confused with one another (as we shall see in 9.3), are murdered or persecuted (see 3.10, 4.10) because they proclaim the end of "this world," of sin, of the prevailing "morality." But in opposing, not a *part* of the law (as the thief, whose theft actually corroborates the validity of the system), but the *totality* and very foundation of the law, they stand outside the structure, lawless, illegal, an *outlaw*. "He has blasphemed. ... What say you? ... to the death!" (Matt. 26:65–6).

The one who has been called, summoned, converted to inaugurate the new order, the new Jerusalem beyond the law, must know how to endure the imputation of outlawry, the charge of "immorality" and subversion: "We have established that this one goes about subverting our nation" (Luke 23:2).

7.7 THE ABSOLUTE PRINCIPLE OF ETHICS

The new legality is based on a new law, which in turn rests entirely on an absolute (not relative), yet concrete (not abstract) principle.

We have already broached this question, in 5.9, above. But I should like to examine it more in depth. The criterion or principle of ethical lawfulness, and moral unlawfulness, is the one I have enunciated above: "Liberate the poor."

An *absolute* principle is contradistinguished from a relative one. A relative principle is one that may be valid today but not tomorrow. An absolute principle governs praxis always and everywhere. Where there is sin (and the absolute non-existence of sin would entail its necessary non-existence, and thus an actually realized, post-historical reign of heaven), there must always be dominated, or poor. The existence of poor who in their death suffer the pain of sin (see 2.7, 2.8) indicates the necessity of the principle, "Liberate *the poor*."

"Liberate "*the poor*" is an injunction addressed to the poor as well—inasmuch as there are other poor, their neighbors, who constitute the locus of the performance of their own service (the fruit of evangelization—see 5.8). The principle "Liberate the poor" implies: (1) a totality, a prevailing *moral* system; (2) an *oppressor* (sinner), the agent of the act of domination; (3) someone just (at least where the relationship of oppressor-oppressed is concerned) who is being treated unjustly.

At the same time, "Liberate *the poor*" presupposes: (4) the importance of keeping account of the mechanisms of sin; (5) the ethical duty of dismantling these mechanisms; (6) the necessity of constructing an escape route from the system; (7) the obligation to build the new system of justice. We are dealing, then, with a dangerous *responsibility.*

7.8 PRINCIPLES DERIVED FROM THE ETHICO-COMMUNAL PRINCIPLE

The absolute ethical principle is respect for the dignity or holiness of the human person, in every place and time. In the concrete, the person of the "rich" cannot be respected "*as* rich"; it is the person of the poor, "*as* poor" or dominated, that calls for respect and a praxis of justice.

In a capitalist society (where workers have no other way to reproduce their life except through the mechanism of wages), or indeed in existing socialist regimes (where it is impossible to eliminate a labor market, hence impossible to eliminate wages as a mechanism), the *right to employment* is directly linked to the absolute right of the poor to life, to existence, to their liberation.

When workers actually earn a wage (the value of their capacity expressed in terms of money—see 11.7, 11.8), then these poor have a right to life, through the possession and consumption of the *necessary basic goods*; food, clothing, housing, health, and the like (Matt. 25:42–3), for themselves, their families, and their children. A society that cannot supply workers with these necessary goods by way of money earned as wages is an unjust, dominating society. It has caught the worker in a structure of sin.

But over and above the necessary basic goods, we find other goods to be necessary as well, so that they too constitute the object of the inalienable rights of the poor (as worthy human persons). I refer to *cultural goods*: science, art, information—minimal cultural objects. And all these goods are "human goods"—that is, the objects of a *free will* (see 17). Realistic, rational, "feasible" planning is opposed neither to freedom nor to democracy. Ethics does not trample on any human rights that may happen to have been included in a moral structure. Rather it establishes them (Matt. 5:17–20).

7.9 ETHICO-COMMUNAL LAW

The illegality of prophets and heroes is not absolute and everlasting. "They act in the manner of those who go to be judged by a law of free men" (James 2:12). How can a free person be subject to law?

For those who have abandoned the hypocritical order of the dominator's social morality, there is the new "law of the Reign" (James 2:8). This law is founded on love: "One who says: I love God, while he hates his brother, is a liar, for one who loves not his brother whom he sees cannot love God whom he does not see" (1 John 4:20). Love of neighbor, of the other as other (see 1.4), is the new law, the *ethical* and *communal* law par excellence. But the demands or concrete content of the *new* law are not written once and for all. The new law can always adopt new content, in accordance with the occasion.

The "association of free persons," free from the past system of oppression—free from subjection to the Prince of this world and his prevailing social legality — is now the subject of the ethical and *communal* legality being constructed in the course of the journey through the wilderness (from Egypt to the promised land, from Babylon to Jerusalem, from the moment of Jesus' resurrection to the parousia). The exigencies or norms of the new legality are the Beatitudes, and their observance constitutes, in the eyes of the world, the "paradox of ethicity." Under the regime of the new ethical, communal legality, Jesus—and the prophets and heroes—can face torture (Mark 15:16–20) and even death (Luke 23:46) in peace (1 Pet. 4:12–19).

In the times in which we live, the prophets, the martyrs, and the heroes must be able to recognize the difference between the prevailing moral legality of the dominator, and communal ethical legality or the legality of liberation. They must be able to endure the social illegality conferred upon them by a system of sin, and proclaim before the principalities and powers of "this world" the madness of the communal legality of the reign of God, the land of promise, the "new land where justice shall dwell" (2 Pet. 3:13).

7.10 WHEN JERUSALEM CAN BECOME BABYLON

And so we arrive in the promised land, the reign of community ethics. But now *ethical principles* and law have themselves become historical, concrete legality, and so are liable to relapse into the condition of a mere prevailing social *morality* (see 5.10).

For Immanuel Kant, author of the *Critique of Practical Reason*, the absolute criterion of practical goodness cannnot include any empirical, concrete content whatever. "Good" denotes the quality of the act that can be elevated to universality—that may ethically be performed by all persons finding themselves in the same circumstances. But the universality of this action depends on the judgment of the very agent who is to perform the praxis. Thus the way is open for a surreptitious elevation of the subject's (European or capitalistic) particularity to the status of universality (validity for every culture and system). With all the "good will" in the world, this subject can perform an objectively perverse action.

But in every human situation there are the poor, the oppressed, who constitute the correlative of sin and the domination of sin. *These here-and-now poor* are *concrete* persons, objectively determinable in real worlds, that of Aztecs, Incas, Chinese, Bantus, capitalists, socialists. There can be no innocent "mistaken identity." Everyone knows, in each *concrete* situation, who are poor and oppressed, who have fewer opportunities, goods, values, rights, and so on. Hence the principle, "Liberate the poor" is absolute (not relative), and nevertheless *concrete* (not universal—with a "universality" that in reality is only particularity with false claims to universality).

But the here-and-now poor can come to be the *there-and-then-rich*, the dominators, the sinful. If I continue to serve them after they have become dominators, let me not attempt to justify myself by saying, "I am still serving the *same persons!*" (which of course I may do in a morality of universality). Those same persons are no longer poor. The principle, "Liberate the poor," is *concrete* and historical. At every moment, then, one must go back and rediscover, *here and now*, the "new" poor.

CONCLUSIONS

Goodness and holiness are not a matter of legality. Jesus destroyed the *old* law, completely fulfilling it in the *new* law of a love that is not just any love, but a love called of-justice, *agape*—love for the other, the neighbor, the poor, *as* other. Many lawful acts are evil, because the laws they comply with are unjust. This is why Paul, as a good ex-Pharisee, opposed the elevation of the old law to the status of absolute principle of Christianity. Faith, hope, and love are the new law. Hence the mere works of the old law do not save. It is faith in the reign of God (as Luther taught) that saves. But *mere* hope, a mere faith-affirmation of the reign, is not enough. *Ethical* praxis (as James teaches) is necessary. The prophets and heroes were outlaws for the prevailing morality in their observance of the absolute, concrete principle, "Liberate the poor."

Chapter 8

Relationships of Producers and Praxis of the People

8.1 STATE OF THE QUESTION

There are those who hold that morality and ethics are essentially ideological. Thus morality and ethics would depend basically on laws, virtues, or superstructural demands (if the last-named category has any meaning). This is a false position. Morality and ethics consist basically in praxis—in real relationships among persons. Morality and ethics are both corporeal, carnal, fleshly. They are *infra*-structural elements (understanding by this term anything of an economic or productive nature, anything connected with life and corporality).

Every day the media carry news stories about workers, corporations, popular movements, and indigenous organizations.

We read in holy scripture:

> Are not the rich exploiting you? They are the ones who hale you into the courts and who blaspheme the noble name that has made you God's own. You are acting rightly, however, if you fulfill the law of the kingdom. Scripture has it, "You shall love your neighbor as yourself." But if you show favoritism, you commit sin. ... If a brother or sister has nothing to wear and no food for the day, and you say to them, "Good-bye and good luck! Keep warm and well fed," but do not meet their bodily needs, what good is that? [James 2:6–16].

Our entire reflection here must remain on the level of corporeal, material, bodily radicality, which is consonant with the greatest holiness, if by holiness we understand ethical perfection.

8.2 "SOCIAL" RELATIONSHIPS OF DOMINATION

When a shoemaker exchanges shoes for bread, a *relationship* between persons arises—a relationship between the shoemaker and the baker. The exchange constitutes a praxis (see 1.2). The production of the shoe or the bread is a *poiesis* (see 1.2, 11.2, 18.2).

These relationships need not be social relationships of domination. They may be communal (8.3). I call relationships between producers *social* relationships of domination when two persons engaged in the process of production are not in a state of equality, justice, and goodness. One of the producers dominates the other. This relationship, maintained in the process of production, is one of inequality, sin, domination (2.2, 3.2). Morality, in the sense of a system of concrete practices (3.6), is situated not only on the level of law (7.2ff.)—the plane of norms or requirements, virtues—but also on that of these real infrastructural, intercorporeal "practical" *social* relationships obtaining among producers themselves.

Even Marxist moralists frequently relegate morality to the ideological plane. Thus they reduce morals and morality to verbal formulations, to obligations of rights and law, to the imperatives of duty—all on an abstract, mental level of mere intention. I should like to register my explicit disapproval of this volatilization of the moral (and by implication, of the ethical). Social moral relationships are actual, infrastructural, practical relationships among producers, within actual, historical modes of production. It is here that the drama of morality (and ethics) is played out.

Because domination, sin, is the relationship that institutionally establishes a definite relationship between persons (2.5), morality is founded totally on praxis, and its norms or exigencies are but superstructural formulations of those antecedent, practical, social, moral relationships.

8.3 COMMUNITY RELATIONSHIPS

In the same way, when the shoemaker and the baker are living in *community*—whether in the utopian community of Jerusalem (1.1), or in our ecclesial base communities, which represent varying degrees of participation in that ancient ideal—and exchange their shoes and bread, they establish an ethical, *community* relationship.

I call relationships among producers—among the participants in a production process—*communal* in virtue of a practial relationship of two or more persons constituting, in justice and equality, without domination, an "association of free persons" (1.5, 1.6, 1.7, 1.9; James 2:12–13). The product of their work in community will belong to all of them—the practice that, according to the unanimous opinion of the Fathers of the Church, must have prevailed among human beings before original sin (2.6).

Ethics is not primarily or essentially a set of norms, obligations, and prophetic maxims—not even in the case of the Sermon on the Mount. Ethics requires, as antecedent condition of its possibility, the concrete, *real* life of the *community*, such as the one Jesus was in the process of founding with his Apostles. It was the praxis of that community that generated the norm, "Happy the poor!" In that community, *factually* and *really*, in *actual* community relationships, the poor were happy, satisfied, treated as persons. And from out of this concrete experience, ethical norms and requirements were derived.

Community relationships of justice, real ethical relationships (infrastructural relationships, in their status as relationships among producers—bodily relationships) are the essence and foundation of ethics, the real starting point of the ethico-prophetic critique. The critique as such may emerge on an ideological level. But it originates on an infrastructural, practical level: that of *community* relationships themselves.

8.4 WHAT IS "CLASS"?

Let us examine that specific instance of *social* relationships of domination (8.2) known as social class. As we know, the question of the "class struggle" (see chap. 16) is a hotly debated one in our time.

Before actually discussing the topic of social class, it will be in order to explain what is meant by it. Had it not been for "original" sin (2.5, 2.6)—if men and women had lived in community (1.5, 1.6)—there would have been no such thing as social class. Social class is the result of sin (16.3–4), in the sense that the dominated class, the poor (2.7), die in life (2.8). (And if there were no *dominated* class, there would be no classes at all, for the constitutive difference of the latter is domination, or a relationship of inequality among stable or institutional groups of persons.) Inequalities—as Rousseau ought to have indicated—are the fruit of sin. It is owing to sin that there are unequal classes.

A "class" is a stable group of persons who, within the practico-productive totality of society, perform a structural function—determined by the *productive process* (*Laborem Exercens*, 11–13)—in the division of labor, in the appropriation of the fruit of toil (11.6). Thus it is the *social* relationships of domination (2.2, 3.2) that determine the dominant and dominated classes. (There are also intermediate classes, auxiliary classes, and so on.) The Aztecs were divided into the dominant warrior classes and the peasants who paid tribute. It was the same with the Incas. Likewise in medieval European society: the feudal lords demanded tribute of the serfs. Today the owners of capital pay their workers a wage, in an unequal exchange of product and money (12.5).

The classes, then, are social relationships of domination inherent in the whole praxis-production process, inevitable in any tributary system—capitalistic, socialistic, or whatever. Each type of social relationship determines distinct social classes in each system.

8.5 WHAT IS MEANT BY "PEOPLE"?

A class is not a people. "People" is a category that will have to be determined with clarity and precision if we hope to be able to distinguish it from other concepts. The "popular question" has not been settled.

"People" is a more concrete, synthetic category than that of the more abstract, analytic "class." The term "people" is ambiguous. A whole nation may be called a "people"—for example, if it is engaged in a struggle with foreigners. This is the populist sense of the word "people": the dominant classes are part of the "people." Or the word "people" may denote only the *oppressed* of a nation, and the oppressing classes will not be part of the "people." I shall be using the word in this latter sense.

Thus a "people" is the "communal bloc" of a nation's oppressed. A people consists of the dominated classes (the working or industrial class, the campesino class, and so on). But it is also constituted of any human group that is either non-capitalistic or that performs class practices only sporadically (marginal groups, ethnic groups, tribal groups, and so on). This entire "bloc"—in Gramsci's sense— constitutes the people: a people is the historical "subject" or agent of the social formation of a given country or nation. The "Cuban people," the "Nicaraguan people," the "Brazilian people," and so forth, are composed of the persons who permeate the respective history of the various practico-productive totalities. Thus we have the pre-Hispanic Amerindians, the colonials, the neo-colonials, and even the members of post-capitalistic societies. Each of these groups is a people.

A people—in the sense of the oppressed classes of a nation— introjects and interiorizes, it is true, the ideology and culture of its dominators. Hence the necessity of evangelization (carried out by prophets—9.3, 19.7) and political organization (effectuated by heroes—9.3, 17.2). The peoples, as the masses, are the dominated; as exteriority, they constitute the eschatological reserve; as revolutionary, they are the builders of history.

8.6 PRAXIS OF THE PEOPLE AS OPPRESSED

As oppressed, dominated, a people suffers the fruit of sin: its members are hungry, without clothing, without housing; they are in pain, they are tortured, they die. As oppressed, they are *"part" of the system*. They are a social class, an exploited "bloc." The wage-earning "class" is precisely the human group whose current domination constitutes the system as such. In the feudal system the serf was obliged to pay a tribute. Insofar as it is brought into being by the social relationship of domination (2.2, 2.5)—precisely as one of the terms of that relationship (1.2, 2.2, 2.5)—a class is *part* of the system.

A people qua oppressed is a nation's social bloc. It includes all such persons as, with their labor, with their life, permit the "rich" (in the biblical sense, as a theological category—sinners, those who rob the "poor") to live. In this sense the people is an alienated, negated "crowd," a mere multitude, sacrificed to the idol (2.3).

The praxis of a people *as oppressed* is an imitative praxis, one that reproduces the system of domination, one that enables the hegemony of dominators to survive, one that consents to the structure that immolates it. As oppressed, popular praxis is negative, alienated, imitative, a praxis of consumerism. As undifferentiated crowd, as passive mass, the people must be politically organized by heroes, and prophetically envangelized in order to be transformed into the collective subject of the reign of God, the agent of a new political order.

The theology of liberation is "second act," or act of reflection upon the praxis of the people, the oppressed classes—the "poor," then, but "poor" in the politico-economic sense, the destitute, the penniless, who must beg in order to live, not poor because oppressed, alienated, "massified." That praxis cannot, it is true, constitute the actual focus of liberation, but it can furnish its starting point.

8.7 PRAXIS OF THE PEOPLE AS EXTERIORITY

This mass, this people, not only forms a bloc of oppressed, a *social* bloc; it engages in communal practices, external to the system (and regarded by the system as trivial, non-existent, unproductive, useless). Precisely *as exteriority*, the people constitutes the "*community* bloc" of the oppressed.

I have already observed the meaning and importance of being "in the exteriority" (4.2, 5.2, 5.6) of the system. Beyond the *totality* of the system that makes the dominated a class, rendering them marginal, or simply ignoring them ("the natives"), the people has an experience of *exteriority*. The "unproductive" aspects of this "bloc," of the people, the aspects that do not generate wealth in the form of profit for capital (12.1), are nevertheless part of the life of the people.

Here I refer to popular culture (18.10). That culture has its language, its songs, its customs, its friendship (a friendship of solidarity), its daily communicativeness and "sociability." The people knows how to establish *community* relationships (1.9). Who belong to the people? The poor who believe in the poor, who help the poor, who love their disgraced brother or sister. All such aspects of the people, aspects exterior to the system of domination, constitute the *positivity* of the people, and the *affirmation* that constitutes the wellspring of liberation (10.6).

Furthermore, there exists a whole *underground* production and economy, likewise exterior to the system. "Underground" is the term used—in the underdeveloped countries peripheral to capitalism—

for denoting the manner in which a people regulates itself in order to survive in a system of exploitation. The value of the underground is that it makes it possible for the people *still* to be there when the moment of liberation struggles arrives. In the underground, eking out their miserable survival, the people learns the cunning of a prolonged war for political, economic, popular, national emancipation.

8.8 A COMMUNO-UTOPIAN PRAXIS AMONG THE PEOPLE

Thus an entire people, as the bloc of a nation's oppressed, is predisposed to a comradeship of solidarity with any member in pain. The "base Christian community" will redouble this natural community quality of that people, by infusing it with "Spirit."

By "comuno-utopian praxis" I mean the actions and relationships of the base Christian communities, "living the reign of God" in a very special manner (1.9, 4.4, 4.6, 4.9, 5.6). These actions and relationships are "utopian" in the sense that they are situated "without": they are *outside* the system. (Thus they are "placeless": Gk., *ou*, "no, not"; *topos*, "place.") The life of the base Christian community responds not to prevailing morality, but to the ethics of the gospel. A people as such, as a historical people, is ambivalent. It contains the best: its exteriority vis-à-vis the system. But it also contains the worst: its alienating introjection of that system.

In a context of this ambivalence, and deep within the ambivalent people itself, the base Christian community asserts the exteriority of the people vis-à-vis the system, its experience of itself as other-than-the-system (in its quality as a *communal* bloc of the oppressed). The base Christian community thus becomes a *place*, a *space*, among the people in which that people, once their consciousness has been raised, will become *authentically* a people, as not-being-(dominating)-system. And in this sense the historical people (the crowd) becomes "my people" (the people of Yahweh), the "people of God" in the sense used by the Second Vatican Council.

True, it remains for authentically popular parties, fronts, or political groupings to organize the people for historical, political tasks. But the "eschatological community" (the base, utopian community), the "church of the poor," retains its purpose, its *raison d'être*: as the subject of a dialectic, the political (5.10, 9.4—9.10) can always close in upon itself and become a moral system of domination. A new idolatry is always possible: thus a prophetic, critical vigilance becomes a necessity.

8.9 A PROPHETICO-COMMUNITY PRAXIS OF LIBERATION AMONG THE PEOPLE

A Cuban Christian militant recently confided to me:

> After twenty-five years of enthusiastic collaboration with the revolution, we Christians have finally understood that we have something to give the revolution that it does not and cannot have in any other way: the *absolute* meaning of life, of service, of love.

The "absolute" is the divine, that which corresponds to God, to eternity, to the holiness of something that will rise, never to die again. It is upon this utopian hope that *the ethical* rests, for it is upon this utopian hope that the Christian faith itself is founded. Here is a hope that no historical revolution can adequately assert.

In the concrete, Christian prophecy emerges from the community praxis of the "church of the poor," the base Christian communities. They furnish the locus or focal point of the people as people. They provide the "whence" of the ethico-prophetic critique of the prevailing morality of domination. The base Christian communities are not exterior to the people, however. They do not impose, they do not pretend to constitute a vanguard. The elitism of those who "know," of the self-appointed conscience or savoir-faire of the people, those who would steer the people, lead the people, is something the base Christian communities must avoid. On the contrary, the base communities must form an "organic" community at the heart of a people. They are part of the people, one popular organ among many, one organizational aspect of the people itself.

Nevertheless the Christian experience does add something to the popular process, to the life of the people. It furnishes eschatological hope. It furnishes the faith that the people is composed of the daughters and sons of God and that God's reign will come. It provides effective love in the form of charity, the option for the other as other. It sets in motion, deep within a people, a current inaugurated by the Spirit (4.2ff.)—a spontaneous groundswell, emerging from nowhere, created without antecedents. This is the transcendent collaboration of the Christian community.

Like John the Baptist, the community prepares the way. And when heroes are moved by their charisms to create something new (and there are surely charisms of the Holy Spirit outside the church as well), the base Christian communities, the "church of the poor," the prophets, are ready and waiting, prepared to contribute their active collaboration.

8.10 LIBERATION PRAXIS OF THE PEOPLE

The theology of liberation presupposes a type of praxis without which it could not exist. Theology is reflection. *Primary theology*, then—basic, or "first" theology (20.9, 20.10)—will consist in the present type of tractate; it explains and describes, engages in theological reflection upon, takes as its starting point, the praxis of liberation undertaken by the people.

The popular praxis of liberation emerges when the people "gets going," when it "gets on its feet," when it begins the process of countering the structures of sin (2.5 – 2.6), when it initiates the struggle against the Satanic work of domination, injustice, sin (2.10). The liberation struggle is the battle with sin, with domination, with injustice and economic thievery, with political authoritarianism, with ideological alienation, with traditional machismo, and so on. When the people launches this struggle, then its praxis, its actions and relationships, are *liberated* from the old institutional bonds. The struggle can consist in revolution (16.7), or its preparation, or its consequences.

There are stable situations in history—situations of permanence and durability (9.6–9.7, 16.6). The present situation in Latin America is not one of these. On the contrary, everywhere around us we see an old process in its death agony and a new historical order being born. Hence the growth of a popular *liberation praxis* against the dependent capitalism suffered by our peoples. We struggle against an exploitation felt in *our* "skin" alone (and not in Poland, Rome, or the United States).

It is the liberation praxis of the communal bloc of the oppressed of the Latin American nations, today, at the close of the twentieth century, that provides the starting point, the "whence," the origin of what is called the theology of liberation (see chap. 20). This theology is the discovery not of individuals, but of an entire generation, a "school of prophets." But first and foremost it has the people as its source, its wellspring, its origin. Liberation theology is popular theology.

CONCLUSIONS

I have not attacked conservative, moralistic positions in this chapter. On the contrary, I have criticized certain leftist elements that disparage ethics, first because they are unable to distinguish it from prevailing morality, and secondly because they situate both ethics and morality in the ideological, juridical, political "suprastructure" (an extremely ambiguous category, to which I refer only in order to reject it). The social or economic relationships of production *include*, in their basic foundation, a practical aspect—a moral or ethical aspect, then. The relationship of one individual's domination over another is itself a practical relationship: it *is* domination, and hence sin. Sin pervades and infects, from the base up, the "material" aspect of production. Thus it is that prophetic criticism of a historically constituted mode of production functions as the antecedent, the "that which determines," where the future mode of production is concerned. And thus Christian communal hope, faith, and love can *determine* the infrastructure of future systems (and Marx himself, in his celebrated introduction to the *Grundrisse*, leaves this possibility open).

Chapter 9

Political Heroism, Ecclesial Martyrdom

9.1 STATE OF THE QUESTION

Many of the problems presented by a communitarian theological ethics can be resolved by bearing in mind the difference between state and church. State and church are two distinct institutions, functioning in the one and only salvation history. But the builders of the new *state* are frequently expected to work with the same mediations employed in the construction of the new *church community*.

It is not always understood that a *theology of the state* is as necessary as an ecclesiology.

Every day the newspapers carry stories of the heroic deeds of men and women engaged in the valiant struggle for liberation in Central America, Africa (Namibia, for instance), or Asia. Our Christian newspapers and periodicals show us the prophets, the heroes, and the martyrs. What is the relationship between the hero and the prophet?

We read in holy scripture:

Before I formed you in the womb I knew you,
    before you were born I dedicated you,
    a prophet to the nations I appointed you.
"Ah, Lord God!" I said,
    "I know not how to speak; I am too young." ...
Say not, "I am too young." ...
But do you gird your loins;
    stand up and tell them

all that I command you.
Be not crushed on their account,
 as though I would leave you crushed before them;
For it is I this day
 who have made you a fortified city,
A pillar of iron, a wall of brass,
 against the whole land:
Against Judah's kings and princes,
 against its priests and people.
They will fight against you, but not prevail over you,
 for I am with you to deliver you, says the Lord [Jer. 1:5–19].

The hero and the prophet are very similar, in their call as well as in their activity, and they are frequently confused. Earlier I referred to Camilo Torres as a hero, and I call Oscar Romero a prophet and martyr. Why? Because the hero and the prophet have different functions.

9.2 SOME NECESSARY DISTINCTIONS

It would be easy to infer that the distinctions I am about to make bespeak a new dualism. But no, I hold to the unicity of history. There is only one locus of salvation history, one universe to house the history of liberation. Nevertheless, we must clearly distinguish between two institutions that emerge in the process of the building of the reign of God.

Let me begin by observing that the hero and the prophet are distinct individuals. By *hero* I understand a politically-minded person who turns his or her life toward the construction of a new homeland, a new historico-political order. George Washington was a hero, as were Miguel Hidalgo and Che Guevara (the last two were murdered before they could see the triumph of the revolution to which they had dedicated their lives). By *prophet* I mean that believing Christian who undertakes a total bestowal of his or her life, in a spirit of consecration, to the evangelization of the poor, to the building of religious, utopian, Christian communities of believers. Heroism and prophecy are both *charisms*, but they are distinct charisms.

Heroism founds the state (in the broad sense of the word—not only the bourgeois state, then, but the pharaonic, the Roman, the Hispanic, and so on). Prophecy founds the church (as a community of believers—see 1.1, 1.5). The person (even the Christian) *as a political person* and member of the state, and the person or Christian *as a Christian*, as a member of the eschatological community, are not formally identical. State and church institutionalize their praxis in different ways, and in different relationships and organizations.

The *heroic death* of the political person must therefore not be confused with the *martyrial death* of the prophet. They may occur together, as when Zealots were crucified with Jesus. Indeed, both persons are put to death for the same reasons. But their praxis, their tactics, their strategies, are distinct. Likewise distinct are the institutionalization they inaugurate and the social or communal entities they organize.

9.3 HERO AND PROPHET IN PERSECUTION AND LIBERATION

Let us examine, in chronological order, four theological, biblical (but at the same time theoretical and abstract), structural stages in the metamorphosis of what Saint Augustine called the City of Abel or City of God into the City of Cain or Babylon (see 3.5, 4.10, 5.5, 5.10).

A heroic death (9.2) is as much the fruit of sin as it is of martyrdom. Both are the product of the praxis of domination (3.10, 4.10), as in the case of the repression, torture, and persecution inflicted on hero and prophet alike by the "*national security* state" of today's Latin America. Egypt and Babylon oppress the Hebrews, Jerusalem murders Jesus, Christendom burns heretics and dissidents, imperialism represses, tortures, murders, and lends money to buy weapons. In all instances, the praxis of domination is domination over the poor, without discrimination between hero and prophet. This is the first stage in the transmutation of the City of God into the City of Satan.

Unless (or until) they are murdered, like Miguel Hidalgo and Carlos Fonseca, or Father Carlos Múgica and Archbishop Romero, the hero and the prophet busy themselves with the organization of the liberation process. The hero organizes the oppressed to the end that they may throw themselves into a process that includes struggle.

Here we have Moses and the plagues of Egypt, Gandhi, or Lenin in the days before the triumph of the Bolshevik revolution (and thus prescinding from any evaluation of the current socio-political or economic content of that revolution). The hero leads the organizations, armed or unarmed, of which a people has need if it is to defend itself and bring Babylon down to dust. The virtues of heroic courage and political prudence join forces to defeat a stronger, better-armed enemy.

The prophet—always hand in hand with the martyr—organizes a church ready for the day of liberation: small communities, with their theologies of liberation, living a life of actual poverty and organized on the model of the "church of the poor."

9.4 THE HERO ALSO BUILDS THE WALL

"Let us rebuild the walls of Jerusalem" (Neh. 2:17). The function of the city wall is defense in wartime. Just as the city is not the temple, neither is the city wall the walls of the temple. In Latin America today we have the example of the Nicaraguans, who must defend their borders against their enemies to the north (5.10). In Europe the Czechs lost their "Prague Spring" through being unable to defend themselves.

A certain anarchism—whether that of the left, which would accomplish the full realization of the utopia of the reign of God here and now, or that of the right, the anarchism of the bourgeois, laissez-faire liberal (like today's neo-conservative), which proposes a perfect market with perfect competition, so as to be able to do without the state—will always oppose the organization of political society. In 1918 the Soviets undertook to develop the Soviet Union on anarchist lines. The effort failed, and in 1921 the New Economic Policy was inaugurated. A certain realism had replaced the anarchistic ideal (17.2 – 17.3).

In order to build walls, bake bread, and beat swords into pruning hooks or plowshares, one must have certain *technologies* available: the "architectonic" technologies, from planning to metallurgy. The hero must turn politician and technologist. Valor in the field yields to technology, planning, and prudence in the political arena. The reign of God needs walls, bread, and plows. Without that which satisfies— the object produced—there is no satisfaction. Not even holy scripture can exist without paper or papyrus, an alphabet, ink, and so on. Concrete technologies, constituting the material, corporeal infrastructure of the possibility of the incarnation of the Word, are now the order of the day. A *theology of the state* is then necessary—a theology of the divine demands (as conditions *sine qua non* of the satisfaction of the hunger of the starving, the clothing of the naked, and so on) a theology of the historical apparatus that produces sacramental objects. Before you can have the eucharist you have to have the *substance of bread* (6.7).

9.5 THE PROPHET ALSO BUILDS THE TEMPLE

Like heroes, prophets shift their activity from life-imperiling combat with the frenzied apocalyptic Beast (the old, repressive state), to the humble construction of daily community. "They went to the temple area together every day, while in their homes they broke bread" (Acts 2:46).

The prophet will be tempted to pine for days gone by, when everything seemed so clear. Repressors had been so easy to detect. But in the lights and shadows of a shift to democracy (as in Brazil in 1985), or in the moment of a revolutionary triumph, when all suddenly profess the victorious ideology (just as all were Marxists in the Soviet Union in 1918, or Sandinistas in Nicaragua in 1980), the deck has been reshuffled, and the latest arrivals are "more Catholic than the pope"—more Leninist than Lenin himself. "Old guard" heroes and prophets risk being overwhelmed by the new champions of "the right way to go about it."

Babylon has fallen. The prophets who excoriated it must now roll up their sleeves and head for the fields to cut sugar and pick coffee. Now their work is to consist in the positively productive daily effort to produce wealth, bread, for the poor, for the people. There is a time to die (a time of repression), and a time to work (in the rebuilding of the temple), and we recall Ezekiel's dream when the people of God still languished under the repression of the Babylonian captivity (Ezek. 40ff.)—a dream that now can become reality (Ezra 5:1ff).

Many who had kept their counsel in Egypt, in Babylon, or under Somoza, suddenly recall, once the revolution has triumphed, that the prophet's role is to "criticize." And lo, the dumb speak. Now we have criticism in abundance, and from every direction. But there is criticism, and then again there is criticism. It is the Dragon and the Beast who are to be criticized. The New Jerusalem is not a legitimate object of crticism. In the New Jerusalem, the first priority is to *work*, to *produce* bread, for the table, for the eucharist. The day of the "work ethic" has dawned, and Fidel Castro, none other, when asked what he means by "practitioners of the revolutionary ethic," points to the nuns of the leprosariums.

This is the second stage in the metamorphosis of the City of God into the City of Humankind.

9.6 THE POLITICIAN: MANAGER OF THE POWER OF THE STATE

Let us proceed with our present abstract, schematic indication of the four stages in the metamorphosis of the City of God (Augustine's *Civitas Dei*) into the City of Babylon (*Civitas Babyloniae*). We have already seen the first two. (1) In the repressive state, the task at hand is the *de*struction of the prevailing system; the hero and martyr will answer the call (see 9.3). (2) In the new state, *con*struction is the order of the day. The promised land, conquered by a Joshua, is to be rebuilt by an Ezra or a Nehemiah (see 9.4, 9.5). (3) The third stage will characterize the state in its classic equilibrium (9.6, 9.7). But then (4) the state reverts to the repression of the Beast (9.8, 9.9).

In the third stage, then, a balance of forces has been struck. The state would appear to have established a classic kind of order, based on hegemony and consensus. There is order indeed, in harmony and unity. Here is the "perfect society." All mortal enemies have disappeared from its midst. The poor are fewer now, and lack any consciousness of their poverty, having imbibed the ideology of newly dominant groups.

Civil society has become "pluralistic"—conveniently enough, for the pluralism in question straddles but a single band of the political spectrum. Here is Hegel's "organic state," lolling in the lap of peace and harmony: its position as economic metropolis of so many peripheral colonies enables it to appease the hunger of its own dominated with wealth extorted from the poor beyond its frontiers. And behold the *Pax Americana* of the post-World War II era. The prevailing order seems so "natural"! More than this: a new "civil religion" springs up—the "American way of life."

Thus the third stage is one of temporary equilibrium. The ethical spirit of the heroes continues to animate the mere morality of the system. A "social teaching" flourishes (see 19.6), demanding certain acceptable "reforms" in the established order. This is where Karl Popper sees a radical reform as the absolute evil: utopia.

9.7 THE ECCLESIASTIC: ADMINISTRATOR OF "RELIGIOUS AFFAIRS"

This time of seeming peace, when prophecy has fallen still, is the calm, stable moment of the priest, the ecclesiastic, the ritual celebrant of the established order. David the king is David the prophet—much more of a poet than a prophet, of course, as one can scarcely prophesy against oneself.

It is at this point that the church begins to regard itself as the "other perfect society," on a par in this respect with the state. Now it insists on its "autonomy" vis-à-vis the state—the latter being fundamentally acceptable now (along with the economic or ideological regime), although it may be called upon to adopt partial "reforms." Capital is found to be in contradiction neither with nature nor with morality. Of course, profit must never be excessive. Land has a rentable value, likewise in virtue of its nature. Of course, the rent must not be unjust. Work may be adequately remunerated by wages—which, again, must be just. Once more the prevailing order has become identified with human "nature." Structural sin (2.5), one would swear to it, exists no more, and the domination and death produced by the sinners smolders in oblivion.

For the church, the state is neither a Babylon to be brought low nor a Jerusalem to be rebuilt (being, after all, so well built). Our third stage is that of the status quo, of the "way things are." The church, in the hands of sacerdotal ministries, celebrates the system, acclaiming rulers, praying for them, crowning kings and emperors, walking shoulder to shoulder with the generals in their parades, and so on. The church is the Church Triumphant, the Church of Christ the King—not the church of Christ the poor one, the one crucified by the state—of Catholic Action that must strive to gain the upper hand in the political contest for influence over the state, over the "powers that be," over the current prevailing order.

In the slow metamorphosis of the City of God into Babylon, then, the clerical conceptualization of the church has come into its own. The prevailing models of church and state are mutually consistent, mutually implicit.

9.8 WHEN THE STATE REPRESSES THE NEW POOR

One of the essential dialectical moments of Jesus' theology of history consists in the principle enunciated in Deuteronomy 15:11: "Never will there cease to be poor upon the earth; wherefore I command thee: Open your hand to your brother the poor one, the needy of the land." There are those who think that capitalism, or socialism, can eradicate poverty *forever and absolutely*. They will doubtless regard this Jesus principle, taken from the Old Testament, as the tenet of a radical pessimism. Nothing could be further from the truth. It is but realism in the hope of the reign of God!

The authentic theologian can never become the ideologue of a party, however authentically revolutionary the party. The theologian will always maintain an eschatological, prophetical reserve, which will announce its presence through a critique stemming from the *new* poor. Any revolutionary process, however just, will inevitably and necessarily produce new poor. Hence the possibility, the suitability, the necessity of the critique in question.

Where there is freedom there may be domination. In fact, there always is. Then sin appears: someone suffers the effects of the domination. And behold, *new* death and *new* poor—new in the sense of different. In the Middle Ages, the poor were those deprived of the protection of the fief: the pariahs of the cities. In capitalism, the poor are those without money (see 12.1ff). In socialism, the poor may be those who have no control over planning, or those without any responsible awareness of the terms of the productive process, or the like (see 17.8), as *perestroika* recognizes. At all events, the state founded by George Washington is now the state governed by Ronald Reagan and by a Congress that votes funds for the overthrow of Latin American governments. Something must surely have happened over the course of the intervening two centuries! The hero has been transformed into the Caesar: Jesus "suffered *under*

Pontius Pilate," we profess in the Apostles' Creed. Pilate was a military official who governed in the name of the reigning Caesar.

9.9 THE CHRISTENDOM MODEL: FUNDAMENTALISM

As we see, we have reached the fourth and final stage of the metamorphosis. We began our ascent with Moses and the prophets, writhing under the power of the Beast in the form of a pharaonic, Babylonian, or imperialistic state. Now, our ascent, our long metamorphosis, is over—and we emerge in the world of Moses' successors. Lo, they have been transformed into the monarchy that represses the poor in Israel or Judah. The exiles of Babylon have returned to Jerusalem, only to crucify the Christ. Suddenly the exiles are the temple, they are Annas and Caiaphas. They are a religion of domination. "Behold ye all this? I solemnly assure you: all of it will be razed to the ground, and not a stone will be left upon a stone" (Matt. 24:2).

An anachronistic, a-dialectical, a-historical *Weltanschauung*—the worldview of conservative, antitraditional, dominative thought—attempts to eternalize a stage in a metamorphosis and falls into sin and abomination (Luke 19:46). *Only prophets are traditional.* They alone discover "the new" to be the willed-by-God. Christendom sprang up by way of an identification of Christianity, the church, with the Roman state (from the time of Constantine or Theodosius), or with the Frankish kingdom (beginning with Charlemagne, A.D. 800). Religion became the bastion of the state, and the pope crowned worldly monarchs "by God's will."

Given this claim that it is Jesus himself who crowns the kings and the dominators, who are those who have to die under the iron fist of the state? How does one distinguish El Salvador's "Christian Democrats" from Christian Oscar Romero? Who holds the place of Jesus now? In Christendom you can murder prophets in the name of Jesus, as occurred in Chile under Pinochet. You can even torture them to death in that name, as occurred in Brazil under Commissar Fleury.

As the heroic state founded by George Washington was gradually transformed into empire, so the brave chaplain of the American Revolution can become the prelate who blesses the weapons to be used against the "communists" of Vietnam.

9.10 THE NEED FOR AN ONGOING DIALECTIC BETWEEN STATE AND CHURCH

Christianity invented the secular state. Before the advent of Christianity, there was no such thing. All states were divine, and of necessity. But with Christendom things would no longer be the same. For the first time in history, the need would arise for a secular state. Christianity found itself unable to do without such a state as its vis-à-vis. The church needed not-to-be-the-state. Accordingly, there must be a state that would not be the church. And the secular state was born.

The eschatological function of the church—essentially a funcction of the "church of the poor" (Pope John XXIII) in its quality as prophetic, ethical, and free vis-à-vis prevailing moralities—is to start the whole of history down the road to the Parousia, the end of history as the return of Christ. All totalization, fetishization, and petrification of a system (and all repression of the heroes and the prophets, whose purpose is to prevent history from continuing its course and direct it toward *new*, more just systems) stunts the growth, delays the arrival, of the reign of God.

The eschatological function of the church is a critical praxis, and one that will not stop short of destroying institutions that embody sin and render it historical (2.5, 2.6). If the church were the state, if ethics were morality, whence would come a critique of the prevailing domination? In order to abide in "exteriority from the state," the church (at least in the base Christian communites, where it keeps company with the poor—the church as the "church of the poor") must not be the state. There has been ambiguity in Christendom between church and state, but never total identity, thanks precisely to the *institutionality* of the church, which has prevented the absorption of the latter by the former.

Heroes and martyrs, politicians and prophets, state and church, are distinct realities, then—both of them necessary for the reign of God, although both are capable of rejecting it.

CONCLUSIONS

Faced with the phenomenon of the metamorphosis of the City of God, we are tempted to exclaim: What good is our activity if the whole process ends up at square one? What point is there in a liberation praxis that will eventually become a praxis of domination? The answer is simple. Nothing in the process is ever the same as before. None of it ever simply repeats itself. All of it is new and unrepeatable: new domination, new poor, new agents, new sinners. Where am I, then, where are we: among the dominators or among the poor? Where will I be casting my lot here and now: with dominators or with liberators? If my comrades in the struggle today are the dominators of tomorrow, that is their affair. You and I shall simply have to mount the struggle against them. The reign of God is *never finished* in history. Ever and again, it *begins* building, here and now, in the praxis of liberation, for us or against us. The important thing is which side we are on, and who the enemy is. Are we with Jesus against the Prince of "this world"? The Parousia, Jesus' return ("Come, Lord Jesus!"—Rev. 22:20) is hastened, indeed realized, in the very praxis of liberation.

Chapter 10

Relative Morality,
Absolute Ethics

10.1 STATE OF THE QUESTION

Catholic theology is particularly concerned to avoid any relativism in moral questions. This attitude is valid where genuinely absolute norms are at stake. But it has also led to the absolutization of relative values, and the "social teaching of the church" (see chap. 19) is a case in point. What is good today can be evil tomorrow—not because the principle of good and evil is relative, but because circumstances can change. (And the first *circum*stance is the *cycle* of the prevailing system as an all-encircling totality.)

The daily newspapers are filled with news of the actions and projects of persons, especially politicians, calculated to fall in perfectly with the intentions and principles of a particular social group. An example would be the United States' Strategic Defense Initiative, or "Star Wars." It is imperative that we learn to distinguish the absolute from the relative in all of these daily events.

We read in holy scripture:

> The spirit of the Lord God is upon me,
>   because the Lord has consecrated me;
> He has sent me to bring good news to the lowly,
>   to heal the brokenhearted,
> To proclaim liberation to captives
>   and release to prisoners,
> To announce a year of favor from the Lord
>   and a day of vindication by our God,
>   to comfort all who mourn [Isa. 61:1–2].

Let us undertake a theological reflection on the *absolute*, universal character of *ethics*. What is it about an authentic ethics that endows it with validity for all ages and circumstances? We must learn to appreciate the relativity of the *relative*, lest we stake the future of Christianity on something destined to pass away with the chrysalis of our times.

10.2 SOME NECESSARY DISTINCTIONS

It is a peculiarity of relativistic thinking to wish to have the relative pass for absolute, and then to reject it because it is only relative. Conservatism likewise maintains the absolute value of the relative (which it controls)—but this time the intent is to be able to assert its everlasting validity. With the relativists we shall reject the conservative absolutes. But against the relativists, we shall register our discovery of an absolute of which they know nothing, owing to their a-dialectical, a-historical, and totalized approach to reality.

In the first place, any "morality" (see 3.2, 3.6, 3.7)—"morality" as the prevailing system—is *relative* to the system itself (as specific entity). Aztec "morality" —what was considered right or wrong in Aztec society—cannot be judged according to the criteria of Roman or Hindu "morality." Torn from its context, the praxis of the Aztec warrior will make no "moral" sense whatever to the Greek or the Hindu—and vice versa. "Moralities" are meaning-totalities (as Hegel explains in his elucidation of the concept of *Sittlichkeit*, or "customs" of a people). Thus, *any morality* is relative to itself, and not susceptible to a comparison with anything extraneous.

In the second place, the "ethical" (see 3.2, 5.3, 5.7, 5.9) carries a demand that will be valid in any system and at any time: "*Never* will there cease to be poor on the land; therefore I command you: Open your hand to your brother" (Deut. 15:11). *Never in history will the poor cease to be*— that is, *there will always be poor*. Inasmuch, then, as we are dealing with a reality that knows no bounds, we easily recognize that the corresponding imperative, demand, *ethical norm*, will likewise be boundless: "Open your hand to your brother." Now we see why "Liberate the poor!" "Feed the hungry!" "Help the needy!" represent *absolute* ethical exigencies—imperatives valid for and in all relative moral systems.

In a word, authentically ethical imperatives *transcend* merely "moral" requirements. They may flow in the same direction as the latter, or merely be compatible with them, or be positively incompatible with them. "Moral" imperatives are empirical, historical, relative, and systematic. Ethical imperatives are transcendental, absolute, and nevertheless concrete (not abstract) (see 5.9).

10.3 RELATIVE MORALITIES

Any culture—in the sense of a civilization, such as the Assyrian or Egyptian, Greek or Hindu, feudal European or Aztec, Bantu or Zulu—contains within itself a *morality*, in the form of a concrete "practical system" or system of practices (see 3.6).

A practical system, or the totality of the practices of a people (or group, or class, and so on), consists in a global structure of interpersonal *relationships* (1.2), held to be normal, natural, legitimate, and good, and obtaining in the family, the economy, politics, religion, and so on. These practical relationships, in turn, are defined by norms, exigencies, imperatives, or moral laws binding the members of the group to their observance.

The system of practices, norms, and relationships in question is stable, is transmitted from generation to generation by upbringing and education, and has its organs of coercion (police, penal institutions, and so on), which have the authority to impose penalties for infractions of the norms of the system. Its moral authorities (from shamans or priests to courts of justice) enjoy the respect of the consensus of civil society. It is impossible for a people simply to discontinue its moral order, codified since antiquity and held to be its by all of the normal members of that people.

Observe: the "practical totality" in question here is *relative*. First, it is relative to itself. That is, it is valid to the extent that it is held to be valid by all: it depends on consent and consensus. It is a tautology. Secondly, it is relative in the sense that it is valid for one group but not for another. It is peculiar to all persons born in such and such precise circumstances, and this differentiates it from any other historical moral order. Thus the opportunities for a transition from one moral practical system to another are few and far between, although from time to time certain aspects of any moral system will "pass on," by actually changing their meaning (as Roman law "passed" into medieval European or modern capitalistic law).

10.4 THE TRANSCENDENTAL IMPERATIVE OF THE GOSPEL ETHIC

"Ethics" (3.2) cannot be understood apart from a reference to "morality." Morality is the "flesh" (6.3, 6.4), the "whence" of the entire ethical operation. In dissociation from an established order, though it be an order of domination, prophetic criticism cannot exist. In the reign of God, where there will be no evil, there will be no prophecy.

It is necessary that there be moral systems. It would be impossible for such systems not to exist. In the order of the incarnation, morality is the culturalization, the concretion, of practical relationships. And social life can be lived only through practical relationships. "Ethics," on the other hand, consists of imperatives that are "transcendental" in the sense that they transcend, "go beyond," surmount, the purview of the established, prevailing, dominant moral order.

The subject or agent of the *moral* order is the *dominant* member of a given system. In feudalism it was the feudal lord. In capitalism it is the owner of capital. The subject or agent of the *ethical* order, on the other hand, is constituted by the dominated members, *the poor*, of that system. In feudalism it was the serf, in capitalism it is the wage-earner, the worker. Ethical imperatives are moral "counterimperatives." If morality says, "Respect the feudal lord," ethics says, "Liberate the serf." The latter imperative "transcends," calls into question, ordains the overcoming of, feudalism. It is an absolute, transcendental, critical imperative.

The ethic of the gospel—or better, the gospel as ethics—is not a morality. It does not propose concrete empirical norms. Nor indeed is it an ethics for one particular time and place: "Liberate the serf." If it were, it would no longer be valid for another, future system. Instead, it proclaims: "Blessed are the poor." The poor are universal. The "poor" in the gospel sense will be present *in any possible moral system*. The gospel "poor" are not this or that type of poor. They are the poor *as such*. Thus the gospel ethic constitutes an *absolute* imperative, not relative to this or that historical moral system.

10.5 MORALIZATION OF THE GOSPEL ETHIC IN CHRISTENDOM

Just as there cannot be ethics without morality (anymore than there could have been an incarnation in the sole person of the Word, without flesh), the ethical critique of a moral system (the Greco-Roman, for instance) de facto generates a *new* morality, a new moral world. Byzantine and Latin Christendom are the prime instances. This new moral order tends to be confused with the ethic of the gospel and thus to deny the authentic gospel ethic. This is the possible danger of the "social teaching" of the church today.

After Jesus, the Apostles, Apologists, the Fathers of the Church, the persecuted church of the poor, the church of the martyrs—all evangelized the Greco-Roman Mediterranean world. The morality of Plato, Aristotle, Plotinus, and so on—Hellenistic morality—like any other prevailing Mediterranean morality, was subjected by that church to a radical critique at the hands of the Christian ethic. But this new Christian world gradually came to regard itself as the City of God. The new civilization thought of itself as the reign of God on earth. And Christendom was born (9.9).

Thus a specious identity was struck between the historical, relative Byzantine and Latin morality on the one hand, and the ever-transcendental imperatives of the gospel ethic. For centuries thereafter, only the saints recalled the non-moralizable transcendence of the ethics of Jesus. But by the end of the Middle Ages, a goodly number of Christians had become the agents of a Christian ethical critique of the feudal world, and had begun laying the foundations of the capitalist world, in the corporations of the "poor" who crammed the medieval cities. Just so, it is our responsibility today, after the example of so many other Christians since the eighteenth century, to voice the Christian ethical critique of capitalistic "morality." So many Christians have identified with the latter in an absolute fashion, thus falling victim to the relativism of a historical bourgeois morality.

The task of Christians in Latin America today, as in the world at large, is precisely to recall the *transcendental* demands of the Christian ethic, which cannot be identified with the morality of capitalism. Moralities disappear. Ethics abides.

10.6 COMMUNAL CHRISTIAN ETHICS

Ethical imperatives are more than practical norms proposed for someone's hypothetical, ideal observance. They are the real, concrete constituents of the praxis and type of relationships actually lived today in the Christian *community* (see 1.1, 1.5, 1.9, 4.6).

The ethico-prophetic critique, voiced "from outside" (see 5.2), comes to us from a *real* (and not merely possible) experience of community (see 1.6, 1.9, 4.6). The reason this critique is capable of rejecting the domination of the prevailing system or its practical norms of domination is not that the prophet is endowed with a brilliant intelligence. No, even the simplest member of the community has the experience of a *community* life. It is this community life that supplies the *affirmative* "whence" of a declaration of the intrinsic connection between the condition of injustice and misery weighing on the oppressed in the system, and that system's prevailing *social* morality.

Any critico-prophetic *negation* of sin, then, proceeds from the *affirmation* of the utopian justice prevailing by anticipation in the base Christian community. This experience of being outside, this "analectic" experience (from the Greek, *ano*, "above, beyond"— beyond or transcending the horizon of the system in the experience of *another* way of living with one's sisters and brothers), is the reign of God *already begun* (1.9). And it is this reign of God that measures the ethicity of any praxis. The community *already* lives, in part, the future system of justice, and from its standpoint in that project (5.2) enjoys the capacity to judge, to condemn, the prevailing morality as perverse.

Communal Christian ethics is something very different from a morality that may have adopted reforms as a result of certain Christian imperatives. Thus the so-called social teaching of the church (see chap. 19) has consisted, until recently, in orientations calculated to *modify*, merely, the prevailing, dominating bourgeois morality. It is not an authentically prophetic ethic. It is only a reformed morality, whose purpose is to avoid "excesses." It accepts the foundations of bourgeois morality, as we shall see. The base Christian community criticizes that morality in a more radical and evangelical way. (This is not to say that the social teaching of the church has no validity.)

10.7 HOW DOES ETHICS CRITICIZE THE MORALITIES?

Ethics is the *affirmation* of life (4.8, 6.7) emerging from the experience of community, the experience of the relationship of a respectful love among sisters and brothers (1.4). If ethics is intrinsically affirmative, how can it be enunciated as *negation*: "You shall *not* kill, you shall *not* steal"?

As we have already observed, the act of killing is a negation of life: a "no to life." This being the case, a no to a "no to life" will be the negation of a negation, and thus an affirmation. The ethical critique is not fundamentally negative. The object or target of its negation is domination, sin, and satanic praxis (3.5, 2.10). It *asserts* the experience of community. It is not *de*structive, but *con*structive. However, it knows that the chrysalis (the old system of domination) has to be superseded for new life to emerge.

Were it not for morality, were it not for institutions, domination would lack the universality inherent in its reality. It would be sporadic, chaotic (see 2.5, 2.6). Ethics steps forward to lodge its prophetic criticism of institutional, historical, concrete sin, on the fulcrum of its affirmation of justice as lived in community (a *utopian* justice, to be sure, for it is lived outside the system). Ethics will have a different content in every age—as many different contents as the number of historical relative moralities it criticizes. Each time, ethics will criticize a different moral content. But its critique will always have the same formal rationale: it will be the *poor* in this particular moral or practical system who are "blessed, lucky, happy." It is they who constitute the criterion of the goodness or evil of institutions— nor must we ever forget that the poor, *here and now*, are Jesus Christ himself: the christological question. Speaking from the depths of the pain, the injustice suffered, the domination that deprives the poor of life in *this* system, the prophet directs a scathing regard upon this system's concrete institutions, denies and rejects these *social relationships*, judges them, and pronounces them, along with the very norms of "morality" that underlie them, *ethically* perverse. The validity of the ethical judgment is absolute, then. And yet it is concrete, inasmuch as *these* poor are distinct from all other poor (a serf is not a wage-earning worker).

10.8 MULTIPLICITY AND EVOLUTION OF MORALITIES

Necessarily, and appropriately, there are *many moralities.* Further: all moralities evolve historically from a germinal stage (in the case of Christendoms, from ethical demands, not by mere domination over other moralities)—subsequently to be swallowed up in the ages of the moralism of an imperial domination (at least in its Greco-Roman phase or the current *Pax Americana*).

It is appropriate, and good, that there be many moralities. They represent a phenomenon of human creativity that has never failed to mold the result of centuries of human experience into these practical totalities. What a marvelous sampler of balance, beauty, complexity, and symbolism we behold in the Inca or Aztec, the Chinese or Japanese, Hindu, and other, moralities! But this multiplicity must not be measured by the yardstick of *another morality.* And this is Christendom's perennial temptation. The Europeans who came to the New World regarded their morality not only as *superior*, but as *Christian.* Thus they were guilty of two errors: their morality was neither superior nor Christian (if by "Christian" we understand the prophetic *ethic* of the gospel).

The moralities of Portuguese, Spanish, English, or North American Christendom are so many different, specific *moralities.* They have been imposed on the Carib, Aztec, Incan, Bantu, Hindu, Nicaraguan, and other moralities by force. Only certain missionaries subjected these "Christian" moralities to the prophetic critique of the gospel ethic. But in doing so, they originated a new, Latin American, morality. The shining example here is that of Bartolomé de Las Casas. He valued the autochthonous moralities (see his *Apologética Histórica*). He subjected them to an ethical critique, but refused to destroy them as moralities.

Moralities undergo evolution. They have a history. It is only in their final stages, in their senility, as it were, that they become tyrannical, external, and authoritarian. It is when they have lost the *élan vital*, the vital thrust, of their youth that they must be subjected to the ethico-prophetic critique.

10.9 TRANSCENDENTAL UNIQUENESS OF THE GOSPEL ETHIC

Moralities are multiple, and subject to an evolution in time. Ethics is *one*, and enjoys permanent validity in virtue of its *absolute* character. It evolves much more slowly. It grows in the continuous exercise of its critique of the historical moralities. Ethical progress, from the "schools of the prophets" of eighth-century B.C. Israel to the twentieth century of our own era has been all but imperceptible. The Hebreo-Christian ethic received its definitive constitution in the good news preached by Jesus. It still had to be made to prevail over specific moralities—a process in which understanding was achieved, and categories implicit in the gospel were explicitly developed.

When I speak of the critico-transcendental uniqueness of ethics, I refer to the fact that ethics is *one* (vis-à-vis *many* moralities); that it is *transcendental* with respect to any and all moralities (the moralities are by definition immanent, intrasystemic); and that it takes its stance *over and against* the morality, negating and rejecting it in any of its dominative, unjust elements (from a standpoint, however, not in the principles of morality, nor even in any previously defined content of its own, but *from* that of *the poor* who are present in the system).

The old "natural law" teaching sought to attain to this pitch of ethical radicality. It never succeeded. "Natural law" had set itself the impossible, self-contradictory task of producing a positive enunciation of universally valid concrete principles from a point of departure in the prevailing morality. (In reality, it only raised the "justice" of that "morality" to the rank of "nature.") Ethics, by contrast, in its capacity as a prophetico-critical *horizon* merely, has no need to define its imperatives positively in advance. It need only negate the prevailing negation, starting from the affirmation lived by the base Christian communities of any age and time.

Accordingly, subjective poverty is an essential of the ethical community. This independence of goods (and institutions) liberates the community from the wealth of the prevailing system, and frees it to criticize the system and give it a new start, to bring in a new moral age.

10.10 THE DIALECTICAL RELATIONSHIP BETWEEN MORALIZING INCARNATION AND CRITICAL TRANSCENDENCE

An ethico-prophetic critique that destroys a moral world originates another world—another, new *moral* world. Moralities are the incarnation of the ethical critique. This is how the moralities of the Christendoms, of European feudalism, of capitalism, of socialism, came to be. The great millenarians of the fourteenth and fifteenth centuries practiced an ethical critique. So did the utopian socialists of the end of the eighteenth and beginning of the nineteenth century. All were Christians.

I use the term "moralizing" to refer to the process that starts as part of an ethical critique, and gradually transforms that critique into a *new morality*. The ethico-prophetical Christian critique of the Greco-Roman moral world, starting from its "outsider" position in the base Christian communities of that day, was transmuted, over the course of the centuries, into European feudal Christendom, or into the Byzantine, Coptic, or Armenian world, and so on. The ethic of the original critique gradually trickled off into a prevailing, dominating morality, with its justification of economic, political, sexual, and other, sin.

This "moralizing" process is not only inevitable, it is needed. Ethics could not exist without morality. It would have to discontinue securing, attaining, institutionalizing its gains in history. *All world history*, until the Parousia itself, will be the scene of ethicity's self-actualization in the moralities.

At the same time, no sooner is a *new morality* constituted, no sooner has it emerged from the matrix of its originating ethical moment, than ethics is back on the scene, once again performing its function of destroying the calcified, the old, and the unjust, and thus launching history once more down its course to greater realizations. Being one, and absolute, ethics reappears through the intermediary of the prophets when the time is ripe, as in Latin America today.

CONCLUSIONS

We have come to the end of the first part of this study. We have covered ten *basic* topics. It will probably have occurred to those using this book that the number of topics in the first part could just as easily have been more or less than ten. Their number is unimportant. The important thing is to have constructed a *minimal*, but indispensable, platform from which to address more concrete, more complex, and more current problems, as we shall now be doing in the second part of this book. Throughout the second part it will be evident that the topics under consideration there are only corollaries of the ten themes of the first part. For some users of this book, the first half will have seemed too traditional and abstract, too timeless, as it were. But I could not have dispensed with a solid foundation erected on the rock of holy scripture and not on personal conjecture. Nor, as a matter of fact, do I make any apologies for the fact that my approach is a *traditional* one. This has been precisely my intention.

As for the last topic of Part 1—the topic just concluded, concerning the plurality of the moralities and the uniqueness of ethics (replacing the classic treatment of "natural and positive law"), I trust that the importance of such a consideration has been shown. In any event its utility will come to light in the course of Part 2.

PART 2

TEN DISPUTED QUESTIONS

Chapter 11

The Ethics of Work

11.1 STATE OF THE QUESTION

Throughout this chapter my approach will continue to be abstract and general. It will be applicable not to the case of capitalism alone, but to the whole of human reality, at least from as long ago as the neolithic age or the invention of money. It will be a reflection on the "community" condition of labor before its transposition to a "social" condition (3.2).

We read, in the daily newspapers, of work, of workers, of production, wages, strikes, money, and so on. What does all of this mean?

We read in holy scripture:

> In the beginning God created the heavens and the earth. ...
> The heavens and the earth and all their array were completed.
> Since on the seventh day God was finished with the work he
> had been doing, he rested on the seventh day from all the work
> he had undertaken. So God blessed the seventh day and made
> it holy, because on it he rested from all the work he had done
> in creation [Gen. 1:1, 2:1–3].

A *theology of work* is the fleshly or material starting point for a communal ethic. Without it a communal ethic would be not only abstract, but unrealistic. Only a theology of work can guide our concrete reflection in the proper direction. Between 1959 and 1961, before the Second Vatican Council, I spent two years with Paul Gauthier working as a carpenter in Nazareth and fishing on the Lake of Gennesaret. It was a spiritual experience, and the aftermath saw the publication of *Jesus, the Church, and the Poor.* The book's title simply lists the three major themes of the *theology of liberation.* The reaction of certain superficial critics notwithstanding, these themes are not fad, fashion, or idle chatter.

11.2 NEED AND LIFE

The point of departure for any reflection on work must be in a stage "antecedent" to the emergence of the phenomenon of work on the human scene (a merely utopian point, to be sure, hypothetical and perhaps a-historical).

Life is action. A living being consumes energy, and that energy must be replaced. Human beings must replace their lost energy, their expended life. They must satisfy their needs (1.7, 4.8–4.9, 6.3–6.7). "Need" is to be defined as any lack of the necessities of life. Need includes hunger, cold, homelessness, illness, and so on. To be "in need" is to open oneself to the world in search of the elements that will satisfy that need. I shall call this openness-of-need *pragmasis* (the Greek word for the "need to make use of something"), and the objects needed *pragmata* (Gk., "things needed, useful").

I shall term the reciprocity between need (*pragmasis*) and the things needed (the useful, the *pragmata*) the "pragmatic circle." If things, the object of use, happen to be at hand, they will supply the wherewithal for the reproduction of life without further mediation. They will be acquired without work, without production. But when the useful object is not within reach of one's need—when it stands outside the pragmatic circle—one must obtain it, extract it, "produce" it. At this point, openness to the world, *pragmasis*, will become a "productive" openness. And *poiesis*, "production," enters the picture. Now the useful thing, the thing needed, is no longer the object of the openness of *pragmasis* alone, the object of need, but becomes the object of *poiesis*, "production," as well. Correlatively, the object of this compound openness of need and production is no longer only the useful (*pragmata*), but the *product* (*poiemata*) of toil. Only in this latter case will there be such a thing as work—the activity calculated to produce, to extract, or otherwise obtain, the non-existent object in order that it be at hand. Work is thus to be defined as human activity set in motion in order to bring into existence some useful object that was previously non-existent or otherwise not at hand. The "productive circle" is not sheerly pragmatic, then. Now women and men must themselves secure the existence of the useful object. That object becomes the product of their work.

11.3 THE PRODUCT: OBJECTIFIED LIFE

The mere object of need, the means of satisfaction that would be available without the mediation of production, is useful, but without "value." *Value* attaches only to the product of human toil. Aristotle (*Politics*, I, 3, 1257) termed this value the "use value" of any object: the quality of a product of work that makes it useful, as a shoe is produced to be worn and walked in.

In order to produce an object, then, we work. This makes our work itself an object. In "working" matter, molding it, "transforming" it—changing its "form" or shape—we render nature the object of *culture*. The object has become a human object. As an object precisely *produced*, it has become *human toil objectified*. Let us call the fact that the object is a product of work, the product *as product*, as objectified work, the "productuality" (not "productivity") of that object.

But if the *work* of the worker has become real in the object, if it has been objectified, then the *life* of the worker has been objectified in it as well—and life has a sacred dignity, because it is a human life, the life of a person—1.3. The "use value" of the object produced is then human life objectified—and nothing less. The use value of an object is "blood" (2.8, 3.10): it is life. It is the circulation of human life from the subject of the work to the object worked, by way of the activity of working. The value of the object produced is ultimately the worker's lifeblood, coagulated.

Thus the "use value" of an object, as objectified human life, is a *sacred* "wealth" or good. Wealth and capital are sometimes identified (see, for instance, *Rerum Novarum,* 15; *Laborem Exercens,* 13). Surely the capitalist's wealth is capital; but there is wealth that is not capitalistic. All use value is wealth: valuable, useful, necessary, positive. Its accumulation against other persons, as in domination, is sin. But wealth in itself is good.

11.4 EXCHANGE AMONG PRODUCERS

For Aristotle, the use of a shoe not as a shoe but as an object by which one can obtain other objects (comestibles, and so on), constitutes that produced object (to which use value attaches in the form of wealth) the subject of another value: an "exchange value."

Thus the objectified life of the subject of work, the objectified life of the worker, can be exchanged for another object, in which some other worker has objectified his or her own life. The shoemaker who has objectified five hours of his life in making a pair of shoes, now exchanges his shoes for the wheat that, in five hours of her own life, the *campesina* has produced. This trade, this exchange, is just: each of its principals has traded off as much as she or he has received. The shoes and the wheat have use value (the shoes to walk in and the wheat to eat), but not for their respective producers (who do not use them, but exchange them). Rather, their use value is value only in the possession of the opposite term of the relationship: the shoemaker will be able to use the wheat to eat, and the *campesina* can wear the shoes to protect her feet while working in the fields. (The relationship in question is a "practical" one—1.2).

To any object, then, an added value can attach, called the exchange value, in virtue of the insertion of that object into the relationship of exchange. The actual terms of the relationship are the subjects of the work that has produced the objects: the shoemaker and the *campesina*. The objects exchanged, the shoes and the wheat, are merely relational mediations.

Diagram 6

Exchange Value

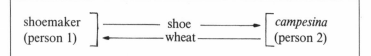

The concerns of *justice* are precisely with this particular species of practical relationship—that obtaining between persons by way of the product of their labors. Justice, then, is concerned with practico-productive, or economic relationships. Ultimately, these relationships constitute an exchange of human life. Circulation of value is circulation of the lifeblood of human beings (Mark 14:24).

11.5 PRODUCT VALUE

Still in general terms (and not yet in the capitalistic sense), the value attaching to a product of human toil resides in its utility and its productuality: the object in question is useful, and it is a product. Before becoming merchandise (the intent of its production when it is produced *in order to be exchanged*), the product is useful. It is wealth. It is the instrument of the satisfaction of a need.

The "value" of the product, then (and we must keep in mind that this value is independent of its function in capitalism), is simply the quantity of objectified human life attaching to that product. It is in complete accord with the Hebreo-Christian concept of "creation" to say that the subject of work, the human person, is the *sole "creative source of value"*: human beings produce, *ex nihilo subjecti*—in the absence of any material substrate (and hence, in due course, in the absence of capital as a material substrate)—what we call "value " (for the moment, in general, or *in abstracto*).

Nature, as mere nature, has no value. It is only matter, potency— the potential material of work. As such it "amounts to nothing." Land "amounts to nothing"—has no more actual "value" than the surface of Saturn—until human work renders it its object, its matter. Land has no intrinsic value. Land as land is without value. It is the agriculture, the work, the human life objectified in that work, that bestows value on land. It is *subjective work* (as John Paul II indicates, *Laborem Exercens*, 6) that furnishes the value of the object. Thus the value of land, like that of any object, is as sacred as human life itself. To rob persons of the value of their product, then, is to kill them (Ecclus. 34:22).

The "product value" is identical with the value of the human labor it represents. By definition, their equivalence is one of total equality. The *price* of the product, for its part, essentially and in the abstract, is merely the value of that product in terms of *money*. The amount of money representing the price of the product ought to be equivalent to the value of the objects needed by workers to replace the life that they have objectified in this particular product.

11.6 PRODUCT OWNERSHIP

The social teaching of the church admits that the natural owner of a product is its producer, the worker. The latter is invested with right of possession and of use. It can scarcely be otherwise if what I have been saying is rational and coherent.

Work bestows on the worker the possession of a thing as one's own right (*Rerum Novarum*, 3). Work produces fruits, and alone adjudicates those fruits to the one who has produced them by working (*Quadragesimo Anno*, 52). Any object possessed is the fruit of labor, and the only legitimate title to its possession, whether as private property, or as public or collective property, is its service to labor (*Laborem Exercens*, 14).

As persons, and persons invested with freedom, human beings are the subject of a relationship of *dominion* over their own life. This is the basis of the right to devote one's life to a cause, even "delivering up" that life (as does the hero or the martyr).

The actual exercise of dominion over one's life implies a number of possible relationships, between the subject of the life and the life itself. It implies the real option to reproduce that life or to suppress it, to objectify it or to recover that objectification. The life objectified by the subject in the product of work is the very life of that subject. This is the foundation of the absolute right of workers to the product of work. It is only through an imperceptible "sleight of hand," as we shall see below (12.6), that workers' ownership of their *own* product is transformed into ownership by *another*, a subject who has performed no work upon that product, a subject who claims the same right to the work of *others* as actually belongs to workers because of their *own work*.

God created the universe for all human beings, bestowing on them the right to the common use of the world. And yet private ownership is exercised over these goods, even when they constitute the necessities of life, despite the Bible, despite the Fathers of the Church, despite Thomas Aquinas (for whom such ownership was legitimate only in the "law of nations," not in "natural law").

11.7 DOES WORK HAVE VALUE?

If the *products* of work have value (and I am still speaking generally, not in a context of capitalism), can *work itself* have any value?

One sometimes hears, when payment for work in the form of wages (11.9) is being discussed, that work has value. But let us keep in mind an essential aspect of the biblical conception of work. If the human person is the most sacred thing in creation, if human work is the image or likeness of the creative act of God, and if "as a person, the human being is the subject of work" (*Laborem Exercens*, 6), then work can have no *value*. As the subject of the highest dignity in creation, and thus essentially and basically the measure and creative font of all value ("all things are measured by the measure of the dignity of the subject"—ibid.), the human being transcends value. One cannot "have" what one transcends. Thus strictly speaking the human being is beyond all value.

Value is a quality or aspect of the product of work, not of the personal subject of that work. Value attaches to a product, to what is useful. A product has value, and in virtue of that value it can be exchanged. It has productuality, utility, and exchangeability. But none of this attaches to human persons as subjects of the work that has produced the product. Neither have they been produced (rather, they have been procreated), nor are they useful (rather, "worthy," invested with intrinsic dignity), nor can they be exchanged (as if they were slaves). One of the satanic practices of slaveholders of the New World, whether in Bahia or Georgia, was the reproduction of slaves. Male and female African blacks were paired for breeding, and slave children were "produced" and sold. In this case the subject of work, and not only the work itself, would have value (as does a cow or a bull). But here a person is treated as a thing, a piece of merchandise, and alienated even before its conception.

Work, then, has no "value" attaching to it, any more than does the subject of the work. Once more, the human being is the "creative source of all value"—a concept essentially in accord with the Christian theology of all ages.

11.8 MONEY AS OBJECTIFIED LIFE

Like the prophets who preceded him, Jesus was altogether conscious of the ambiguity of money. "How hard it will be for the rich to enter the reign of God!" (Matt. 19:23); "One cannot serve God and mammon" (Matt. 6:24); ". . . the mammon of iniquity" (Luke 16:9). Why this mistrust of money? Why this negative view of "mammon"?

Shoes can be exchanged for wheat in virtue of the exchange value (11.4) attaching to each of those products respectively. To the one— the shoes, for example— a *relative* value attaches (a value relative to the wheat). Thus it can be exchanged for the other term of the exchange, in this case, the wheat (whose value is *equivalent* to that of the shoes). But then, say, a table could be exchanged for x amount of wheat, a chair could be exchanged for y amount of wheat, whereas a house would bring z amount of wheat. Wheat could be measured out in quantities equivalent, respectively, to the values of all the other products of work, and thereby itself constitute the measure of all those values. Were it actually to function as such a universal equivalent in real life, wheat would by that very fact be constituted as *money*.

Money, in its basic definition, is the value of some product of labor (or indeed some abstract value as such) determined by convention to function as the measure of all other values. But just as the value of all products of human work is human life objectified, money also represents human life. If with x amount of money I can eat, survive, for a month, then x amount of money represents as much life as I live over the course of a month. To accumulate money is to accumulate human life. For a desert ethics of shepherds and bedouins, or of the prophets of Israel, accumulation was hoarding, and perverse: "'Let no one attempt to keep anything over for tomorrow.' But they paid no attention, and sought to keep something over for the morrow, so that putrefying maggots emerged in it to spoil it" (Exod. 16:19–20).

Money affords the possessor the opportunity to accumulate, to amass, the wealth that is the life of others. If there were no money, one could still steal, but thefts could not be cumulative. They would be "discontinuous," perpetrated as single points in time and space. They could not be institutional. Money is the bloodthirsty god Moloch or mammon, and the blood for which it thirsts is the blood of human life.

11.9 WORK CAPACITY AND WAGES

The institution of wages has flourished even beyond the pale of capitalism—for example, among the ancient Greeks or Hebrews. "Pay not a just wage, and shed blood" (Ecclus. 34:22). What is a wage? How are a worker's wages determined?

A wage is simply the price of the usual value of a worker's capacity for work. Price is the expression in terms of money of the value of a thing. Money (11.8) is a product (or series of products) whose value (or series of values) is designated by convention as the measure of other values. When price was expressed in gold coins, the number of coins representing the value of a thing (the price of the thing) was the expression of its value in gold. The amount of human life objectified in the production of shoes or wheat was regarded as "tantamount," precisely, to the "amount" of human life objectified in the obtaining, the extraction and refining, of that much gold. The gold was the *measure* of the wheat or the shoes.

Thus money fixes the value of the "work capacity of workers" (*Laborem Exercens*, 12)—not of their work, which has no value, being the "*creative* source of all value." What is "work capacity"? Work capacity is potential for work in the sense of Thomas Aquinas's *potentia* or Aristotle's *dynamis*. Whether or not workers *can* work depends on whether they have eaten and rested, have good health and a strong body, clothing, housing, and education. It further depends on whether they have a spouse and children (the latter being the workers of the next generation), and whether they eat, are educated, and so on. All such elements constitute the *conditio sine qua non* of workers' *potential* (capacity, *potentia*, strength) for actual work.

In other words, in reality a wage does not purchase the subject or agent of the work (the human person, created by God and procreated by human parents, by the human race). A worker has dignity, but no value. Thus the person of the worker can only be "gratis." The wage purchases only the work capacity or potential of the worker. The value of this capacity does shift to the product as part of the "product value." But the "value of the integral product" also includes the *new* value created by the subject of the work. When men and women work, they not only reproduce the goods necessary for their subsistence; they create, *ex nihilo* (out of nothing, as far as any pre-existing, underlying matter is concerned), new value, out of their creative subjectivity alone. It is owing to this act of creation that there is "progress" in the history and development of humanity. The "product value" of an object produced is equal to whatever amount of the life of workers it objectifies. As the creation of workers, as the fruit of the toil of these particular human beings, the product is the property of the workers who have produced it.

11.10 AN ETHICO-PRODUCTIVE COMMUNITY

The "life cycle" (4.8), in terms of both human nature and justice, is the locus of the consumption of energy by the human person as a living being. This living being suffers need; and thereupon performs work; and thereupon is satisfied with the product of that work—by consuming, and thereby recovering his or her objectified life with interest (for in working the worker has created *new* value).

Were it not for sin, were it not for domination and theft, it would be easy for individuals to constitute "living communities" (*Laborem Exercens*, 14), like the ecclesial community of Jerusalem (1.1), or like the later communities of cenobites who held all things *in common* (in the East, as well as among the Latin Benedictines with their motto, "to work is to pray," or like the Jesuit, Franciscan, and other "reductions" (independent communities) of colonial Spanish and Portuguese America. All of these communities were "commun-ities" indeed—entities in which life, production, and consumption were practiced in common. In these historical utopias, these "associations of free persons," the product was originally communal.

Here the "face-to-face" of the community of persons (1.5), the practical or ethical relationship, functioned as the "whence" of any decision-making as to the production of products for life and living. The "*subjectivity* of society" was guaranteed:

> By the subjectivity of a society we mean the ideal or factual attitude of a society guaranteeing each and every member of the community, in virtue of their own work, full title to co-ownership in the great workshop in which they commit themselves in union with all their peers [*Laborem Exercens*, 14].

In such a community, all workers are "conscious of working on something of their own" (ibid., 15). Full individuality is actualized in full community.

In this type of community of production, the worker ought to enjoy full, conscious awareness of, and bear full responsibility for, the productive process, from its original planning to the last decision taken regarding the product. In this type of community, one could genuinely "speak of socialization" (ibid., 14).

CONCLUSIONS

The hardest questions are simple when stripped to their bare essentials. A *theology of work*—and thus of course the ethics that forms part and parcel of this theology—must accept fundamental biblical principles, not excluding those expressed in the "social teaching of the church." It has not been my intention to contribute anything new to the content of the theological ethics of work. I have sought only to establish the starting point for an ethical critique of the prevailing, dominating morality of Latin America, the peripheral world, and the developed capitalist nations themselves.

Chapter 12

Ethical Critique of Capital

12.1 STATE OF THE QUESTION

I have come now to the central topic of the ethical theology that is the subject of this book. I continue, however, to deal on an abstract, general level. I am still speaking of *structural sin in general*—institutional sin stripped to its essentials. Only later shall I apply my findings to the more concrete levels of this sin. I am reflecting on the "social mechanism of sin," then, to use the words of Pope John Paul II in Mexico in 1979, but in its most general sense—in its basic *reality*.

We read in the daily newspapers that such and such corporations or institutions have made investments, that such and such a wealthy person is "worth" so much capital, that there is a crisis in the "capitalistic system," or that the value of merchandise has dropped on the market. What theological meaning attaches to all of this?

We read in holy scripture:

> As for you, you rich, weep and wail over your impending miseries. Your wealth has rotted, your fine wardrobe has grown moth-eaten, your gold and silver have corroded, and their corrosion shall be a testimony against you; it will devour your flesh like a fire. See what you have stored up for yourselves against the last days. Here, crying aloud, are the wages you withheld from the farmhands who harvested your fields. The cries of the harvesters have reached the ears of the Lord of hosts. You lived in wanton luxury on the earth; you fattened yourselves for the day of slaughter. You condemned, even killed, the just man; he does not resist you [James 5:1–6].

The words of Saint James will provide us with the theoretical (theological) horizon of an unmistakable situation of injustice whose cries to heaven are even more deafening today than when these words were written.

12.2 THE "POOR" TODAY

The "poor" constitute the majority of the population of the nations of the world, especially in the "peripheral" world. Let it be noted, however, that I am still speaking in general, or "essentially." I am speaking of the "poor" in their basic confrontation with the "rich"—with the vested interests of the system (any system, not just a capitalistic economic system).

The "poor," in their anteriority or exteriority, are those who emerge into the society of the prevailing system from a community that has been dissolved—for example, the Zapotecs of Oaxaca in Mexico, who must come to Mexico City in order to find work. The dominating system has destroyed their previous way of life. It has expelled them from the place where they had lived in security, with legitimate wealth, with their family, relatives, nation, history, culture, and religion. They are the *pauper ante festum*—the poor who find themselves standing wistfully at the door of the feast that is about to make them its main dish.

The "poor"—still in the negative sense—are those who, in the face-to-face of the person-to-person relationship (1.3) must confront the person possessed of money. And yet they have not sold themselves. They are poor because they have their own corporality to sell (6.4), their bodiliness, their skin, their "hide," in their absolute nakedness, their radical poverty—without food, clothing, housing, health, protection. They are but miserable beggars. The word "economy" comes from the Greek *oikos* and *nomos*, and means, etymologically, "law of the house." The homeless, then, are nothing, non-being, worthless, to the economists of domination. The "poor"—this time in the positive sense of the word—are the miserable unemployed, precisely in their carnality, their fleshliness. They ask the person with money, the capitalist (or abstractly, capital) for work. And yet they are subject, the creative subject, of all possible value. These starving poor, who beg for work, for a wage, are the very Christ of the *ecce homo*. And yet it is they who constitute the foundation and groundwork of the whole current system of domination. They abide only on the outside,"thrown into the ditch and robbed." But there is no Samaritan to help them.

12.3 SIN AS THE SOCIAL RELATIONSHIP OF DOMINATION

I have shown that praxis is a relationship (1.2), and that the praxis of domination or sin is a *social* relationship (2.5), being the breach of *community* relationship (1.5, 4.6, 12.2). When that relationship is institutionalized (2.5–2.6), it becomes real and historical. In this section I propose to speak (in abstract, very general terms—considering sin in its ultimate essence, then) of the fundamental institutional sin of our time.

Standing in the "face to face" of the person-to-person relationship (chap. 1) are, on the one hand, the "poor" and, on the other, those who have the money to pay for the work the poor perform (the "rich," then, in the sense of the biblical category). But the persons in this relationship do not face each other as did Moses and God, or the Samaritan and the poor victim of the robbery on the road to Jericho—that is, in infinite respect for one another's otherness (5.2). Instead, in the interpersonal relationship under consideration, one term is constituted by a wretched individual who must go begging in order to eat, dress, have a house or health, and so on; and the other is the person who has money (and we ask: from what source? by what means?) and who wishes to increase the amount of that money thanks to the other person. The money ($—see Diagram 9 p. 161) must increase ($') and adopts the other as the mediation of that increase. It instrumentalizes, reifies, alienates that other (2.2). The prince of "this world" has commenced his praxis (2.10).

The person having money proposes to the poor person (the individual who has already been *violently* coerced, with the violence of the injustice that has destroyed his or her community of origin—16.7) a contract, an exchange (11.4). Thus a *relationship* is struck between the two: I give you money ($—Diagram 9) and you give me your work, which, purchased as commodity, now becomes my property, for I am the one who had the money. Correlatively, the one who had work to offer exchanges it for money—receives wages (W) (see 11.9).

But there is a subtle *inequality* in this exchange, invisible both to the one who has the money and the one who offers the work. This is a *social* relationship (8.2) because it is a relationship of domination, of injustice. Invisibly, imperceptibly, it is sin. Why? Because the person having the money uses the *person* of the worker while paying only for that person's *work capacity* (11.9). The employer makes use of the whole worker, makes use of the "creative source of value" (11.9, 12.2), though paying only for his or her "upkeep." It is as if someone wished to purchase an automobile by paying only for fuel and servicing. I receive the "creative subject" gratis, and pay only for what is needed to keep that subject from dying, to keep it working. As creators in the image of God, inventors by nature, obviously human beings will produce a value equivalent to the value of their needs (which is the value of the money they are to be paid in wages! 11.8) in a certain time, and then will go on to produce beyond this limit. Thus the value of the product (11.5) produced by the worker will acquire a "more-value," *more life* and more reality than the value of the wages received. In other words, the worker will give more life than he or she receives. This is an injustice, a *social* relationship of domination (3.2), a sin.

12.4 WHAT IS CAPITAL?

The word "capital" has a great many meanings. It derives from *caput*, Latin for "head." To have a great many sources or "heads" of profit was to have a great deal of "capital." Many understand "capital" as money, others as goods, and so on. Let us examine this question.

In the social teaching of the church, capital is a "fact": "neither can capital subsist without work, nor can work subsist without capital" (*Rerum Novarum*, 14). These documents generally identify capital with "wealth." More precisely: "Capital, inasmuch as it constitutes a set of means of production, is only an instrument, or instrumental cause" (*Laborem Exercens*, 12). It has been a long road from *Rerum Novarum* (1891) to *Laborem Exercens* (1981). The teaching now is that all capital is the fruit of work: "All of the means of production, from the most primitive to the ultramodern, have been developed gradually by the human being.... [They are] the fruit of work" (*Laborem Exercens*, 12).

Pursuing the line of thought I have undertaken, the concept of "capital" could be understood as extending beyond money or commodity to the means of production as well. But—and this is sometimes forgotten—work, purchased and used (over the course of an eight-hour day, for example), as it is taken up or subsumed by the capital that has employed it, itself becomes capital—specifically, the value-creating aspect of that capital. Finally, the product, too, which is value before being commodity, is capital.

In terms of Aristotle's concept of movement (*kinesis*), then, we may understand capital as the *subject of value in its movement of growth*. Value *passes through successive determinations*. It moves from money to work (wages), then to the means of production, then (in virtue of the interplay of the latter two moments) to objectification in the product, then (as the product enters the market) to commodity, and finally (as the merchandise is sold) to money once more ($—Diagram 9). But this time the amount of money has grown, has become more money, surplus money ($'), as profit has accrued to the original amount. This entire, circular (or rather, spiraling) process, like some great, organic maelstrom, is capital: the growth of value, "valorization."

12.5 THE POOR AS WAGE-EARNERS

In a biblical sense of the word, the "poor" are the dominated, persons murdered by sin (2.7–8). The "poor" in the economic sense are the wretched, those left lying by the side of the road, those living outside the system. Biblically speaking, the "poor" are the exploited: they are Job suffering the results of the praxis of domination, writhing under the satanic praxis of the sinner.

Torn from their original *community* (8.3), their former source of security, the poor have been thrown on the "labor market" (12.2). In the "world of commodities" (*Laborem Exercens*, 7: "work was understood and treated as a kind of merchandise"), the poor, in their absolute nakedness and radical poverty, sell their "skin" as a thing. "The primacy of the human being vis-à-vis things" (*Laborem Exercens*, 12) has gone by the board. Now they are isolated, solitary *individuals*, without a community, in a dominating *society* (3.2), where they attain to their "sociality" only to the extent that they toil in the workshop or are bought and sold *on the market*. Whether in the workshop or on the market, they continue their individual isolation.

Once workers have sold their work, they are no longer their "own," but the property of another. Now they are "made other" ("otherfied") alienated, the object of sin and exploitation, and this in an institutional manner (2.5) thanks to the social division of labor. Now their work must be sold daily. The only alternative is starvation. Like some great god (2.3, 12.10), capital fills every corner. There is no possibility for the reproduction of the worker's life without the participation of capital. There is no "work ... without capital" (*Rerum Novarum*, 14). Now we have "work for hire," the obligatory alienated *social* relationship that demands of workers that they sell themselves for a wage that pays them *less* life than the life they objectify in the product destined to be possessed by the owner of money. "Work for hire" is the name of the institutional sin of our time. It has held sway for the past several centuries of human life on earth. Thus work for hire is the "original" sin committed against the worker (2.5)—committed by the "rich" (in the biblical sense) upon the poor.

12.6 ACCUMULATION OF "SURPLUS LIFE"

The theological syllogism is a traditional one. Workers objectify their life in their product (11.3; Ecclus. 34:21). Their wages, being in the form of money, are vehicles of value, which is life (11.9, 11.8). But the value or life objectified in the product (11.3) is greater than that received in wages. (Otherwise where does the profit come from—the difference between $ and $'—Diagram 9?) See 12.3.

Some identify profit as a difference in value between the value of merchandise sold and the payment received, which payment would somehow be greater than the value of the commodity sold. In that case, the seller steals from the purchaser (commercial injustice). But then, in becoming buyers in their own turn—in buying the products needed in order to produce their own--sellers (and workers themselves can sell their work for more than the value of their work capacity) are robbed in turn, and everything "comes out even."

The objection might be raised that employers earn their profit by the work they perform. No, work is recompensed precisely through a wage, which employers can and should receive (in some decent proportion to the wages the workers are paid). Anything left over—called "profit"—is the fruit of the *work of the non-owners* of the capital invested—for which they have not been paid—not that of the capital itself, and therefore does not belong to the owners or stockholders.

But does capital not "earn" a profit from the risks it takes? No, risk is not a principle of the creation of value or earnings. (This is not the place for the rehearsal of and response to every possible objection. Suffice it to have sketched these two.)

The secret of the great idol of capital lies in the fact that the profit gained in exchange, in the circulation I have sketched, is based on the "surplus life" acquired by capital in the productive process by paying *less* by way of wages (x life) than the value produced in the product by the worker (y life—11.3). And James protests in advance: "Here, crying aloud, are the *wages* you withheld from the farmhands who harvested your fields. The cries of the harvesters have reached the ears of the Lord of hosts" (James 5:6) The social relationship is unjust and sinful, and this is why "your wealth has rotted" (James 5:2).

"Capital springs from labor, and bears the marks of human toil" (*Laborem Exercens*, 12). It is made up entirely of the accumulated life of the worker. Workers have been dispossessed of the fruit of their toil in advance (11.6), and day after day, by reason of the structural sin of our time, continue to be stripped of the "surplus life" they produce—the difference between their wages and the value of the product. This surplus life is absorbed by capital. "Capital cannot subsist without work" (*Rerum Novarum*, 14).

12.7 THE INSTITUTION OF INVISIBLE SIN

Thus in its more comprehensive, broader sense, at least, if not indeed in its strict sense as well, capital is a *social* relationship of domination, a certain relationship of unequal exchange among persons, a *practical* (1.3) or *moral* (3.6) relationship, with respect to work or its products—a *productive* relationship, then (1.2, 8.4), an economic exchange in both the anthropological and the theological senses of the word (11.4, 1.6, 6.10). But this relationship is stable and historical. Therefore we are dealing with an altogether particular "*social* institution."

The prince of "this world" (2.10) employs his mechanisms in all invisibility. Neither his existence nor his machinations are any longer the object of anyone's belief. Thus he can act with impunity. The "good" bourgeois person (3.7, 3.8, 3.9)—indeed the "good" worker (the virtuous, punctual, "responsible" worker), because the dominated at times introject the dominant morality (8.6)—are actually *good* and moral in the eyes of the prevailing morality (3.7). The *social* relationship of domination, which is the unjust essence of capital, is accepted by the owner of the capital and of the work as "natural" (3.9). In all tranquility of "moral conscience" (3.8), the owner kills the neighbor.

Thus this *institutional sin* is very subtle. It is invisible. It is "absent in its very presence." It conditions the existence of us all (2.5): it determines one of the terms of the *practical* (1.2), *social* (8.2) *relationship*. (To be sure, the determinism in question is relative. I reject the oversimplification of a determinism that would preclude the possibility of a "conversion"—4.3.) It is in this sense, as well as by reason of its nature as wealth or means of production (as for the social teaching of the church), that capital is a social, historical *institution* of injustice, and hence a praxis of domination. Capital consists of the accumulation of the surplus life unjustly extracted from the worker.

The structural sin of any age has always been invisible to the prevailing morality of that age (3.6), and bourgeois morality is no exception. But the task of ethics, of prophecy, is to render that sin visible, after the example of Bartolomé de Las Casas: "All have sinned. It is gravest injustice."

12.8 THE PERSON OF THE WORKER AS "NOTHINGNESS"

Capital has no misgivings about its own divinity. It pretends to produce profit *ex nihilo*, out of nothing. Its idolatrous (12.10), fetishistic nature blinds it to the origin of any of the value that it contains, that it has accumulated. It actually believes that it has produced that value. The person of the worker is regarded as nothingness in the process.

Only God creates from nothing. Out of infinite, unconditioned freedom, God has created the entire universe. But capital pretends that it too has created something out of its sheer spontaneity. It has created profit, it cries. Of course, for this to hold true, the worker must be reduced to nothing. And surely enough, for capital, the worker who does no work—who is not the subject of "productive work," of work that yields surplus life (12.6)—does not "count," does not constitute a "social class" (8.4), is not made use of (exploited), and hence cannot have been subsumed by capital (12.4). Such a worker is outside, is no-thing.

For capital, furthermore, the wage-earner is "virtually poor" (*virtualiter pauper*). *Before* being purchased, the wage-earner is nothing. *While* being used, the worker is an alienated aspect of capital (in a social relationship of sin). *After* being used, when no longer needed (for example, when technology has stepped up production and decreased the number of wage-earners), the worker is a miserable beggar (even with welfare payments or unemployment benefits in developed countries; in peripheral countries the worker simply starves to death in some urban slum or outlying shantytown).

Constituting a social relationship of domination—being sin—capital shows no mercy. It cannot commiserate, it cannot accord any consideration to the dignity of the person. It can have no recourse to any ethical yardstick. It does not hear the voice of the other (4.2). It has "hardened its heart."

12.9 BLOOD CIRCULATION

Capital, then, is ultimately value (11.5)—but only in the strictly capitalist sense of value. Value attaches to something useful (use value is its material base) produced by human work (productuality) in order to be sold as merchandise (exchangeability is essential to value).

Ultimately, then, capital is "value" *moving* or circulating through its successive determinations—money, wage-earning work, means of production, and so on (12.4)—and growing, thanks to the "surplus life" it extracts from the worker (12.6). The Bible styles this value "blood": "Who does not pay the just wage spills blood" (Ecclus. 34:22).

Blood is the seat of life (2.8). Without blood an organism dies. But workers objectify their life in the product of their work, in the value of their product (11.3). And so their death occurs: objectified life has not returned to the producer. Instead of a "circle of life" (11.2), the movement of value is transformed into a "circle of death" (2.8). It continues to be life—but it has become the *life of capital*. For, as we have seen, the life of capital, like the circulation of blood, is a continuous circulation of value, which is transformed from money into wages or means of production, then into product, then into merchandise, and so on, and finally into *more* money, "surplus money." O blessed profit, "made" on the altar of the murder of "the innocent" (James 5:6)! "To divest the poor to offer sacrifice"—to the idol, capital—"is to murder the child in the presence of its father" (Ecclus. 34:20).

Thus value follows its life course through the successive determinations of *industrial* capital to become *profit*; then through the veins of *commercial* capital to reach the status of *commercial profit*; thereupon to arrive at the condition of *financial* capital, which gains *interest* through the investment of money alone. Interest is the sin of usury transfigured to the virtue of saving. Behold the bourgeois virtue of economy (saving, hoarding), condemned by the Fathers, the church, and justice itself (15.2–3). All of this value is simply and solely the *life* of workers dispossessed of their property.

12.10 IDOLATRY CONSUMMATED

Our reflection is theological. Accordingly, evil is seen and interpreted *sub peccati lumine* ("in the light of sin"). In its origin and essence, capital is a social relationship of domination. Therefore the consummation of its "morality" (3.8), and its total justification, rests upon its ready capacity to consign the other term of the relationship to oblivion. Capital's self-absolutization, its claim to utter singularity, isolation, and existence *ex se*, its denial that it is beholden to anyone or anything, constitutes its character as a false god and an idol (2.3).

The sin of Adam, we learn in the Book of Genesis, consisted in seeking to be "as God." Capital, too, denies its origin (the toil of the worker), pretending that its increase, its growth, its profit, emerges from its own entrails (rather than being extracted from the worker in the form of "surplus life"). It owes no one anything, then. All value produced, regardless of its actual source, belongs to capital. Capital has negated the worker as the "creative source of value," absolutizing itself instead. "Work has been separated from capital, and counterposed to capital ... almost as if they were two autonomous forces" (*Laborem Exercens*, 13). And this "separation" has fetishized capital, and alienated it from work.

Indeed, to "separate" capital from work as a self-subsisting profit-making entity, and work from capital as a self-subsisting wage-earning entity, is to forget that "*all capital* is objectified work" and therefore *only work*. We do not actually have two terms here. We have one only: *work*, now as objectified (as capital), now "living work" (as the life of the personal subject working here and now).

Once capital is absolutized—idolized, fetishized—it is the workers themselves who are immolated on its altar, as their life is extracted from them (their wages do not pay the whole of the life they objectify in the value of the product) and immolated to the god. As of old, so today as well, living human beings are sacrificed to mammon and Moloch. Only, today the oblation—and it alone—permits the dominant class to enjoy the surplus life of its victims. "Woe to you rich. You have received your reward" (Luke 6:24).

CONCLUSIONS

The theology or ethics of liberation interprets reality *sub pauperum lumine*—from the point of view of the poor. My conclusions may seem exceedingly hard, unilateral, and apocalyptic. In my view, they are simply ethical, evangelical, and realistic. Jewish theologian that he was (however some may be at pains to deny it), Jesus draws the conclusions generated by his premises. He did not cringe or fall back before them, cost his life though they might. Not without reason "must this man suffer much, be rejected by the elders, the chief priests, and the doctors of the law, be executed" (Mark 8:31). Our ethic cannot be a reformist morality (3.6, 3.2). This does not mean that it will be practicable on the present level of abstraction. ("Abstract" or "essential" does not mean "unreal." However, abstract conclusions cannot be practiced without concrete mediations.) All tactics are possible within the framework of ethical demands. But they may not violate ethical principles (5.3, 5.6–7, 5.9) through the utilization of the moralizing, received tactics of the day. Such tactics may not be adapted to the prevailing system. One must distinguish between the tactics demanded by the practice of prophecy or ethical criticism, and a reformist betrayal on the part of those who accept the tenets of the system of domination in the name of the reign of God.

Chapter 13

Ethical Critique of Dependence

13.1 STATE OF THE QUESTION

Still very abstractly—if more concretely than with the considerations of the preceding chapter—I now turn attention to yet another essential aspect of sin. Having examined the "international *social* relationship"—the vertical relationship between capital and labor—let us consider the horizontal relationship of competition obtaining among the particular supplies of capital of the various nations.

We read about North-South relationships in the daily newspapers: we hear that UNCTAD meetings have been broken off, that the rich nations are forcing the poor nations to pay for their crisis, or that the rift is widening between the nations of the North and those of the South.

We read in holy scripture:

Woe to the rebellious children,
    says the Lord,
Who carry out plans that are not mine;
    who weave webs that are not inspired by me,
    adding sin upon sin.
They go down to Egypt,
    but my counsel they do not seek.
They find their strength in the pharaoh's protection
    and take refuge in Egypt's shadow;
Pharaoh's protection shall be your shame,
    and refuge in Egypt's shadow your disgrace.
When their princes are at Zoan
    and their messengers reach Hanes,
All shall be ashamed

of a people that gain them nothing,
Neither help nor benefit,
    but only shame and reproach [Isa. 30:1–5].

Here we have an apt characterization of the situation I am about to describe. To the sin of chapter twelve is added a new sin, so that we have "sin upon sin," superdetermination, superdomination, superexploitation. The expression "sin (*jatha't*) upon sin (*hal-jatha't*)" indicates that our considerations are about to shift to a more concrete, more real, more complex level.

13.2 SOME NECESSARY DISTINCTIONS

Capital (12.4, 12.9) is not of a piece. It is cloven, divided, differentiated. There is capital and capital: this branch of capital and that, this sector and that, this nation's capital and that one's. Only in the abstract, only as a single concept, is capital one. In the concrete it is multiple.

Here we must invoke the species of *analogy* that Thomas Aquinas called "proper proportionality." First, what I have said of capital in general, I now apply to the various kinds of capital under consideration as they stand in opposition to one another. We find individual supplies of capital operating in mutual confrontation. They are in "competition" with one another. If capital is a "*social relationship*" (12.3), two or more supplies of capital in confrontation will constitute the terms or a *relationship of relationships*. The relationship obtaining between capital and labor is *vertical*—a relationship of exploitation as sin (12.7). The relationship obtaining between two supplies of capital is a *horizontal* one—that of competition.

The horizontal relationship among supplies of capital is manifold. First there is the relationship among the branches of capital (between the metallurgical industry and the chemical industry, for example). The branches of capital can *compete*. One may be more profitable than another; or one may be more profitable during one period of time, and another during another. In analogous fashion, capital may be divided into "sector one" (the produced means of production, such as machinery and technology—this will be constant, fixed capital) and "sector two" (as, for example, consumer or agricultural products, terms of a relationship with wages—circulating capital). An individual supply of capital as a whole will have branches, sectors, parts, dividing it further through a division of labor.

Then, once more in analogous fashion, capital is divided along international lines, with the total capital of one nation pitted against that of another in a relationship of competition, or those of nations having their respective total aggregates of capital more highly developed (in the *technological* component of value, then) standing in opposition to the supplies of capital of less developed nations, the stronger against the weaker (in terms of *accumulation*), the central against the peripheral (in terms of the *spatial* hegemony of a capital first to develop in *time*), and so forth.

13.3 THE NATION AS POOR

Still in terms of our analogy: just as a particular supply of capital has a subject of appropriation—a person, the capitalist—so also a total national capital has a subject of appropriation: a bourgeois class. Beginning with the Renaissance this class rose to the status of the hegemonic one in the West, and set up the nation states, first in Europe and later in the Third World, so that "men of all countries ... are now citizens of an independent state" (*Pacem in Terris*, 42).

Despite the danger of its fetishization—as in Nazism and Fascism—the "nation" is the "great society to which one belongs on the basis of particular cultural and historical bonds. ... The culture of a determinate nation ... [is] a great historical and social incarnation of the work of all generations" (*Laborem Exercens*, 10). Despite the criticisms we may level against it, the nation continues to be the spatial, politico-historical, cultural, linguistic, and even religious horizon within which peoples live and dwell.

Consequently, corresponding to the vertical relationship of class (that between capital and labor), we have a horizontal relationship as well, and one of worldwide dimensions. One can "set in relief the problem of *class*, especially," as Pope John Paul II says; but one can also bring "the problem of the *world* into the foreground ... the worldwide sway of inequality and injustice" (*Laborem Exercens*, 2). Here sin acquires a world dimension, and the suffering Job of the Bible becomes the *poor nation*.

By "poor" nation I understand the victim of (politico-military) domination, the ideological (cultural) hegemony of another nation, and economic exploitation (by way of the transfer of surplus value). Poor and impoverished, "the hungry peoples call out to the opulent peoples" (*Gaudium et Spes*, 9).

13.4 THE INTERNATIONAL SOCIAL RELATIONSHIP

As I have said (12.1), because capital is a social relationship, competition among national supplies of capital will constitute a relationship of relationships. Both relationships are relationships of domination: the first by the very nature of capital, the second—the one now under consideration—in its quality as a relationship of dependence. That is, both relationships are relationships of sin. In the latter we have "sin upon sin," in the form of the *exploitation of the exploiter*. Let us examine this question.

We cannot escape the fact that "the poor peoples always remain poor, and the rich become gradually richer" (*Populorum Progressio*, 59), a fact that Medellín attributes to the following causality:

> We wish to stress that the main culprits in our situation of economic dependence are those forces that seek unrestrained profit, and thus pave the way for economic dictatorship and the "international imperialism of money" (condemned by Pius XI in *Quadragesimo Anno* and by Paul VI in *Populorum Progressio*) [*Medellín Document on Peace*, 9e].

Praxis is a relationship among persons (1.2) or among nations (or their supplies of capital). The praxis of domination is sin (2.2). The "*international* social relationship" of domination among nations (or among their supplies of capital, even where the relationship is one of competition among dominators) is an "*international* sin," then, a world structure of evil, the structure of the domain of the Prince of "this world" (2.10), and it causes the death of entire nations (2.8), the *poor* nations (2.7). This complex structure determines its agents, and is inherited historically (2.6). It is the most fundamental social sin of our age (2.5), despite the fact that it is the least visible (3.9).

If there is sin in the social relationship of capital, by which one person appropriates the life of others (12.6), now we have the sin whereby entire nations transfer *their life* to other nations, through the intermediary of complex mechanisms by which the total capital of poor countries is lost, annihilated, delivered over to other countries.

13.5 WHAT IS DEPENDENCE?

Medellín speaks of "dependence." This concept appeared in the social sciences in Latin America only in the mid-1960s, and has not yet attained the status of a clearly constituted category. But we may say that it denominates the abstract or essential law determining the type of international social relationship obtaining between the total national capital of a central (developed) nation (or nations) and the total national capital of a peripheral, underdeveloped nation (or nations)—a law whose ultimate content consists in the *transfer of the surplus value* (the surplus life) of weak capital to strong capital.

This is sin, this horizontal domination of one total national capital over another, weaker, and undeveloped national capital, in the international relationship of competition; this is *sin upon sin*, dependence. At its most general, basic, and abstract level, dependence will be the universal law as applied to the particular case of mercantile or free-trade colonial or imperialistic domination. Thus it will be operative in the phenomenon known as transnationalization (14.3). "Dependence" will thus denominate the theft, the unequal exchange, the sin, of the appropriation of the human life of another nation through the transfer and appropriation of its surplus value.

How is this transfer effectuated? In the first place, the "highly industrialized nations" (see *Populorum Progressio*, 57), in virtue of the greater technological resources at their disposition, can produce products at lower cost, put them on the market in less developed countries for a price above their value, and reap extraordinary profits. The less developed nations, on the contrary, must market higher-cost products (less technology having been employed in their production), lower their price to below their value when they are placed on central markets, and reap so little profit that these nations simply transfer their surplus value, their surplus life, to the developed nations, annihilating their own work and impoverishing themselves. Various factors convert this abstract "law" into a concrete tendency, and in certain cases actually transform it into a two-way street.

In its essence, then, "dependence" in ethical theology denotes a structural international sin by which the poor peoples lose *life*.

13.6 THE POOR NATION: A PEOPLE AND ITS DOUBLE EXPLOITATION

The poor capitalistic country (I shall speak of the socialist countries only in chap. 17)—poor even though capitalistic—is exploited through its bourgeois class (socially) and its total national private capital (economically). Without the transmission of which I have been speaking—without the transfer of surplus value from poor capitalistic nations to rich ones—the surplus life of a people cannot flow abroad. That is, if a poor nation is either a pre-capitalistic one, and therefore unexploitable, or a post-capitalistic one, which would therefore no longer allow itself to be exploited, so that there were no transfer of surplus value, then neither would there be a transfer of surplus life.

A peripheral total national capital is weak (because it transfers its surplus life and thus fails to build itself up), underdeveloped (because it is a latecomer technologically), and politically dominated (by security forces). A peripheral total national capital will therefore have to increase its exploitation of its workers (in the capital-labor, or vertical, relationship) in order to *compensate* for the loss of competition with other, central capitals (in the horizontal relationship). Thus the separation between the rich and the masses of the oppressed generates an ever more violent, bloody, repressive scenario.

The dominant bourgeois classes (the "rich," 2.7) must compensate for the transfer of their own surplus life by extracting even more of the life of the masses than before. Their productivity is low, for they have little technology (constant or fixed capital, depending on the level) at their disposition. Thus they must super-exploit the wage-earner, the "poor," by demanding more speed and effort in the workplace, as well as by imposing a minimal alimentary regime—tortillas and beans, rice and manioc, "bread and water." And so the *poor of the poor countries* become the genuinely miserable mass of the planet.

Thus the "peoples" are the *social* and *communal blocs* of those in the poor nations who are oppressed by super-exploitation. But these masses today are the subjects or loci of a universal conscientization with regard to the international, basic structural evil of which they are the victims. Their *consciousness* (4.2) is the clearest consciousness in present world history. As the subject, the host organism, of total suffering, they are the subject (agent) of our planetary future as well.

13.7 "SURPLUS LIFE" TRANSFERRED TO THE CENTER

The fetishistic essence of world capitalism is most clearly seen in the transfer of the life of the worker of a peripheral country to a central country via the supplies of capital between competition:

> Perhaps the greatest problem of our days is the one that concerns the relationships that ought to obtain between the economically developed nations and the countries still in the process of developing economically. The former enjoy a *comfortable life*, whereas the latter suffer the most grievous scarcity [*Mater et Magistra*, 157].

This transfer of "surplus life" is a concrete, horizontal channel (that of competition, 13.2) through which value passes from one total national capital to another. It is procured, in its essence, vertically (through the accumulation of capital in the form of work, 12.6), by way of the super-exploitation of peripheral workers. It is domination over a dominator who exploits still another victim of domination.

Theologically, "dependence" is the name of the international sin by which peripheral peoples are sacrificed to the fetish of world capitalism. Not only the laboring or agricultural class, but ethnic groups, tribes, and other marginal groups have their lives (their life, their work) immolated on the altar of a fetish (2.3, 12.9, 12.10) that today wears a global face. But the channels of this domination occasion no explicit consciousness of their nature or overt responsibility for their injustice (2.9). They operate through rigid structures, seemingly objective and objectively justified, whose origin no one remembers and whose rectification no one can imagine. And indeed, within the framework of the capitalistic rationale, no solution is possible (3.6).

To export the product of a poor country and sell it for a price *below* its value is to immolate *human life* to the international fetish in the form of profit. For a poor country to import a product and sell it for *more* than its value is likewise murder: it is the theft of the life of the poor, who use their money (their life—11.8) to purchase *less* life (in the form of products) than the life they have objectified in their wages.

13.8 THEOLOGY, POPULIST AND POPULAR

It was in the mid-1960s of our century, in Brazil, Peru, Chile, and elsewhere in Latin America, that the "poor" were first discovered as a *class*. Here, in Latin America today, were the "poor" in a truly biblical sense of the word (2.7, 12.2, 12.5, etc.). At the same moment, the "poor" were being identified in Argentina, Uruguay, and elsewhere, as the *people*. Despite the ever-present threat of "populism," this latter outlook (8.4–8.5) was adopted, from about 1973 onward, by all currents of thought in the theology of liberation.

I define "*populist* theology" as the theology that speaks of liberation, but does so in a context of *national* liberation—which would be unobjectionable (13.2, 13.3), were it not for the fact that it identifies the "nation" with the "people" (13.6): that is, it includes in the concept of "people" the dominant classes, especially the bourgeoisie. This is precisely the tenor of the Latin American "populisms"—those of Vargas, Cárdenas, Perón, Apri, and the like. These represent the capitalistic project of an anti-imperialist national liberation to be effectuated under the aegis and inspiration, and in the interests, of the industrial bourgeoisie. Certain theologies sustain this position, and these currents take an anti-socialistic line on "liberation."

At the other extreme there have been—and there still are today—theologies for which "liberation" is a process to be spearheaded by a "working class." What meaning could such a conceptualization possibly have in Guatemala, El Salvador, or Nicaragua? A certain dogmatic, abstract, classist theology rejects as "populist" any position that is not totally abstract. Here the "poor" are the wage-earners alone. This sort of "Marxism" is bookish and amateur.

A *popular* (neither populist, then, nor simply classist) theology of liberation defines its protagonist—the "people" (8.5–8.10, 13.6), the historical subject of the nation—as a bloc of the oppressed that excludes dominant classes, a bloc restricted to the "poor" in the political and economic sense of the word: working classes, ethnic groups, tribal groups, other marginalized groups, and even a petite bourgeoisie that has been "converted" (4.3)—the biblical "children of the pharaoh" (Exod. 2:10).

13.9 LIBERATION FROM SIN TODAY: ESSENTIAL LEVEL

Here as well, two extreme positions are to be avoided. Some think of sin as an *exclusively* religious phenomenon, played out *only* in *direct* relationship with God (2.2). The abstractive, monophysitic mentality betrayed by such an approach mars the August 1984 "Instruction" on the theology of liberation. It implies that there can be no such thing as sin on a profane, secular, economic, or political level. At the opposite pole there are those who think that sin is *only* to be found on these concrete levels.

Both positions are in error. Sin, as the domination of one person by another (2.2), is effectuated in praxis: in the action of domination and in the social relationship of the alienation of the other. In the concrete (and this distinction is neglected by the "Instruction") sin is an economic, political, sexual, ideological, or similar, domination. In the abstract (basically, or metaphysically)—inasmuch as everything finite and concrete is a creature of God and hence to be found within the order of the reign of God (1.8), as its affirmation (1.9) or negation (2.3)—all concrete domination, albeit profane, will always and at the same time be sin *against God*: against God's creatures, God's sons and daughters, or God's divine Son (and hence a matter for christology)—James 2:14–26; 1 John 4:19–21.

One of the concrete, historical, and *social* (3.2) dimensions of "sin today" is that it is a *social* relationship of inequality and domination—the relationship that I have denominated strictly (and if it were only "wealth," or "means of production," or any other partial element, my judgment errs—12.4) *capital*—wealth amassed by means of the blood extracted from the life of the poor.

On this abstract, fundamental, or essential level, liberation in a *dependent* Third World means the defeat of this alienating, sinful "social relationship." Historically, concretely, and essentially, *liberation* today is a dissolution of, emergence from—a gigantic *exodus* from—this "*social* relationship," where the poor are the victims of murder (2.7–8).

13.10 LIBERATION FROM SIN TODAY: WORLD LEVEL

Liberation (from sin) on a concrete level can be sexual, ideological, political, or economic liberation. It can be liberation, for example, from the social relationship that constitutes the essence of capital. But this concrete liberation, simultaneously and intrinsically, in virtue of its transcendental relationship (its creatureliness with respect to the Creator and its redeemability with respect to potential redemption in Christ), is religious, eschatological liberation as well (inasmuch as it constitutes community, 1.5; struggles with sin, 2.5, and with Babylon, 3.5; serves, 4.5; satisfies the poor, 4.9–10; sanctifies, 5.9, and liberates the "people of God," 8.10).

Poverty today, on its essential level, is the fruit of sin as the specific social relationship of capital and labor (12.3). But on a more concrete level—on the world level—sin has the name of dependence: sin is the transfer of surplus life from one nation to another (13.7). Liberation in this second sense is "national" liberation, yes, but not in the "populist" sense—rather in the popular (13.8). Liberation is deliverance from the sin of the horizontal international social relationship in which life is extracted by way of competition among supplies of capital—thanks to, and simultaneous with, deliverance from the sin of the vertical essential social relationship in which life is extracted by way of the relationship victimizing the wage-earner (12.5, 13.10). A "national" liberation consisting only of a breach with the social relationship, to the benefit of the national bourgeoisie, is only populist, superficial, and fictitious. The reality of the oppression of a poor people, by way of the relationship between capital and labor, abides.

A peripheral nation enjoys authentic national liberation only when it is effectuated in tandem with a liberation from the social relationship of capital and labor—in other words, only when national liberation is characterized by the "promotion of a more humane world for all" (*Populorum Progressio*, 44), and a genuine concern for "full human perfection" (*Gaudium et Spes*, 86).

CONCLUSIONS

I have dwelt on only one concrete level of sin—the structure and mechanism of sin on the world level, the relationship of domination imposed by the Prince of "this world" in the form of competition among the supplies of capital of the various nations occupying their several stations in the international division of labor (that is, executing their precise assignments in the process by which sin designates some as dominators and others as dominated). A theological community ethics must call things by their name. Precious little has been forthcoming in the way of prophetic denunciation of these levels. No ethical judgement has been pronounced upon the prevailing structures of our idolatrous world, which, with impunity—indeed, with a tranquil Christian conscience—plays with the very life of so many millions of human beings.

The extraction of wealth from underdeveloped, peripheral countries whose capitalism is weak and dependent is the immolation of human life to the cannibalistic, demoniacal, invisible god Capital. No one sees him, hears him, knows him, or blames him. Many Christians are the very agents of this monster, the Beast, in its appropriation of the lives of its victims. These Christians think they offer worship to the God of the poor of Israel, to the poor Jesus of Nazareth, in their Sunday liturgy. But they continue to offer weekly worship to the Monday-through-Friday god of their factories, their fields, and their private properties, which continue to swell with the surplus life of the poor, the life of a Christ crucified anew.

Chapter 14

The Transnationals

14.1 STATE OF THE QUESTION

Let us now proceed to an even more specific level of sin. Moving beyond the *essential* level (that of the relationship beween capital and labor) and the *world* level (that of dependency, or competition among national supplies of capitals), let us turn our attention to a still more specific phenomenon—one that presupposes the other two.

In the course of the competition among total national capitals, certain of them gain the upper hand over developed and peripheral supplies of capital alike. They extract surplus life or surplus value from both.

We read in the daily newspapers of the latest exploits of the transnationals. We see that Fiat or Volkswagen profits have shot up, or that the General Motors budget is larger than that of entire nations. We are bombarded with Coca Cola, Ford, Shell, and Datsun ads. Philips is an international giant in electricity, Nestlé in foodstuffs. These are facts.

We read in holy scripture:

There was a rich man who had a good harvest. "What shall I do?," he asked himself. "I have no place to store my harvest. I know!," he said. "I will pull down my grain bins and build larger ones. All my grain and my goods will go there. Then I will say to myself: you have blessings in reserve for years to come. Relax! Eat heartily, drink well. Enjoy yourself." But God said to him, "You fool! This very night your life shall be required of you. To whom will all this piled-up wealth of yours go?" That is the way it works with the man who grows rich for himself instead of growing rich in the sight of God [Luke 12:16–21].

In bygone times, the sin of accumulation was a "little" sin. Major accumulation was impossible. In our times, the financial capacity for accumulation, for the extraction of the life of others, is practically infinite. Thus we find the magnitude of the misdeed incomparably greater. After all, today we are dealing with "sin upon sin."

14.2 SOME NECESSARY DISTINCTIONS

It may appear to be a matter of great complexity, but we shall have to acquire a clear notion of the double role played by the so-called transnational corporations, and their consequent need of the capital of central and peripheral nations alike. Without this capital there could be no transnational profit.

First of all, *capital* "in general"—on an abstract or essential level—must be distinguished from "world" capital—the capital that operates in the world market. By world capital I mean the sum or empirical totality of all of the supplies of capital in the world—all of the supplies that exist, added together and considered as a unit. "Total world capital" is the sum total of human life objectified in a given moment of world history and accumulated within the capitalistic system.

The component parts of this total world capital are competitive. Hence we must distinguish *central, developed capital* from *peripheral, underdeveloped capital.* These are the essential analytic concepts of which we shall have need in order to construct our other empirical concepts. The total *capital* of any given central *nation*—the United States or Japan for instance—constitutes a *part* of this total central, developed capital.

Indeed, "transnational capital" (whether the totality of the capital of all transnational corporations taken together, or the particular capital of any one of these corporations), is, in the main, *part* of the capital of a *central* nation (or nations) that penetrates the ambit of the peripheral, underdeveloped total capital of a given dependent nation (or nations). Thus we must distinguish between the national capital (of a central country) that may be engaged exclusively *within* the market of that country, from transnational capital emerging from *beyond* its borders.

A peripheral nation, for its part, can be the seat or locus of great private national capital, petty capital, and state capital—the component parts of a peripheral total national capital.

14.3 TRANSNATIONALIZATION OF PRODUCTIVE CAPITAL

Being basically part of central capital, then, these enormous conglomerations are able to control asymmetries among nations, technological levels (including the administration of entrepreneurial or financial management), and salaries. Their purpose is to boost the rate of surplus value and profit. Were nations to disappear—were national markets, with their country-by-country differences, to disappear—the transnationals that profit by the prevailing situation would also disappear.

Until the time of the Second World War (1939–45), "central capital" transferred beyond its borders was used only in non-primary productivity or let out at interest. From then on, however, it began to play the role of *productive* capital as well—the factory, the productive process—outside its national borders. Under the pretext of reducing the need for imports on the part of the southern nations, and thus affording the possibility of an accumulation of currency, productive central capital was transnationalized into the dependent countries. Thus the fourth and last step was taken in the development of a North-South relationship of capitalistic "dependence."

In the first stage (see Diagram 7), capital destined to become "central" accumulates wealth by commerce and colonial thievery. In the second and third stages, this central capital "sells" industrial products produced in factories located within the *central* country.

In the fourth, transnational, stage, central capital locates its

Diagram 7

Historical Stages in the Development of Dependence

Colonialism		3. Imperialism	4. Transnationalization
1. Mercantilism	2. Free Trade		

factories (the productive stage of capital) within peripheral countries.

14.4 SUPPORT NATION AND HOST NATION

With the transnational supplies of capital (of General Motors, General Dynamics, Siemens, Toyota, and so on) now deposited partly beyond the borders of the central country, the relationship between transnational capital and the "*support* nation" (between General Motors and the United States, for example) is made "flexible" or it is diminished. But it by no means disappears. This relationship has need of the protection or "security" of, for instance, the United States (in extreme cases, by application of that ultimate instrument of coercion, "armed intervention"). Furthermore, the greater part of the "profit" flowing from the foreign investments in question is transferred to the "*support* nation," where it vitalizes, transfers life to, the population of the central country (even to the dominated classes of the "center").

The "*support* nation" is constituted of the totality of the population of the state or country where a given transnational capital has originated. The level of "patriotism" exhibited by this capital is outstripped by its need to increase in value, to realize profits, to accumulate more capital. Hence the frequent complaint, voiced by the population of the central country itself, of a lack of national solidarity on the part of the transnationals. Before it is North American, German, or Japanese, transnational capital is *capital*.

By contrast, the transnational reinforces the relationship of its capital with that of the "*host* nation"—Mexico, Brazil, or Argentina, for example. Until now these peripheral nations have simply provided a market. But now they are the preferred locus of "labor power" (thanks to low wages), of raw material (which is frequently cheaper to obtain there), and of underdeveloped banking, as well as the point of departure for sales to the home market (*in* the host country) and the export market (*from* the host country).

In the second and third steps in the development of its dependence—the stages of free trade and imperialism—the peripheral nation has indeed spent its currency in the "purchase" of central industrial products. But it was relatively free with respect to central capital itself. Now, however, the *productive phase*, in the form of factories, for example, has penetrated the peripheral country like a Trojan horse. Now foreign capital has access to political power, massive advertising and other propaganda, and the cultural configuration of thousands of workers. Suddenly foreign capital is no longer exclusively an economic force in the peripheral country. Now it has ideological and political power as well.

14.5 HOW DOES TRANSNATIONAL CAPITAL EXTRACT SURPLUS LIFE?

Far from suppressing differences between central and peripheral nations, transnational capital actually needs them (13.2). It simply could not function without a difference in, for example, the technological components of the value of capital (more developed in some nations and less developed or underdeveloped in others). If the "law" of dependence is ultimately the determination of a transfer of surplus life (13.7), the case of transnational capital will constitute a specific instance (with variations) of the *over*transfer of surplus life or value—and at the expense not only of a weak peripheral capital, but of the central supplies of capital, to the extent that they happen to be in competition with the transnational capital in question.

Where supplies of underdeveloped capital are concerned, transnational capital can place products on the market of a peripheral nation at lower prices (13.5) and thereby make excessive profits (overaccumulation due to unequal competition), thereby proving the centro-peripheral aspect of the "law" of dependence. But inversely as well, where developed central capital is concerned, transnational capital can place products on the central market at lower prices simply by importing them from the periphery, where both wages and material components are cheaper, and once more reap excessive profits.

As we see, reduced to its essence, the phenomenon of the transnational corporation is the verification of a special corollary of the "law" of dependency: the transfer of surplus value from the periphery to the center. There is no such thing, then, as a single world capital. The notion is empirically contradictory, for we would then be dealing with a unique, solitary capital that would have no competitors. Nor are national markets abolished, even though transnationals circulate their products within themselves. We have the transfer of surplus value from the periphery to the center (thanks to the unequal competition between central and peripheral capital, and the transfer of profit to the center), and we have the annihilation of the various non-transnational supplies of central capital. We have concentration.

14.6 WHERE IS THE INJUSTICE?

One might ask, by way of objection, where is the injustice? Where, in the following triple relationship, is there anything unethical? (1) We have the relationship obtaining between transnational capital and underdeveloped capital (in the form of excessive profit). (2) We have the transfer of surplus value (surplus life) from the periphery to the center. (3) And we have the relationship between transnational capital and developed central capital (excessive surplus profit: the concentration of capital). What could be immoral, what could be sinful, about this complex mechanism? It all seems a mere product of technology, administration, and human intelligence.

Once again, evil is invisible (12.7).

Even if the capital-work relationship (3.9, 12.5) is taken to be "natural," and even if the extraction of surplus life from the periphery (13.7) is likewise "natural" (in any case both, although

Diagram 8

Triple "Social Relationship" of Domination Established by the Transnationals

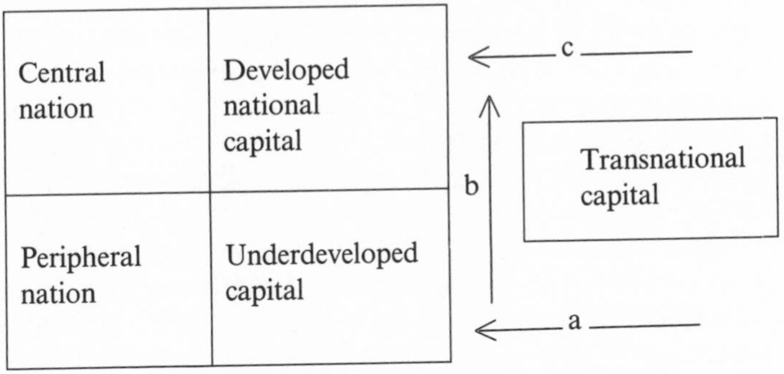

antiethical, are perfectly "moral" for the bourgeois system—3.6), there is still plenty of room to speak of injustice or sin in many forms.

In the first place (Diagram 8, arrow a), transnational capital competes with peripheral capital on an unequal basis, for we are dealing with a situation of classic "dependence" (steps 2, 3 of Diagram 7). Because it wields a better technology, and produces products at lower cost, transnational capital produces merchandise at a lower price or of better quality. In the second place, far from creating employment opportunities, transnational capital actually wipes out traditional sources of production. The twenty employees of a Coca Cola distributor throw thousands of others out of work— fruit vendors (who had put fruit juice on local markets), employees of small soft-drink companies, and so forth. We are dealing with *unequal competition* in the market of a peripheral country.

14.7 SECOND INJUSTICE: OVERTRANSFER OF SURPLUS LIFE

The second aspect (Diagram 8, arrow b) represents the alleged "loan" of technology to "replace imports" and thus spare the exportation of currency. In reality it is converted into a channel for the extraction of life, and one of unprecedented proportions. The transnational corporations develop and fine-tune new methods of removing wealth from the poor nations. As a result, instead of "developing," as the blueprints of "developmentalism" expect them to, the poor nations grow ever more deeply impoverished.

Functionally, the transnational corporation consists of a circulatory exchange between a *parent company* and a *peripheral subsidiary* (Ford Detroit and Ford Buenos Aires). The question is *how* to "send" currency (money with an international value—for example, American dollars) from the subsidiary in the peripheral country to the parent company in the central country. This currency, this *money*, we recall, is human life (11.8).

One way of doing so consists in making "payments" by the subsidiary to the parent company—often enough fictitious or unnecessary, and in any case massive. For example, production plans are "sold," and at a high price. Or "royalties" are paid. Or the parent company can be asked for international "loans" (countersigned by the peripheral state): interest will now have to be paid on this "credit" (actually an investment by the transnational corporation in the peripheral country). Or the subsidiary can "buy" parts from the parent company—state-of-the-art technology, and correspondingly expensive (indeed, artificially overpriced).

Another way of transferring peripheral surplus life is by "exporting," to the central parent company, products manufactured by the peripheral subsidiary. The parts of a Volkswagen motor will be sent from Brazil to Germany to be assembled and sold. In this case the product is underbilled—sold for less than its actual value, by billing it either at less than cost, or even at cost but thereby at a price below its "product value," which will include gratuitous surplus life (11.5). Furthermore, the "market price" in the central country will be a great deal higher than it would have been in the peripheral country by reason of the low wages paid the peripheral worker. Thus we have a direct transfer of surplus value from the peripheral country to transnational capital—from the periphery to the center without the necessity of passing by way of market or circulation. The surplus value is "produced" in the periphery, but "realized" in the central market.

Here, then, is a concrete case of broadened, enlarged "dependence," accompanied by a corresponding increase in the degree of "invisibility." Sin loves concealment.

14.8 THE THIRD LEVEL

In "dependence," taken as a whole, the sum total of the profit of a total central capital is equal to (and is the realization of) the transfer of surplus life from a total peripheral capital, as we have seen. Now, in turn, the transfer of surplus value from the peripheral subsidiary to the transnational central parent company is equal to the profit obtained through the advantage of transnational capital over the merely national central capital (keeping in mind the products "exported" from the periphery)— arrow c in Diagram 8.

Transnational capital has at least two competitive advantages over other supplies of capital in their native land. First, the transnational corporation acquires *money*, profit, from its subsidiaries (by way of overaccumulation) that it is able to use in research, advertising, and so on. Coursing through its body is the blood of the workers not only of the central country, but of the peripheral countries as well. The transnational corporation has become an international idol (12.10).

Secondly, the peripheral product has been produced at a lower "cost price," thanks to the lower average wage in the periphery (and so at the "price" of the hunger, poverty, and death of the overexploited peripheral worker). This product can therefore be offered for sale at a more favorable "market price," occasioning "extraordinary profit" in the game of competition with merely national central developed capital.

As we see, in the case of the transnational corporation as well, *homo homini lupus*. The transnational victimizes the human being of periphery and center alike. Universal competition extracts unjust gain wherever it can. And it is more than clear that without "dependence" there would be no transnationals. Transnational capital is "overdetermined" sin: "sin upon sin." How childish other forms of domination now appear—including those described in the Book of Revelation! The whole of the wealth ever stolen by the Roman empire was dozens of times less—if indeed comparison is possible—than the accumulated value of General Motors. That apocalyptic Beast is an innocent kitten by comparison with the "beasts" of our time.

14.9 ARTERIES OF LIFE

By way of summation, let us turn our attention to the complex, invisible "arteries" by which the "blood of the poor" circulates in the capitalist system at the close of the twentieth century.

First (chap. 12), the life (surplus value) of the worker flows vertically (without returning) from the worker to capital. This is the essential, abstract relationship of the phenomenon in question—the "*social* relationship" that has constituted the sin of the modern age, first in Europe and now throughout the world.

Secondly (chap. 13), on a more concrete level, the developed, central capital extracts life (surplus value) from underdeveloped peripheral national capital, obliging the latter to exploit its workers even more intensively, and thus enabling central capital actually to improve the quality of life of the workers of the central countries (even enlisting them as accomplices). The "*international* social relationship" of sin is thus less visible and more complex than the "*social* relationship" of sin.

On a third level—more complex and more specific than that of either of the two preceding levels—a *part* of the developed central capital now establishes a *direct* and essential (hence without the intermediary of circulation and merchandise, as heretofore) capital-work relationship with the peripheral worker (while seeking a reduction in this worker's wage), without abandoning the level of *competition*. While still competing with peripheral and central supplies of capital, it simultaneously effectuates an "overdetermination" of the "law of dependence" through the transfer of surplus life from the periphery to the center—no longer merely through the unequal exchange determined by the differing organic composition of the two supplies of capital, but thanks to a wage difference as well. Thus we have a direct increase in the rate of surplus value (that emerging from the "wage – work" relationship) as the basis of a new increase in the rate of profit. All this permits a disproportionate accumulation of human life by transnational capital vis-à-vis that of all non-transnationalized individual capital or branch of capital. And structural sin makes a quantum leap.

14.10 "CIVILIZING" POWER OF THE TRANSNATIONALS?

Certain writers—Michael Novak, for example—make a Christian apologia for the transnationals. We are told they are the great producers of goods and services, the creators of wealth worldwide, the inventors of technology, and the roaring engines of human progress. The old logic of the industrial revolution, the logic of the invention of the machine, springs to life anew in the current age of the technological revolution.

If the transnational corporation actually placed its enormous concentration of technological and financial capital, with its fantastic skill in planning and administration, at the service of humankind, it would be the greatest benefactor of humanity the world has ever seen. But the fact is that this gigantic conglomerate operates in the service of capital alone. Its exclusive aim is the augmentation of surplus value and capitalistic profit. As a productive, effective cell of capital, the transnational corporation is subject to the limitations of the phenomenon that subsumes it and incorporates it into its logic: capital.

Operating as it does in the sole interest of an augmentation in the rate of profit (and hence functioning in the relationship obtaining between all profit and all capital, and in that relationship alone), so that its all-compelling interest is the basis of all profit and all capital—surplus value, surplus life—the transnational is simply incapable of responding to the urgent, basic needs of the peripheral world. On the contrary, if it hopes to boost its profits, it must expend all its energy and apply all its sophisticated technology to the production of superfluous goods—luxuries, fashions, the distortion of national crafts and technologies, and so on—thereby precisely impairing the production of the goods and services required by the great majorities. It also reduces the number of workers required for the production of its goods and services, through the application of advanced technologies—but fails to raise wages, for the labor pool remains the same.

Far from being instruments of "civilization," the transnational becomes the universal vampire, extracting blood, "surplus" human life, from the periphery of the capitalist economy. "Thou shalt not steal. Thou shalt not kill." And yet theft and murder only penetrate more deeply and spread their tentacles even further as they become technologized and universalized. To boot, they now do this in the name of democracy, liberty, and civilization. Humanity's mighty potential benefactor has become its pitiless predator.

CONCLUSIONS

As the reader will easily believe, these brief pages have been insufficient even for a rough sketch of the questions confronting us, to say nothing of an exhaustive attempt at an answer. My only intent has been to initiate a discourse to be followed, step by step, in specific theological tractates. My treatment of the transnationals, however, has served to exemplify the sort of specific subject that must occupy the concern of a theology of community ethics, inasmuch as it has shown that this institution of domination (and hence of sin) operates in the interests of the Prince of "this world," as a mechanism of the "sin of the flesh," or the "law of sin." Will it not therefore be in the interests of the reign of God to oppose its machinations? Is the liberation of the poor from these "*social* relationships" of sin not a matter precisely of theological concern? Are not these profane structures, these economic and political structures, also the great Babylon? Will not the attempt to fetishize "religous" sin or otherwise separate it from "secular economic structures" be the hallmark of a theology of the concealment of sin—a theology of domination, then?

Chapter 15

International Loans and Weaponry

15.1 STATE OF THE QUESTION

Let us consider another aspect of the transnationalized structure of sin/domination. Our new considerations will bear not only on the productive level of this sinful domination, but on its financial or monetary level as well.

We read in magazines, and in all our dailies, of huge international loans that have been made to poor nations. How did this come about? In 1967, world capitalism entered a state of crisis. The demand for goods and services in the central capitalist countries had suddenly dropped, resulting in restricted production. But this caused unemployment, so that now still less money was available to consumers for goods and services. And the vicious spiral proceeded apace.

Now financiers needed a new way to use the money left over from production. One of the ways they found was to lend it irresponsibly to needy countries. Another way consisted in increasing arms production. And so we have two types of investment that reproduce not life, but death.

We read in holy scripture:

At the end of every third year you shall bring out all the tithes of your produce for that year and deposit them in community stores, that the Levite who has no share in the heritage with you, and also the alien, the orphan, and the widow who belong to your community, may come and eat their fill; so that the

Lord, your God, may bless you in all that you undertake.

At the end of every seven-year period you shall have a relaxation of debts, which shall be observed as follows. Every creditor shall relax his claim on what he has loaned his neighbor; he must not press his neighbor, his kinsman, because a relaxation in honor of the Lord has been proclaimed. ... If one of your kinsmen in any community is in need ... you shall not harden your heart nor close your hand to him in his need. Instead, you shall open your hand to him and freely lend him enough to meet his need [Deut. 14:28–15:2, 15:7–8].

In Hebrew and Christian tradition, for the Fathers of the Church, for the popes, for Thomas Aquinas, the lending of money at interest was regarded as *contra naturam*, against nature, a sin: usury. Accordingly, it was condemned. Since Calvin and Knox, however, the practice has become universal. Just so, it is "against nature" to produce instruments for the murder of one's neighbor: weapons. Yet Christian countries are the primary producers of these instruments of anti-life.

15.2 SOME NECESSARY DISTINCTIONS

The question of international loans, then, is a current, central issue for theological ethics. The whole operation might appear to be "natural," moral, objectively planned out in advance and scientifically executed. But we must understand, first of all, that capital has many "members," parts, or functions. The human body has a digestive, circulatory, and locomotive system, all in the unity of one comprehensive system. So also capital has a variety of dimensions, different products, various movements, apparently contradictory but actually bound up in the unity of its overall organic life.

Thus we must distinguish industrial, commercial, and financial or monetary capital. *Industrial* capital is capital tied up in wages and means of production (factories, the productive process that culminates in the industrial product). Its profit arises from an unjust "*social* relationship" (12.6), inasmuch as workers objectify *more* value in the product than they receive in wages. To put it another way: the product is worth more than the money or value that the capitalist has invested in its production. Industrial profit is the worker's life, robbed. This is sin.

Commercial capital, for its part, is capital that is no longer tied up in production itself. Capital buys merchandise with money and sells it at a *higher* price than it has paid for it. What is the source of this "commercial" profit? It is simply a part of industrial profit. That is, commercial profit is merely a part of the surplus life for which workers have not been paid. (We must not think that this profit comes out of consumers' pockets, even though consumers pay a price *above* the value of the merchandise.)

Thus commercial capital, as well, is participation in sin, the sin of industrial injustice.

15.3 INTEREST ON CAPITAL

Financial capital sells money. Without producing products or selling another type of merchandise, financial capital nevertheless "turns a profit" in the form of interest. From what source might *financial* capital draw its "profit," or the interest it gains by delivering over or selling money? The relationship between this surplus money (interest) acquired by the financier, the banker, and the life objectified by the overexploited peripheral worker is now so remote that it might appear nonexistent. At last we have the total absolutization or fetishization, the perfected idolatry, of capital. Capital is a god, representing itself as having proceeded from nothing (*ex nihilo*).

We must understand, then, that the wage-earner's surplus life (12.4), the time of his or her unpaid work, passes through the "blood vessels" of capital until it coagulates (2.8, 3.10, 11.2) as interest on money lent. (If we consider money simply in itself, we shall never be able to explain where the interest comes from.)

Industrial capital must "transubstantiate" its merchandise into money as quickly as possible, in view of the time factor inherent in the cycle of capital. Time is of the essence. The more quickly industrial capital sells its merchandise, the more quickly it will be able to invest its money in a new cycle of capital (that is, the more quickly it will be able to pay wages and buy the means of production for new products/merchandise). One way of accelerating the sale of this merchandise is to sell it to commercial capital.

Another way for industrial capital to have the money for its product more quickly is to buy this money from monetary or

Diagram 9
Phases of Capital

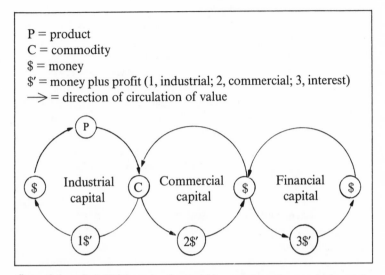

P = product
C = commodity
$ = money
$′ = money plus profit (1, industrial; 2, commercial; 3, interest)
—→ = direction of circulation of value

Industrial capital   Commercial capital   Financial capital

1$′   2$′   3$′

financial capital. Without having sold its merchandise yet, industrial or commercial capital already "has its money back"—the money for that anticipated sale. But this anticipation, the bridge across this time gap, has a price. How is this price paid? It is paid by delivering over to financial capital some part of the industrial (or commercial) profit obtained once the product is actually sold. But this "profit" is purely and simply unpaid (and hence unjustly obtained from the worker) surplus work or surplus life. The interest on a loan, then, is once more a participation in the structural sin of capital as such (12.4).

15.4 MONEY CREATING MONEY?

For Aristotle the creation of money by money was an act against nature (*Politics*, I, 1, 1258b). Similarly, we read in Deuteronomy: "You shall not demand interest from your countrymen on a loan of money or of food or of anything else on which interest is usually demanded" (Deut. 23:20). And Saint Thomas added: "The Jews were forbidden to lend at interest to a brother ... whereby we are given to understand that usury extracted from *anyone* is sinful"

(*Summa Theologiae*, II–II, q. 78, a. 1, ad 2). Until the sixteenth century it was traditional to identify lending at interest, or usury, as sin. It was avarice, and avarice was a vice. Calvin, as we have said, permitted loans at interest.

How can capitalism have arrived at an interpretation so far removed from Christian tradition? An ideological process of fetishization is the culprit. Capital was absolutized. The process was rather as follows. Capital was identified with wealth, and regarded as a factual *given* (12.4). The "*social* relationship" of inequality or injustice (12.3) that lurked here remained undetected. Thereupon profitability was ascribed to capital without further ado, as proceeding from or attaching to its essence naturally—as something simply belonging to it (with a wide variety of explanations).

But once capital and profit had come to be regarded as factual givens, exempt from any ethical judgment, the "original sin"—the injustice constituting their essence (12.5)—was concealed. And once this had been accomplished, a further step could be taken. Instead of being invested in *industrial* production (whence the surplus value was actually extracted), money could be invested in *commerce*. If money in the form of industrial capital (Diagram 9) makes an (industrial) profit (1\$′), why would not this other money (commercial capital) also make a profit (2\$′)?

Finally, why would not actual, financial money make a profit (in the form of interest—3\$′), just as other money (that of industrial or commercial capital) makes its profit? Thus profit would appear to emerge "from nothing" (*ex nihilo*), and be justifiable on the basis of the sheer existence of capital.

15.5 THE NEW MOLOCH

The current international monetary system based on the dollar originated in 1944 at Bretton Woods. Shortly afterward the International Monetary Fund and the World Bank were born. These institutions were founded for the purpose of making loans to underdeveloped or poorer countries so that they might buy the products of wealthy countries.

As already indicated, from the moment of the beginning of the crisis of capitalism in 1967, and especially since the "great recession" of 1974–5, a great deal of monetary capital simply "floated."

Overproduction (or a weak market; poverty; lack of money) produces recession. Money that would have been invested in production was instead lent at interest. The floodgates of interest were opened in the United States as well. Big interest attracted big capital (oil capital, Eurodollar capital, and so on).

But the day of reckoning arrived: the interest came due. How did the banks acquire the necessary money to pay the high interest rates they had promised their clients? By lending the money invested in them at still higher rate. Thus money was lent to Third World countries (via their corrupt governments, and with the monetary mirages of the Chicago School of Economics, for example, shimmering before their eyes), but in such a way as to attract it back to the center (by selling off superfluous, stored merchandise, or even simply by offering corrupt peripheral bourgeoisies bank accounts in the central countries).

As we know, Mexico, Brazil, Venezuela, and Argentina alone were $300 billion in debt by 1983. Mexico was to pay $12 billion in annual interest beginning in 1984 (a country whose dominant class kept some $70 billion in North American banks). A Mexican worker earned about a dollar an hour that year. Twelve billion human "life-hours"! A half-million persons sacrificed annually to the god Moloch (calculating the average working life of a laborer at eight hours a day for forty-five years to support a family of four). Human blood spilled in torrents, in sacrifice to the modern Huitzilopochtli (the god to whom human victims were immolated)!

15.6 NEW TRANSFER OF SURPLUS LIFE

Forgotten is the sin piled upon other structural sins: "sin upon sin." Compound sin hides in the shadows, never to be seen. When all is said and done, who pays the interest on international loans?

Money is merchandise or a sign of merchandise (gold, for example). It is universal equivalent *value* (11.8). The value residing in money is that of objectified work: the value of money is the value of the time of human life that such and such an amount of money could acquire in order to reproduce this life (with food, clothing, housing, health services, and so on). But money cannot of itself produce more money. How, then, is "more money" made out of bank interest? How does money "make" surplus money? As we have seen, interest on loans is paid with part of the value proceeding from industrial profit.

In the case of international loans, where could peripheral capital (state as well as private), still as feeble as ever, obtain the money to pay the interest on this debt? In the last analysis peripheral capital's only profit comes from the application of peripheral industrial capital itself. But the profit on industrial capital is only the realization, on the level of circulation—the realization in money in the market—of the surplus life that has been acquired on the level of production thanks to a wage that has *underpaid* the value objectified in the product by the worker who produced the product. In other words it is life stolen from the worker (unpaid-for surplus life) by over-exploitation—which permits peripheral capital to make a profit and pay the interest on its international loans.

In conclusion, then: it is the workers, the dominated classes, the marginals who pay the interest on the loans that central and peripheral capital find so necessary if poor countries are to have the wherewithal to buy from them, if the dominating classes of the peripheral countries are to have the means to make their profit. And at long last an enormous and very complex mechanism, a gigantic "*social* relationship" of domination, appears, based exclusively on the exploitation of *life*—based on sin.

15.7 WAR AS BUSINESS

For the pre-Socratic Greek philosopher Heraclitus it was "war," strife, contention that generated all things and systems. "War is the origin of all," said this philosopher of domination. In the same fashion, capital thinks: competition, this death struggle waged by all against all, is the source of life and wealth. Indeed, in the United States today, for example, war is a *business*. A number of gigantic corporations (among them Lockheed, General Dynamics, McDonnell Douglas, Boeing, United Aircraft, and Grumman) billed the Pentagon more than $10 billion (as much as 88 per cent of their sales) in the years from 1961 to 1967. And in doing so they made incomparable profits, for they were in a monopoly position.

Military expenditures have multiplied twenty-five times since the turn of the century. Since 1945 they have quadrupled. In 1982, $650 billion, or 6 per cent of world production, was spent on arms. In

1986, 36 per cent of the U.S. national budget went for arms. One could think that war were the locus of great scientific progress, to borrow Hegel's concept. In 1968 the Massachusetts Institute of Technology received $119 million from the Pentagon, Johns Hopkins University $57 million, and the University of California $17 million (the "mandarins of the Empire," sneered Chomsky). The hope was that these investments would yield "great benefits for humanity." A mirage.

The destructive capacity of today's nuclear weaponry outstrips that of conventional armaments thousands of times over. For the first time in history, and the first time in the life of our planet, we face the possibility of the *total extinction* not only of the human race, but of all life on earth. The human species is at the mercy of a force too great for it. Should that force be activated in error, or by a fanatic or terrorist, or by way of a "preemptive strike," it would drag us all down to death. Christian ethics faces the possibility of our suicide as a species, and the North American bishops addressed this threat in their pastoral letter of 1983, *The Challenge of Peace*.

15.8 SINFULNESS OF THE ARMS RACE

The "arms-race complex" represents sin, and this in various aspects of its structure. In the first place the industrial production of arms is an activity performed by capital in order to make profit. This profit, as we have seen (12.5–6), is extracted from arms industry workers and scientists as "surplus life." "The population lives on weaponry."

In the second place, in the United States for instance, the arms race syndrome takes on a particular physiognomy (see Diagram 10). The fulcrum of all the other relationships is the unit formed by the Pentagon with the weapons industry. The Pentagon assigns 80 per cent of its contracts directly to industrial corporations without public bidding. A good part of the citizen's budget, then, is spent on instruments of destruction without any competition. It is all done behind the public's back. This is another aspect of the sin in question.

The Strategic Defense Initiative, or "Star Wars," which the Reagan administration has proposed to Congress and the countries of Western Europe, would compound the sin. It would call for unheard-of expenditures incurred for the sake of enormous new

Diagram 10

The Arms Industry, U.S.A.

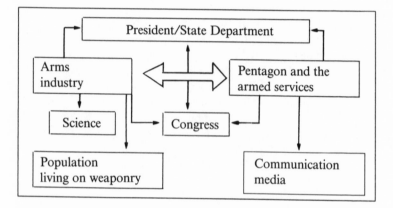

profits on the part of the weapons industry. In 1968 President Reagan's home state of California hosted 17 percent of the war industry, followed by Texas (where so many chicanos are pressured to work in war factories) with only 9 percent. The North American episcopate went so far as to say that "those who in conscience decide not to participate in defense activities will find support in the Catholic community" (*The Challenge of Peace*, IV, C: "To the Men and Women of the Defense Industries").

Worst of all, poor countries fall into the same vices. There are countries with workers who earn less than $200 per year, and nevertheless the government invests less in agriculture than in military activities.

15.9 UNPRODUCTIVE INVESTMENT: INSTRUMENTS OF DEATH

The implicit contradiction of weapons production carries the seeds of its own rejection. Let us consider a few figures:

	Military Spending: Percentage of National Budget, 1966	Percentage of Rate of Increase of Production, 1950–65
United States	8.5	2.4
West Germany	4.1	5.3
Japan	1.0	7.7

Source: Melgan, *The Capitalism of the Pentagon, p. 296*

The difference between the figures for the United States and Japan is arresting. The United States *wastes* on weaponry what Japan spends *usefully* on increased production. Evidently there is a direct correlation between military spending and negative economic effects.

After all, weapons (instead of Isaiah's plowshares) are tools and means precisely for the elimination of life. A plow is a tool for working the land—for acquiring the "bread of life" that produces life as it is consumed. Jet fighters, bullets, nuclear warheads detonated or stockpiled, reproduce no life, serve no useful purpose. They all represent a recessionary, inflationary investment, producing crises in production and consumption, and wiping out wealth acquired by the blood of the worker and bought with the work of the people.

Military production in the United States grew by 2.3 percent in the first half of 1983, and industrial production fell by 1.6 percent. There is evidence that military expenditures currently exert a harmful effect on the productivity of labor. Such expenditures compete for scarce resources with capital employed in civilian industries just when they are being so mightily pressured to increase their level of production in view of the threat posed by international competition, especially by Japan and Europe.

Hunters used their weapons to hunt animals. They needed to eat. But soon they were using them to wage war—to hunt their human enemies. And "the military" was born. Jesus "died *under* Pontius Pilate"—a military man—as have nearly all the martyrs ever since.

15.10 ARMED MIGHT OF THE BEAST

In the Book of Revelation the Beast is invested with power; and all of its might is in weaponry:

The dragon conferred upon it its power. ... Who shall be able to *fight* against it? It has been permitted to *wage war* against the anointed and vanquish them, and has been given authority over every race, people, tongue and nation [Rev. 13:2, 7].

When all is said and done, the strength of the Prince of "this world" (2.10)—the way in which Satan in fact exercises power—is through coercion by the instruments of death, coercion through weaponry. The martyr's "cross" (3.10) is the actual use of the weapon that kills the innocent, the people (an innocent civilian population fanatically defined in advance as "the enemy").

There would be no *real* sin if it were not effectuated by the use of arms. It was Pilate's soldiers, once more, who crucified Christ.

The sin of the violent murder of one's neighbor by the use of weapons of war is intimately bound up with economic and social injustice. The mighty, the dominators, must control the oppressed,

Diagram 11

The Bread of Death

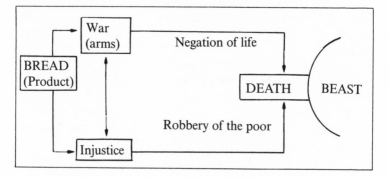

must keep them subdued, keep them "pacified," by means of weaponry. "Bread," that biblical symbol of all productivity, has become the "bread of death" (see Diagram 11).

The circle of death is complete. Sin is domination, and as domination of the life of the other (2.2) it is the extraction of surplus life (12.6). But now this structure of sin (2.6) must be guaranteed. It must be endowed with permanency. Weaponry and military power constitute the highest court of the effectiveness of sin. Arms and armed might are the ultimate demonstration of the power of the reign of the Prince of "this world." The torture of heroes and martyrs, then (9.3), and their actual death on their "cross," is the consummation of sin upon earth. And yet this torture and death are also the means by which the glory of the Infinite is made manifest. Crucified by the military power of his age (the Romans), Jesus manifests the absolute contradiction of history.

CONCLUSIONS

In this chapter I have been able to draw two conclusions from the behavior of the social relationship known as capital. First, loans are made at interest under the pretext that this profit is earned by the intrinsic value of capital itself. Secondly, this capital, as productive industrial capital, is invested, not only in useful products but in destructive ones as well. For capital, however, it is indifferent whether it is "bread" or weapons that are produced. Value (the life of the worker) can be objectified (11.5), and profit gained or surplus life accumulated (12.5), in either or both. The surplus value of the product, whether it be food, a plowshare, or a weapon, is profit; and though profit mean the death of the worker, it is the life of capital. Here the social relationship of sin appears in all its brutality.

Interest is ultimately the surplus life of the poor, distributed by industrial capital in financial, monetary capital. War, the war of domination, is coercion of the poor on the part of the Beast, whose end and aim is to keep them locked up in the structures through which others can extract their surplus life. Institutional violence, then, is the other face of sin. Here sin shows its true face. Off comes the mask.

Chapter 16

"Class Struggle,"Violence, and Revolution

16.1 STATE OF THE QUESTION

We frequently hear in the church, both in the documents of the social teaching of the church and in the mouths of individual Christians, that neither the class struggle nor violence may be approved or practiced by Christians. Like so many other questions, however, this one too is fraught with confusion, both terminological and conceptual, especially at the theological level.

The daily newspapers carry news stories of strikes, worker demonstrations, and police repression of these expressions of a struggle on behalf of workers' interests. We likewise read of wars, guerrilla actions, air highjackings, and attempts on the lives of industrialists or politicians. All around us we see violence, and sudden social change.

We read in holy scripture:

> I saw no temple in the city. The Lord, God the Almighty, is its temple. . . . Nothing deserving a curse shall be found there. The throne of God and of the Lamb shall be there, and his servants shall serve him faithfully. They shall see him face to face and bear his name on their foreheads. The night shall be no more. They will need no light from lamps or the sun, for the Lord God shall give them light, and they shall reign forever [Rev. 21:22, 22:3–5].

For the Christian, the reign of God is to be the perfect community

(1.5). In the reign, injustice, social classes, inequalities, sin, violence, will be no more—only a continuous movement from the new to the newer, from discovery to exciting discovery. Revolution will no longer need to be fostered; it will be ongoing and permanent. After all, in perfect love, newness prevails; no structure is ever needed but the ongoing creativity of new structures. And this is to be "forever," as our text from Revelation tells.

16.2 WHAT IS MEANT BY "CLASS STRUGGLE"?

It has already been explained, if in very abstract and introductory fashion, what "classes" are (8.4). Their existence is undeniable. All through the history of human societies, from the neolithic age to the urban civilization of today, humanity has been stratified in classes. Obviously the classes of capitalism cannot be those of feudalism, nor of a slave society, nor of tributary regimes of the most varied types, nor of socialism, and so on. But classes are a *fact*.

Neither—as we read in the Vatican "Instruction" on the theology of liberation (1984)—can one deny "the *fact* of social stratification, with the ensuing inequalities and injustices" (IX, 2). Here, then, is a first meaning of the expression "class struggle": the tensions, contradictions, and practical confrontations that de facto exist among these "social stratifications" or classes of society.

Thus the historical *fact* of a struggle among the classes is as patent as the *fact* of the classes themselves. What some are so concerned to deny is the "theory of the class struggle as a fundamental structural law of history" (ibid.). It will be in order, then, to engage in a theological reflection on the difference between the *fact* of the class struggle and the *theory* of that struggle.

At once we encounter two contrary positions. Some simply deny the existence of classes or of class confrontation or struggle, despite the objective evidence. Many Christians are prone to adopt this ideological stance. But at the other extreme there are those who, driven by a purely anarchistic zeal for complete destruction, are desirous of revolution for the sake of revolution, and hence exaggerate class contradiction in order to foment hatred among the classes. Both positions are obviously wrong and to be rejected. The community ethics of a Christian theology sees things differently.

16.3 CAUSE OF CLASS DISTINCTIONS: SIN

Had there been no sin—had Adam not fallen—there would be no classes. It is as simple as that. But this is altogether different from denying the *current* existence of classes. Theologians who would deny the current existence of classes deny precisely the current existence of sin. In other words, they are theologians of domination: they attempt to conceal domination by declaring it non-existent, prematurely proclaiming the eschatological nature of the reign of God when the structures of the reign of "this world" still prevail. Thus they confound God with Satan.

It is because there is sin—because there is domination of one person over another (2.2ff.)—that some appropriate the product of the work of others and thereby—institutionally and socially— establish an inequality of class. Inequality, historical and hereditary injustice, the death of the poor (2.8), the existence of a *dominated* class (after all, if there are classes, there must be at least two—in fact there are always many more—and if there are at least two classes, then at least one must be more wealthy than the other, leaving the other poor, poor because dominated)—is *always* the fruit of sin, of domination, of forgetfulness of the fact that one's sister or brother is the manifestation of God in history and is Christ himself—Christ who in his bodily need lays claim, as a matter of justice, to the bread stolen from him.

If the existence of a dominated class is the fruit of sin, then in the reign of God, where "nothing deserving a curse shall be found," there will be neither sin nor sinner. Nor, then, will there be classes. The reign of God will be a *classless community*, the positive utopia of Christian hope.

To assert, therefore, the existence of classes is not only not anti-Christian, it is *essentially Christian*: it is the simple assertion of the existence of social sin (3.6) and Satan. To deny the existence of classes is to deny the existence of Satan. Such a denial is a serious fault, and a fault committed by a good many Christians.

16.4 CAUSE OF THE CLASS STRUGGLE: SIN

If it be admitted that the existence of classes is the fruit of sin, then the *fact* that these classes counter and oppose one another, the fact of their struggle, must likewise be the fruit of sin. But let us be very clear: the precise element of this struggle that is the fruit of sin is the struggle of the *dominating class* to exercise its domination over the underclass, the dominated. The *sinful* struggle is the domination. After all, the suffering endured by the dominated classes is the effect of the struggle of the sinner (the dominator, the "rich" as a biblical category) to dominate the poor (the underclass, the biblical Job).

When the dominated class suffers in silence, and patiently endures, the contradiction and opposition of the classes will not appear openly. The sin of the dominator will remain invisible. This is the hour of the "hegemony" of the dominating class. For the time being the "struggle" is *latent*, not actual and current. This is the "classic" age (9.6), when "it would appear" that there is no injustice. Many a Christian would like to see this situation eternalized, in the hope that the latent struggle will never surface, in the hope that the prevailing "harmony will be prolonged in peace." What such Christians fail to understand is that the prevailing "harmony" and "understanding," the apparent "reconciliation," is predicated and based on *an unjust relationship*—the sinful relationship of domination. In other words, a "peace" is preached that tolerates the sin of the domination committed by a dominating class *now* oppressing the dominated, the impoverished—oppressing those who must live in misery *now*.

If the poor, the dominated class, become aware of this sin, of the domination exercised upon their person, their structures, their group—if this exploited class gets up on its feet, demands its rights, and defends its life, then, and only then, does anyone presume to judge the "class struggle" as a *theory*, as ethical sin, as the interpretation beyond the raw fact. The "judges" forget that the struggle of the poor is directed *against sin*, whereas the struggle of the rich is *against the person* of the poor.

16.5 THE REIGN OF GOD: WITHOUT CLASSES OR STRUGGLES

It is often forgotten that the struggle of the rich, of the dominator class, is the very praxis of sin: that it is the struggle of the Prince of "this world" to establish his lordship. This class struggle passes itself off as the very "nature" of things, and morality guarantees its goodness (3.6). But the truth of the matter is that the struggle of the poor, of the dominated class, is the very praxis of the reign of God: it is struggle *against* sin, against domination, struggle to establish the

New Jerusalem (5.5). The first struggle is perversity and sin. The second is good, holy, and virtuous. The first is morality. The second is ethics (5.3).

Sin, the cause of class differences, struggles to maintain those differences. Here is the struggle of the dominators to dominate (a struggle waged by their armies, their police, by Pilate, by Herod, by the crucifying soldiers). Holiness, which strives to establish the reign of God, struggles with sin, that it may eradicate class differences, and, in all justice, strike an equality among persons. Holiness is the love that struggles, that "divides everything on the basis of each one's needs" (Acts 2:45). Sin builds inequality. Holiness builds the equality of the reign of God.

After all, in the reign of God, in the "face-to-face" of the community-without-differences—or rather with the sole difference of the fullness of each member's personhood in proportion to the degree of his or her commitment in history—"the night shall be no more": there will be no work, no economics, no ecclesial or political structures, no ideologies, no sin, no classes.

The construction, here and now, of this *classless community* is the construction of the reign of God *here and now*—in the realization that, in history, in *this* history, this perfect community can never be realized completely, but is always inaugurated when two persons constitute community in its name, or when some inequality is eradicated in the name of justice.

16.6 REFORMISM AND DEVELOPMENTALISM

Let us face facts. First, the concrete, simple daily "changes" that we make very rarely touch the essence of our structures. In the second place, it is almost impossible that it should be otherwise. The fact is that it is very difficult to go beyond mere "reforms." Even the social teaching of the church, in its central aspect, merely proposes the reform of already existing systems (19.6). But this is not reform*ism*. By "reformism" we must understand the extreme position of those who regard reform as the only thing *ever* possible. Franz Hinkelammert has shown that Karl Popper's thinking is "reformist" in this negative, pejorative sense. But the frank, realistic admission that one must live in a situation that is merely "reformable" because reforms are the only thing actually possible here and now, is simply the daily practice of the prudent, realistic, even revolutionary militant who knows full well that revolutions are not a daily occurrence.

In this same spirit of realism, the development of productive forces, the development of a society's wealth, should be the ongoing intention of those who opt for the poor and the oppressed. "Development" enables the needy to have more goods so as to fulfill their needs—provided, of course, that the development in question is a *human* development, not merely the development of capital, as it is in most cases in Latin America, Africa, or Asia. "Developmentalism," on the other hand, is the pretense that the *only possible development is capitalist*, and that therefore money must be borrowed, and technology—the technology of the transnationals— employed.

With the collapse of populism, Latin American nationalistic capitalisms decided in the second half of the 1950s that the only hope for Latin American development lay in borrowing North American capital and technology. Ten years later the error of this notion became clear: instead of development, we had a still greater dependence, and the still wilder flight of our own capital—a greater loss of "surplus life" (13.7) than ever before.

"Reformism" is a mistake, a sin against the reign of God. Its only ambition is the everlasting reproduction of the *same system*. "Developmentalism" is a transgression against the Spirit, for it believes only in *current means*, which are those of the system. It lacks the patience to seek new paths when necessary. It places its only hope in the "means" offered by the Prince of "this world."

16.7 DEPENDENCE, BREACH, AND REVOLUTION

Let no one think that an ethics of liberation is revolutiona*ristic*. Revolutiona*rism* would be that anarchism that, here and now, before all else and always, come hell or high water, in season or out of season, would launch a revolution. Quite the contrary—only the patient, the humble, only those who hope, like our oppressed peoples over the years, the decades, the centuries are called in the *kairos*—the "fullness of time," the "Day of Yahweh"—to work the mighty deeds of the heroes, the prophets, the martyrs.

Our situation of dependence in the underdeveloped, peripheral nations (13.5) points to a double sin: the social relationship of capital with workers (12.3–5), and the relationship of the developed North with the underdeveloped South (13.3). When the *kairos* is reached, the struggle with sin will no longer consist in the implantation of reforms. It will launch an attack upon the very *essence* of the structure of sin.

It is this breach with *essential structures*, which is possible only at rare moments in history—having ripened and matured over the course of centuries, suddenly to materialize in a matter of mere weeks or months—that is called "revolution." Cromwell's revolution in England in the seventeenth century, or the French Revolution in the eighteenth, or the Russian or Cuban revolutions in the twentieth, are *essential* social changes. In our own case, in the Latin America of the close of the twentieth century, the "*social* relationships" of domination that we have found to be constitutive of capital and dependence are being breached and dissolved, whether by way of the struggle with sin waged by the workers (as a class) against capital (the capitalists), or by way of the struggle of the poor countries with the rich nations—in other words, in a "class struggle" against the sin (13.9) constituted by the vertical capital-labor relationship, or in a "struggle for national liberation" against the sin (13.10) constituted by the horizontal relationship of a developed country with an underdeveloped country.

Revolution is essential breach with the structures of sin—sin as injustice, sin as anti-community, alienative, social relationship. Such a breach or rupture is necessary and possible only at certain moments in the multicentenial history of a people. It is a "once and for all" happening, perceived and exploited by the heroes and prophets of a people only once every so many centuries.

16.8 VIOLENCE

As Paul VI declared in Bogotá, Colombia, on August 23, 1968, "violence is neither evangelical nor Christian." Of course, the pope was referring to the violence of force, in Latin *vis*, the coercion of the will of others against their rights, against their justice. He spoke of the violence of sin. "It is clear," said Medellín, "that in many parts of Latin America we find a situation of injustice that can be called *institutionalized violence*" (*Medellín Document on Peace*, no. 16). This is the more visible violence, the violence of every day, the violence of sin (2.2), institutional violence (2.5), the violence that produces weapons (15.10) or obliges the poor to sell their work (12.3).

This violence, that of the Prince of "this world," is frequently practiced with the consent of the oppressed. There is an ideological hegemony and domination in which the poor *accept* the system of domination, as something natural, as an obvious, eternal phenomenon (3.9). But the moment the oppressed (oppressed classes, oppressed nations, the poor) get on their feet, the moment they rebel, and oppose the domination under which they sweat and strain—this is the moment when *hegemonic* violence becomes *coercive*. Oppression becomes repression. All repression is perverse. There can never be a "legitimate" repression, as a certain conservative, right-wing group of bishops and others in the Latin American church say there can be.

Confronted with the active repression or violence of sin, many adopt the *tactics* or stance of "non-violence," as Mahatma Gandhi in India, Martin Luther King, Jr., in the United States, or Miguel D'Escoto in Nicaragua. This courageous position cannot, however, be elevated to the status of an absolute theoretical principle, an exclusive strategy for any and all situations. To the violence of sin the martyr opposes the valor of the suffering servant, who builds the church with his blood (9.2–3). But this martyr, this prophet, is not the political hero.

16.9 JUST DEFENSE AND A PEOPLE'S RIGHT TO LIFE

The exact contrary of the repulsive, unjust violence of the oppressor is the active *defense of the "innocent*," of the oppressed poor, the repressed people. Saint Augustine teaches us that it is a requirement of charity or Christian love to *re-act* to unjust violence: "matters would be still worse, after all, were malefactors to lord it over the just" (*The City of God*, IV, 15). Saint Thomas likewise teaches that struggle is not sin (*Summa Theologiae*, II-II, q. 40, a. 1) if its cause is just. Further, he adds, "force is repelled with force" in the case of defending *life* (ibid., q. 64, a. 7).

The church has always held the "just war theory" where the authority of governments is involved, even in the Second Vatican Council (*Gaudium et Spes*, 79). But it happens that an innocent person or a people can be oppressed, repressed, colonized by a government. In that case the war is not a war of one state with another, but a liberation struggle between oppression and the defense of the innocent. Joan of Arc against the English, Washington against the established order, the *Résistance française* against Nazism, Bolívar or San Martín against Spain, Sandino against the North American occupation—none of these heroes (9.3) represented the established *governments* of a state (9.8). They have their legitimacy in virtue of their *just cause* and their *right intention*, in virtue of their right to employ *adequate* means (even arms, as a "last resort") for the defense of the people—keeping in mind the principle of due proportion, of course, and not using more force than necessary to attain the realistic ends at stake. These are precisely the requisites that church tradition, including Saint Thomas, has always demanded for the use of force in defense of the innocent, the poor, the oppressed, in order that the use of force be just and legitimate. The Sandinista National Liberation Front, for example, complied with these requirements in its struggle with Somoza. And yet its members were labeled "subversives," "violent," and so in. In his Peace Day Message of 1982, Pope John Paul II asserted: "In the name of an elementary requisite of justice, peoples have the right and even *the duty* to protect their existence with *adequate means*" (no. 12). Peoples, then, and not merely governments, have this right and duty, and the means they are allowed to employ are "adequate means," in other words, even force of arms when necessary as a last resort to "repel force," as Saint Thomas put it—the force of sin and oppression.

But although the hero has need of "adequate means" to build the *future* state (9.4), the prophet and the martyr never need these means to build the present church, the Christian community (9.2). But political heroes cannot be forced to use the same means as do prophets and martyrs. A Camilo Torres will be a hero and an Oscar Romero a martyr. Their historical options were different. But both options can be legitimate. The political *legitimacy* of the actions of citizen Camilo will be judged by the future liberated state, not by theology or the church. In two encyclicals the popes condemned Latin American emancipation from Spain in the early nineteenth century. They committed the error of venturing into politics, and thus overstepping the bounds of their specific authority. Heroes are judged by heroes (7.6). Nor must we forget that there is such a thing as the charism of heroism, bestowed by the Holy Spirit.

16.10 REVOLUTION, MORALITY, ETHICS

I have already observed that daily life is a tissue of innumerable little repetitive acts, including, at best, "reforms," that may or may not enjoy transcendence (become institutional). Thus we have Christian moralities (3.6)—prevailing moral systems that have taken their inspiration in Christianity, like the moralities of medieval European or colonial Latin American Christendom. Today, however, Latin America is caught up in a special stage of its history: that of its second emancipation. The first Latin American emancipation was its deliverance from dependence on Spain and Portugal, in the early years of the nineteenth century, or, in the Caribbean, from England, France, or Holland. In the first emancipation the agent and beneficiary of the revolution was the Creole oligarchy. Today, in the second emancipation, the subject or agent is the people of the poor as the "social bloc" of the oppressed (8.5).

As already indicated, revolution is not part of a people's normal experience. A revolution takes centuries to mature and materialize. But when a revolutionary process does break out, as in Nicaragua beginning in 1979, certain Christian ethical principles can function as norms to regulate and guide that exceptional praxis (5.6–7). The poor are the subject (agent) both of the reign of God, and of the revolution of liberation being conducted in Latin America here at the close of the twentieth century. Thus there will be an *essential* change in structures here. Prevailing "*social* relationships" (see chap. 13–15) will give place to other, more just structures and relationships (although they will *never* be perfect in human history before the Parousia, the Lord's return—Rev. 22:20).

As Moses abandoned the *morality* of Egypt only to find *ethical* norms to guide his praxis (5.9), so the heroes of the future homeland, along with the prophets, who frequently become martyrs (and this is why there have been so many martyrs in Latin America since 1969— because there are prophets), must have at their disposal a Christian ethics of revolution, a community ethics of liberation, an ethics capable of justifying "the *struggle* for social justice. This struggle must be seen as a normal dedication of the genuine good," says Pope John Paul II (*Laborem Exercens*, 20).

CONCLUSIONS

It might appear that the Christian may not theologize upon such current questions as class struggle, violence, or revolution. Those who do theorize upon these themes only too obviously do so in terms of their own ideologies, quickly taking sides in order to justify their daily praxis, be the latter one of domination, indifference, liberation, or what have you. But all these questions must be examined dispassionately, in the light of the principles sketched in part 1 of this treatise on community ethics.

Sin produces ethical discrepancies between persons—between dominator and dominated, hence between the dominating class or the "rich," and the dominated class or the "poor" (the oppressed as a social bloc). To deny the existence of classes is to deny the existence of sin. To deny that dominators struggle to institutionalize and eternalize their domination is the earmark of a naive mentality—if not of the bad faith of connivance. To deny the dominated their just right to defend their lives, defend the innocent, and rescue the people, and to call this defense sin, stigmatizing the "class stuggle" as "hatred and nihilism" (for it is, after all, a movement to an*nihil*ate sin), is the praxis of a theology of domination. Just so, to regard the revolution of the poor as "sin," and the institutional violence of coercion and repression practiced by the dominators as the "nature of things," is to establish a diabolical morality and call it gospel. Values today are reversed, and the worst of principles and movements are presented as the Christian ethics of Jesus, the ethics of the gospel.

Chapter 17

Ethical Problems of Contemporary Socialism

17.1 STATE OF THE QUESTION

Once a revolutionary process has been initiated, a profound social change must follow, in the form of an institutionalization. But any institution opts for a certain type of praxis and rejects others (5.10). The New Jerusalem dreamt of by the exiles of Egypt, the utopia that slaves yearned for, can come to be the very organism that represses and murders the prophets and Jesus. Christians, therefore, without becoming fifth-columnists or anarchists, and yet without skepticism or automatic rejection of any and every process of change, will always maintain a certain critical exteriority, an "eschatological reserve," that will afford them more realism and political prudence.

Each day the newspapers carry reports of protests against restrictions of freedom in socialist countries—in the Soviet Union, in Poland, in Tibet. We read of the violence, the absence of democracy, the bureaucratism, the totalitarianism, and the out-and-out brutality of the "eastern bloc" or "iron curtain" countries. At all events, for some Christians at least, Christianity and socialism *as practiced today* are intrinsically incompatible. Christianity and socialism are as different as day and night.

On the subject of "institutionalization" holy scripture teaches:

> The rights of the king who will rule you will be as follows: He will take your sons and assign them to his chariots and horses, and they will run before his chariot. ... He will use your

daughters as ointment-makers, as cooks, and as bakers. He will take the best of your fields, vineyards, and olive groves, and give them to his officials. He will tithe your crops and your vineyards, and give the revenue to his eunuchs and his slaves. ... He will tithe your flocks and you yourselves will become his slaves [1 Sam. 8:11–17].

The dialectical prophetic community, set in confrontation with the tributary institution of the king, becomes, as we have seen (9.6, 9.10), a demonstration of the tension that must obtain between the struggle with sin (waged by the prophet) and the institution (which will always have something of domination, something of sin, about it).

17.2 THE INSTITUTIONALIZATION OF SOCIALISM

I am not speaking, at this point, of the socialism of the Jesuit "reductions" of eighteenth-century Paraguay, which certainly underpinned and served as a utopia for the bourgeois socialism of the same century. Nor am I thinking of the utopian Christian socialism of a Saint-Simon or a Weitling. Indeed, I do not refer to the socialism proposed by Marx or Engels. My discourse in these paragraphs bears upon no ideological or theoretical movement at all. Rather I am speaking of *de facto socialism*—socialism as it has actually existed in the Soviet Union since 1917, socialism as we see it today in China, Vietnam, Angola, or Cuba, the socialism of today's Poland, Hungary, or Yugoslavia. I am speaking of real, concrete socialism. Of course the differences among the various socialisms are legion. But I shall proceed in my customary fashion, and obviate this potential difficulty by limiting my discourse to an abstract, general, essential level.

De facto socialism did not spring full-fledged from the Czarist regime in the Russian October Revolution. It is a matter of historical record that, in the years from 1917 to 1921, the "Soviet" revolution strove to implant a so-called natural economy, one that would transcend the law of value, and do without money, prices, or a market. In a word, the Soviet revolution attempted to realize the Marxian utopia.

But in 1921, Lenin himself was forced to recognize the ineffectiveness and failure of many of the elements of the Soviet utopian project. On that October 17, Lenin acknowledged:

> There can be no doubt that we have suffered a very serious defeat on the economic front..... The challenges of the economic front are a good deal more formidable than those of the military front. ... This defeat has been manifested in the higher spheres of our economic policy .... [We] have not succeeded in improving our productive forces. ... In its direct approach to the tasks involved in organizing the economy ... the communist system has retarded the growth of our productive forces, and was the principal cause of the deep economic and political crisis that we suffered in the spring of 1921 [*Selected Works*, 12:176–7].

Actual socialism, then, will have to reckon, after all, with market, money, wages, and prices, with the so-called law of value, and so on. *Something new* had appeared on the face of the earth, something undreamt of and unimagined. The new system was not the re-establishment of capitalism, to be sure. But neither was it communism. It was simply "de facto socialism"—socialism as it really exists.

17.3 ... AND THE "LAW OF VALUE" ABIDES

In 1928–9 the Soviet Union inaugurated centralized planning and the socialist system of property—the latter replacing the old institution of private property and legitimated today by *Laborem Exercens*, 14: "... Common access to the goods destined for humankind ... the *socialization* of certain means of production." But individual workers, far from being members of a *community* (which the "Soviets," anarchists, and the like, longed to establish), have forever after been regarded as an abstraction, as a kind of discrete, autonomous "producer," the subject and object of various mercantile relationships. In other words, the "transmission belt," as Isaac I. Rubin called it, is still "value," which continues to link the work remunerated by an enterprise in wages, the wage received, the subsequent purchase of merchandise produced by other enterprises, and so on. Even with regard to production itself (17.4), the "law of value" maintains its status as the required point of reference. Money is still the means of purchase: the value of merchandise continues to be expressed in its price. True, the distribution of productive agents—the division of labor—is determined beforehand by *planning*, as are production quotas and the price of merchandise. But it is *value*—the character of the product precisely as something produced for the market (albeit for a socialist market—11.5)—that affords the commensurability, the relationship, and exchange, of all the terms of the socialist economy.

Thus it comes about that, from the revolutionary process responding to real ethical exigencies (5.6), a new *morality* (3.6) arises. I am not suggesting that the moralities of capitalism and of socialism are more or less the same, any more than I would equate eighteenth-century capitalist morality with the feudal reality it replaced. The chimerical "third way," some "other way out," is anti-historical. The "Christian way" is politically nonexistent. In asserting the qualitative superiority, for the underdeveloped Third World, of an economy based on planning (and admitting its unavoidable imperfection, its everlasting perfectibility) rather than on a "perfect market equilibrium" under the law of the growth of the profit rate, I simply desire to recall, as do theologians of liberation, that *no* real, historical system can escape de facto constitution as the prevailing system. Every system will produce its *morality*, its practical legitimation (3.7). This explains (not: justifies) Stalinism.

17.4 THE RATE OF PRODUCTION GROWTH

The supreme commandment of Christian love is to "give the hungry to eat." But to this purpose "bread" must first be produced (6.7). The first intent of a revolution that has overthrown the exploitation and poverty of the wage-earning class has necessarily and essentially been not merely to effectuate a change in the regime of appropriation (that of the means of production, and even of the distribution of goods), but, earlier still, to attempt to *increase* the availability of the existing "satisfiers," the objects of the people's need. The capitalist rationality is essentially governed by growth in the "rate of profit"—meaning growth not only in the gross quantity or total amount of profit, but also in the ratio of surplus value or surplus life to the total capital employed. The new rationality of socialism is based on the growth of the economic "rate of production"—again, an increase not only in the gross quantity of the product, but also in relative productivity. This second principle of rationality is much more humane. It seeks to measure the economy from the standpoint of the human needs of the majorities (and thus employs the product, the "satisfier" as its yardstick), rather than exclusively from the standpoint of potential profitability, or accumulation (in terms of valorized realization) of capital.

Nevertheless, the rate of the economic growth of production is *still a market criterion*. I am not saying that it is capitalist. Production, in terms of the totality of products, cannot be measured physically. It must be measured in terms of the value, the price, of the products. On the basis of the law of value, albeit consciously controlled, socialist planning has utilized the rate of increase of production as its criterion of evaluation. This formal, mercantile criterion, which is not the "*direct* satisfaction of needs" (although that satisfaction is its limit), can become the new mystification of a factor that is not the actual human being—*living work* as a person, as Marx would say. *Laborem Exercens* is correct, then, in warning against "the danger of considering work ... a mere anonymous *force* needed for production" (no. 7)—or, still more clearly: "the sources of the dignity of work are to be sought principally not in their *objective* dimension, but in their *subjective* dimension" (ibid., 6). The sin of capitalism is to have taken work—which is an actual, living human being—and turned it into merchandise. The sin of socialism is that the human being is transformed into an "instrument of production" (ibid., 7) of the *social*—but not the *communal*—whole.

17.5 INDIVIDUALITY IN COMMUNITY

Laborem Exercens frequently criticizes aspects of socialism on the basis of Marx's own theoretical principles. The encyclical speaks of "subjectivity," for instance. Marx called it "individuality." Let us use the same method.

In the *Grundrisse* (1857–8), Marx puts forward certain propositions with a decidedly non-Stalinist ring:

> Free individuality founded on the universal development of individuals in the subordination of their communal productiv-

ity ... as social patrimony, constitutes the third stage.... *Communal* production ... is subordinate to individuals, and *controlled* in community fashion by them as a patrimony [of their own].... [It is a] *free* exchange among individuals, associating on the basis of community appropriation and *control* of the means of production. This last association has nothing of the arbitrary about it. It presupposes the development of material and *spiritual* conditions [*Grundrisse*, 1974, pp. 75–7].

Marx speaks not of a "collectivity" (*Kollektivität*) but of a "community" (*Gemeinschaft*). His would be a "communitarian," not a collectivistic, thinking. Furthermore, contrary to general misconceptions, he identifies the perfect community as the full realization of the particular *individual*, or subjectivity fulfilled. This is the utopia of an ethical thinker whose criticism must be leveled against socialism today. Marx's utopia has not been realized. It retains its challenging currency.

Full "individuality" or "subjectivity" calls for total community participation at every moment. In the first place, community is constituted of the "face-to-face" of its component individuals. Secondly, just as there can be no community without individuals, so neither can there be fully constituted individuals without community. In mere *society* (3.2)—and I am speaking of a socialist society at this point—the isolated, solitary, abstract individual (in a different manner than in capitalism, however—12.5), would not be a *really* realized individual. In the *society* of real socialism, then, the individual will require the organization of the *community*-as-subjectivity (11.10), the utopian horizon of a community constituted in the exercise of *democratic* freedom, full *participation* in or conscious personal management of the productive process, *control* in planning—in the total *responsibility* of fulfilled members of a human, organic community, and a human community that means to move toward the future, not to return to the past.

17.6 SOCIALIZATION OF THE MEANS OF PRODUCTION

As for the social teaching of the church on this point, *Laborem Exercens* initiates a new approach to the question of property. Now the basic criteria are: work and the human person:

One may speak of the antinomy between work and capital ... but behind the one and the other are human beings—concrete, *living* human beings: on the one hand those who perform work *without being owners* of the *means of production*, and on the other hand the entrepreneurs who are the owners of these means [*Laborem Exercens*, 14].

Human beings are the owners of the fruits of their labors (11.6). God is the creator of nature. On the basis of these two principles, the traditional teaching of the Bible and the church is that "the right to private property [is] subordinate to the *right to common use*, to the universal destination of goods" (*Laborem Exercens*, 14). This teaching had been obscured over the course of a number of recent decades by a certain absolutization of *private* property. But no Christian can take scandal from the Pope's teaching that "the socialization, in appropriate conditions, of certain means of production" (ibid.) is not only feasible, but positively to be recommended. To be sure, certain requirements must be observed in order to have the *full realization* of this socialization. The socialization of certain means of production is not being criticized, then, but rather its perfection is being called for:

> One must keep account of the fact that the simple withdrawal of those means of production [the withdrawal of capital] from the hands of their private owners *is not sufficient* to socialize them in a *satisfactory* fashion [ibid.].

How may these means of production, this capital, be partially or unsatisfactorily socialized? The "administration and control" of the socialized means of production, the pope explains, may remain in the hands of a group of persons:

> The group responsible for direction may fulfill its commission in a satisfactory manner.... But then again it may fulfill its commission in an unsatisfactory manner, by reserving to itself a monopoly over the administration and disposition of the means of production.... And so the mere transfer of the means of production to the ownership of the state, within the collectivistic system, is certainly *not equivalent* to the *socialization* of property [ibid.].

As we see, then, the social teaching of the church no longer criticizes socialism *from the standpoint of capitalism.* It now points to the shortcomings of socialism *on the very premises of Marx.* To be sure, the principle remains a Christian one, however fully it may coincide with the thought of the historical Marx: "One may speak of socialziation only when the *subjectivity* of society has been assured" [ibid.].

17.7 CONSCIOUSNESS OF THE PRODUCTIVE PROCESS

Socialism is defined from the standpoint of work. But it is "living work" itself, and its rights, that constitute the concrete, real source of the *ethical* critique of de facto socialist *morality.* Marx himself demanded, for the full realization of individuality, the worker's exercise of a conscious control of production. Hence the protest of the working world in actual socialist societies that it is deprived of an adequate "awareness" of the productive process itself. This protest is not only a practical, but a theoretical necessity as well. *Laborem Exercens* speaks to the point:

> Workers want more than remuneration for their work. They also want society to consider the possibility that, *even while working on something owned in common,* they could enjoy the awareness of working on something of their own, right in the productive process. This consciousness is snuffed out in them in a system of excessive bureaucratic centralization, where they feel themselves to be no more than a gear in the transmission of a mechanism whose "driver" is "upstairs somewhere.". . . The socialization of the means of production, if it is to be *rational and fruitful,* must take workers' complaints under careful advisement. Everything possible must be done to ensure, even within this [socialist] system, that persons be able to maintain a consciousness of working on something of their own. [*Laborem Exercens,* 15].

It is understandable, then, that certain theologians working within a socialist state, such as Józej Tischner in Poland, should ascribe such importance to the "meaning" of work. The question of "meaning" has a direct relationship to the realization of full individuality, full human subjectivity, responsible, free, cheerful participation in the personally managed construction of a better community, in the production of the "bread" to be "divided ... on the basis of each one's need." Unfortunately, planned production has often simply excluded any *conscious* participation on the part of workers in the productive process, as if the two were incompatible. This is one of the sins of socialism—socialism as actually practiced. Instead of being a "living community" of joy, the "great workshop" or factory becomes the melancholy place of abstract "production." It is not a place where "working men and women can participate in the management and control of their companies' production" (*Laborem Excercens*, 8).

Marx himself anticipated the plight of individual freedom under the despotism of a production that would simply ignore it. Thus he criticizes certain utopian socialisms:

> The bank, then, besides being the universal buyer and seller, would be the universal producer, as well. It would actually be ... the *despotic government of production* and the administrator of distribution.... The Saint-Simonians made the bank the papacy of production [*Grundrisse*, 73].

Marx demands that the "material process of production" be in the hands "of persons associating freely who have subjected it to their *planned* and *conscious control*" (*Das Kapital*, I, 1, 4).

17.8 PLANNING AND AUTONOMOUS ENTERPRISES

The socialist rationality far surpasses the capitalist rationality with regard to the real exercise of the right to work, to the annihilation of unemployment, and so on. *Laborem Exercens* teaches:

> In order to guarantee employment for all ... they must provide for *across-the-board planning* for the availability of concrete work.... They must attend to the correct and rational organization of such availability of work. The responsibility for this comprehensive solicitude rests ultimately on the

shoulders of the state. But this must not entail a unilaterally implemented centralization on the part of public authorities. Rather it is a matter of a *just and rational coordination*, within whose framework the initiative of persons, of autonomous groups, of centers and work enterprises, must be guaranteed, while keeping account of what has been said above about the subjective nature of human work [no. 18].

We must be very careful not to misinterpret the Pope here. He is not directing the members of a socialist society to return to the capitalist system. He is simply defining the terms of a struggle for a more humane, more just, more democratically socialist system.

In order to overcome the imbalance of the capitalist market (the "socialist market" is another matter), planning is once again indispensable. In 1939 L. V. Kantorovitch proposed the theoretical framework of a "total planning," a planning that would be "perfect" within its parameters. Neo-liberal capitalism criticizes all planning, simply on the grounds that perfect, total planning is impossible. But perfect planning is not the issue. What is at stake is *approximative* planning. Inasmuch as perfect, total planning is empirically impossible, socialist planners must admit the existence of, and ascribe a relative autonomy to, the productive *enterprise* itself (just as capitalism tolerates the state as a lesser evil). In other words, a tension, a contradiction obtains between planning on the one hand, and the socialist mercantile decision of the relatively autonomous enterprise on the other. The plan stipulates to the enterprise how much and what the latter must produce (its "goals"), as well as how much it may consume (its "costs," or the ratio of its expenditures to its product). The enterprise makes its decisions within those limits. But it can make these decisions in terms of its *own* goal of such-and-such an increase in its rate of profit. And so intermediate institutions appear between the central plan and the entrepreneurial level of the implementation of that plan. This phenomenon is referred to as a "conscious control of the law of value."

As we see, the new socialist economy, with its new concepts, such as "consistent prices," "calculated prices," "revenue prices," "planned prices," and so on, poses new ethical problems. Ethics may endorse the plan as a rationality that strives to create an economic balance superior to that of the liberal capitalist market, while nevertheless insisting on the rights of the enterprise—"that great workshop, as it were ... those living communities" (*Laborem Exercens*, 14).

At the same time, ethics will remind the autonomous enterprise of the importance of eliminating the implicit selfishness of exalting the increase of the rate of profit ("maximal profit"—ibid., 17), even in the Yugoslavian regime of "self-management," over the common good of the socialist society as a whole—and hence over and above the plan. After all, only the latter can regulate the relationships of the whole.

17.9 AMBIT OF NEGOTIABLE CONFLICTS AND DEMOCRACY

"Democracy" is not an attribute of capitalism. Quite the contrary, democracy can be realized more fully in socialism—within the necessary limits of historical situations. The popular sovereignty to which the socialist state must be subordinated—in other words, "socialist liberty, or a human freedom in a socialist society" (Franz Hinkelammert, *Crítica a la razón utópica*, p. 251)—"can only be realized in the hypothesis of a criterion of demarcation between planning and business autonomy" (ibid.). The social teaching of the church today, though admitting the legitimacy of "a reasonable planning and an adequate organization of human toil" (*Laborem Exercens*, 18), nevertheless insists on the importance of the concrete realization of workers' freedom in the exercise of an autonomous personal management of the productive process. But the socialist regime has failed to create and institutionalize the political organs by which workers and self-managed enterprises can defend their rights or register the conflicts that inevitably arise, where it may well be possible to "negotiate" a problem without impugning the legitimacy either of the state as a whole or of the system. "An excessive bureaucratic centralization" (*Laborem Exercens*, 15), a so-called democratic centralism, has not afforded citizens *sufficient political room* to express their concrete individuality, their full subjectivity. Freedom to express their ideas, freedom of religious conscience as a public act, dissidence within the limits of justice, personal management—these are things not easily institutionalized in a state or nation committed to "total planning."

This is a sin that socialism, socialism as it is really lived, must give up. I make this assertion not in the name of capitalism—not to urge a return to the past—but in simple recognition of the need of reform, for the sake of the future of socialism itself. Christian prophecy, coming out of three thousand years of tradition that began with Abraham of Ur of the Chaldeans, has a word to say in the building of a new socialist society, especially in Latin America.

17.10 MYSTIFICATION OF TECHNOLOGY AND SOCIAL PROGRESS

But perhaps the basic criticism to be made against certain socialisms (Stalinism, for example, which is far from being a dead letter at the present time), is that they conjure up the image of a utopia consisting of a simple projection of its own self-image into an unlimited future, where total planning, by way of a development *ad infinitum* of science and technology, in a demiurgic optimism with respect to social progress and the perfection of society as an economy of production, leads to the construction of a new fetish, a new apocalyptic Beast. Here future communist society is simply socialism without flaw or blemish, intact and immaculate, without problems or contradictions—the "reign of a god" on earth, the absolute justification of socialism and the total denial of its historical crises and contradictions. "Dialectical materialism," as the pantheistic ontology of an eternal, infinite matter, is the central ideological—nay, philosophical— support of this mystification.

For the realization of this "perfect society," an immense development of productive forces is necessary, an unprecedented technological and scientific development. Marx explicitly placed the "kingdom of freedom" *beyond* all sovereignty of need, *beyond* any *possible* mode of production. Mystified socialism, by contrast, asserts the "technological myth": the possibility of realizing this ideal. In this case, "perfect planning" and the infinite development of technology are the only conditions required for this communism—which is nothing but the "idea" of present-day socialism projected, in anticipation of a correction of its current contradictions—the "god" of Feuerbach, the "perfect idea of humankind."

The concept of "communism"—which in Marx was a utopian, not a factual, concept, a horizon (an ethical limit *in function of which* its non-reality in the prevailing system can be criticized)—is suddenly transformed into an immediate, *historical* goal justifying the institutionalization, with all its contradictions, all its inescapable injustices and sins, of socialism. And behold, Stalinism.

CONCLUSIONS

Far be it that I should be seeking some "third alternative" between capitalism and socialism—as if I championed "another way out," a politico-economic system that would be neither capitalism nor socialism but the "Christian solution" to the economic and political questions of humankind. A concrete, positive Christian economico-political project does not exist. An ethical or prophetic criticism exists, but this is at most a moral criticism or a demand for reforms— not a positive "third way" political project. On the other hand, we are not simply indifferent where a choice between capitalism and socialism would be concerned, especially for Latin America. We as Latin Americans suffer under capitalism. Ours is the misfortune to have to suffer capitalism in its essence (capital itself—chap. 12), dependence (chap. 13), the transnationals (chap. 14), and so on.

Socialism may well be a more rational system for righting the imbalances of the capitalist market system with its unemployment, overproduction, hunger, exploitation, and so on, all the product of the triumph of growth in the rate of profit as the sole criterion of praxis and rationality. By contrast, application of the criterion of a growth in the rate of economic production, under a system of approximative planning, would appear to be a better solution for the present imbalances. But in itself it will never be the reign of God on earth.

Chapter 18

Ethics of Culture and Ecology

18.1 STATE OF THE QUESTION

The twin questions of ecology and culture as material for ethical reflection present a set of problems partly transcending the prevailing division of the capitalist and socialist worlds.

Humankind appeared on our tiny planet more than three million years ago (although *Homo sapiens* has been in the picture only in the last two hundred thousand years). In the course of the intervening ages, the human being has progressed from the condition of an altogether rare, land-locked species, having neither wings to fly nor fins to swim, to rule over all the earth. We have domesticated, systematically consume, and preserve in our zoos or tolerate in our "natural" parks (which, being parks, are not natural), practically every species of brute animal.

We read in the newspapers every day that the European forests are dying, that birds can no longer migrate, that the fish of the Mediterranean and of other waterways in industrial countries are perishing, that environmental pollution in Mexico City has reached deadly levels, that a lethal gas has escaped in India, that contamination from a nuclear accident poses a threat to human life in the cities for hundreds of miles around. Our gigantic technological and scientific miracles turn against us, and our lives hang in the balance. Further: as we know, a self-styled universal culture is dominating and extinguishing autochthonous cultures, ethnic groups, tribes, and peripheral nations—whole peoples, as in Latin America, Africa, and Asia. Along with nature, the cultural diversity of humanity is disappearing from the globe.

We read in holy scripture:

In the beginning, when God created the heavens and the earth, the earth was a formless wasteland, and darkness covered the abyss, while a mighty wind swept over the waters.

Then God said, "Let there be light," and there was light. ... "Let us make man in our image, after our likeness. Let them have dominion over the fish of the sea, the birds of the air, and the cattle, and over all the wild animals and all the creatures that crawl on the ground." ... God looked at everything he had made, and he found it *very good* [Gen. 1:1–3, 26, 31].

When God created all things, everything was "very good." What have we done with God's creation today, then? And what have we done with the entire cultural production of humanity before us?

18.2 PERSON, NATURE, PRODUCT: *POIESIS*

We have seen (1.2) that *praxis* is the person-to-person relationship: it is a "practical" relationship, an action between two human beings. In passing, we have briefly observed that *poiesis* is something else again: the person-to-nature-to-product relationship. *Work*—the relationship of person-to-nature-to-product—is a "productive," manufacturing relationship, the relationship precisely of work (11), in virtue of its third term: the product. The work relationship is a triple relationship, then, with each term determining different questions (see Diagram 12).

Diagram 12

The Threefold Work Relationship

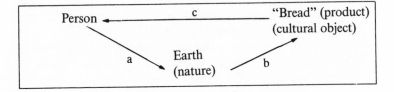

The person-to-nature relationship can be one of mere "abiding," the locus of our "abode"—a relationship of passivity, admiration, and knowledge alone. This will be our theoretical, contemplative culture (arrow a). Only when the person-to-nature relationship becomes a work relationship—a relationship of the transformation of nature through human activity—is the relationship extended to a term constituting a human, cultural, no longer merely "natural," product. Now we have a technological, productive culture (arrow b). The movement from nature to product is a productive, technological process, implemented in our day by science. The distribution or consumption of the product (arrow c), for its part, is the moment of the "subjectification" of what human beings have in part objectified. This movement represents not objective culture (which would be material or symbolic cultural objects), but modes of consumption, of use, of satisfaction—subjective culture or customs, from culinary pleasure to the joy of the religious or spiritual.

Morality and ethics (3.2) both form part of this relational triangle, each with its own practical determination of it. Because relationships with nature and product are mediated by or addressed to *other persons*, they always have a *practical*—a moral or an ethical—status. The ecological question (nature precisely as our *oikia*, as humanity's "house and home"), and the cultural question (the "cultivation" of the earth), are human, practical questions, then.

18.3 "MOTHER EARTH"

From the time of the ancient Inca *Pachamama* in Peru, the *Cuahtlicue* of the Aztecs in Mexico, or for that matter the Roman *Terra Mater*, the *earth* has always been regarded by agricultural peoples, colonial planters, even nomads, as the mother of life, nourishment, and fertility. The earth is the radical, organic soil *where* one lives and *whence* one lives. From her motherly bosom spring the Andean potato, Central American corn, and wheat and grapes for the bread and wine of the Mediterranean.

In its natural fertility, the earth is the material origin of basic wealth—the origin of primordial, primary "use value." Without so-called natural things, human beings would be unable to perform any work at all. All work in the last analysis is the trans-formation—changing the *form*—of the matter born of earth.

Passively then—the earth as landscape, as the place where we eat, dress, and dwell, the boundless horizon, nature rustic, wild, and chaotic—the earth is the nature that touches our skin, the place where we make our *dwelling*, our *eco*logy. This is the origin of the dialectic of person and cosmos, the phenomenon of nature as *habitat*.

From this earth, then, we gather wood, for we have discovered fire: wood is warmth now, and safety, and light. In this earth we find a cave, and it is our house. We find a large stone there, and it will be our door. We find the fruits of the earth, and they become our nourishment. Here are the animals, whose shepherds we shall one day be, herding them to replace our protein or to clothe ourselves with their hide. Nourishing, welcoming, protecting, motherly earth! Earth, lovely nature, splendor of dawns and sunsets, beauty of mountain streams, of the singing of the nightingales, of the terrible, bounding sea! Earth, mother of the sweet-smelling rose.

18.4 DESTROYING THE EARTH

Sin is the destruction of the work created by God. God's most perfect deed is the human person. But the earth, too, is the work of God. Its destruction is the annihilation of the locus of human history, of humanity, of the incarnation, and hence the gravest of ethical misdeeds.

The earth was once a garden, a Paradise. Today it is one great refuse heap. What species has done this? The human. No longer do we rest on the bosom of our *Terra Mater* in love and respect. No longer is she our "Sister Earth," as she was once upon a time for Saint Francis of Assisi. "Brother Sun," for his part, is hard to find in Mexico City, decked in his mantle of smog.

The earth, as sheer material, as purely exploitable, unlimitedly destructible, as a source of income, as a cause of a growth in the profit rate, or even in the rate of mere production, is now but another aspect of the human *dominative* act. This change of attitude toward the person-to-nature relationship, culminating in the industrial revolution, now issues in the delusions of today's national state regarding the "promise" of transnational capital. The hotbed of this entire phenomenon is an aggressive society that destroys natural ecology, a society for which the corruption of nature is an intrinsic aspect of the process of its domination of human beings, the poor, the subjected classes, the peripheral countries.

The transnational corporations locate their most contaminating industries, and exercise the least safety precautions, precisely in the underdeveloped countries. Factory waste kills the fauna and flora of the oceans, pollutes the atmosphere with asphyxiating gases, and wipes out the natural producers of oxygen (such as our forests, or ocean algae). The developed countries rob the periphery even of its oxygen! After all, they consume more than they produce. The Club of Rome announces the extinction of non-renewable resources, and the response is an augmentation of the contamination. The gigantic ecological collapse looms. The time draws near when, as if by an act of cosmic vengeance, nature will exterminate the species *homo* from the face of the planet. Inextricably intertwined with the sin of economic and political injustice, the sin of human domination, is the very death of nature. And yet, as we know, "the one who grasps for the sword, dies by the sword."

But the growth of the profit rate will hear no reasons. It would rather *extinguish life* than see its own death, the death of capital.

18.5 ECOLOGY AND LIBERATION

Nuclear war (15.5) and the death of the natural life of our planet would appear to be foretold in the Book of Revelation (6:1–8; 9:13–21). At any rate a like cataclysm is surely the work of the Beast (2.10; 12.10). Still, it is the poor who must bear the brunt of it.

Nature—the earth, its biosphere, its atmosphere, its waters—lies mortally wounded. Nor does the gangrene creep over it in an even process. Rather the process is organic: the center will offer more resistance to the crisis, whereas the periphery, the poor nations, will be the first to die. The crisis is a world crisis, but responsibility for it lies with the politicians of a military-industrial complex that destroys nature. The persons responsible are those in authority in the developed powers of the center, which with 30 percent of the world's population contaminate more than 90 percent of the earth.

That industrial center will never decree a reduction in its own profit growth—perhaps not even in its production growth. This would mean the end of a system whose very essence is inscribed in the parameters of an irrationally accelerated growth rate. Or will some technological miracle regenerate the destroyed ecological balance? It is scarcely likely. Rescue, if there is to be rescue, may well arrive by other routes. Is a new attitude toward the relationship between the human being and nature still an option for a capitalism in its current stage of development? Will not poorer, less destructive, less consumer-oriented, more economical, more patient, more popular models of the relationship between the human being and nature, models more respectful of the earth, now appear only among peoples whose degree of technological contradiction has not attained the level at which we find it in developed central capitalism? Will not a breach with the destructive system be realized only when person-to-person relationships are redefined? Once peripheral peoples are liberated, will they not have an effect on the North-South relationship, and the person-to-nature relationship as well?

18.6 CULTURE

The theology of culture is a chapter of the theology of work (which we have examined in chap. 11), and both are constitutive parts of our theology of liberation:

> When with the work of their hands or with the assistance of technical resources human beings cultivate the earth that it may produce fruits and come to be the worthy dwelling place of all the human family ... they personally accomplish the very plan of God [*Gaudium et Spes*, 57].

The Bible calls the fruit of toil "bread," suggesting a eucharistic sacramentality, satisfaction as nourishment, and the essence of human culture (see 1.6, 4.9, 6.7, 6.8, 6.10). Culture is first of all agriculture: the cultivation of the earth as the "working" of nature. Work is the very substance of culture, its ultimate essence, its basic determination, in the sense that its very being, as *actualization* of the human being, is a *way of producing human life*. Work is the self-production, the creation, of human life. Before being objects, indeed before being "modes of consumption" of these cultural objects, culture is a *way of working*.

On the one side, culture is *material poiesis* or production of objects, the productive technique (technology, art), as well as the systematic totality of the instruments of work or of objects produced. This is material culture. The work-earth-bread relationship, then (creative human action, nature, product), is the essential material level of culture: the eucharistic "bread."

On the other side, culture is *symbolic poiesis* or production, the spiritual expression of material production. Any material cultural object is a *symbol* as well, and a symbol must always bespeak a relationship to the material (be it only to the basic need to eat, to enjoy sexual love, and so on—the profoundly *fleshly* dimensions of human existence and thus the most symbolic dimensions of all).

The symbolic totality of a people is that people's spiritual culture. The dialectical synthesis of culture is constituted in the life modes or lifestyles (the *ethos*) that make up the totality not only of production of material, symbolic objects, but of the mode of consumption lived by the community in the unity of history as well—the totality of the community's attitudes toward its values (the values emerging from a generative "nucleus" of meaning for a given concrete human group).

It is in this sense that the incarnate Son "has spoken according to the culture proper to different ages" (*Gaudium et Spes*, 58a). "But at the same time the church, sent to all peoples of every time and place, is not bound exclusively and indissolubly to any race or nation. ... It can enter into communion with various cultural modes" (ibid.).

18.7 CULTURAL DOMINATION

Sin on the level of culture, of which the church itself cannot be exonerated, having de facto identified itself over the course of so many centuries with Western culture alone (the phenomenon of *Christendom*), is the domination of one culture by another.

Culture, especially African and Asian, comes in for a great deal of discussion in contemporary theology. The issue is surely a crucial one. But we must discard a certain theological "populism" (13.8)— an "ethnotheology" of sorts, which claims to work exclusively from the level of culture, ignoring the political and economic spheres altogether, and understanding "culture" only in the "symbolic" sense of popular culture. We may not thus allow ourselves to forget the contradiction prevailing among the *plurality of existing cultures*. Latin American or African "culture" is not one but *many*, and contradictory, with hegemonic cultures dominating others in a structure of sin.

At least from the sixteenth century onward, Spanish and Portuguese culture, and later English, French, and Dutch, and finally North American (18.8), engulfed the peripheral cultures by conquest and colonization. Aztec, Inca, Bantu, East Indian, Chinese, and other cultures were dominated and annihilated, or relegated to the supposed status of barbarism, savagery, and bestiality. Their gods were demons, we heard, their symbols sorcery, their traditions ignorance and falsehood, their dances indecency and immorality.

The modern European Christendoms, Catholic and Protestant alike, proclaimed to the human history of the Third World the witness of an obliteration of alien cultures, the annihilation of the neighbor, of the other, in the name of Christianity. The scandal is universal, and the day of judgment, sentence, and reparation yet to dawn. But there are other sorts of cultural sin as well—some of them more recent (18.8), others in the national order (18.9).

18.8 TRANSNATIONAL CULTURE

An invisible, forgotten *cultural domination* accompanied the expansion of the transnationals (chap. 15) in the period beginning in 1945. A self-styled "universal culture"—the Coca Cola culture, with its blue jeans and other "modern necessities"—is penetrating the Third World in all its breadth and depth. Both the "needs" and the means of their satisfaction are exported to the Third World, whose peoples, in all but total helplessness, contemplate not only the domination of their states, their armies, and their economies, but the destruction of their cultural objects, their customs, their symbols, the very meaning of their life. The destruction is a *spiritual* one. "The advent of urban-industrial civilization also entails problems on the ideological level, threatening the very roots of our culture" (*Puebla Final Document*, 418).

It is only too clear that a *bourgeois culture* of the dominating classes in the peripheral countries establishes an organic connection with this pretended universal culture, in order to seize control of education, the media, the organisms of scientific and technological research, and the universities. The "universal culture" is the "new Enlightenment" of those who regard themselves as "cultivated" because they are familiar with mechanisms imported from the

European and North American cultures and superficially implanted in peripheral countries. In the nineteenth century these were the liberals in Latin America. In the twentieth they are the developmentalists.

The church itself is profoundly involved in this whole problematic, not only by reason of its worldwide presence, but because the churches of the central countries of capitalism are hegemonic within Catholicism and Protestantism, and transmit willy-nilly the guidelines and models of their cultures of origin. Thus a cultural domination frequently employs the church itself as its tool and instrument.

18.9 POPULAR CULTURE, RESISTANCE, AND CULTURAL CREATION

The authentic national culture of a dependent, peripheral country is now split into two opposing factions. It bears on its bosom the mark of cultural domination. The culture of the elite dominates the culture of the masses (whom it controls), dominates the culture of the oppressed classes (whom it rejects), and finds itself in continual tension with the "*popular* culture."

The popular culture (for the authentic meaning of "people" see 8.5–10), basically structured around daily *work* (as "productive work" in the laboring and rural class; as "unproductive" work from the viewpoint of capital, in the ethnic groups, tribes, marginal groups, and other sectors that preserve their "outsideness"—8.7), is the nucleus of the people's practice of the centuries-old resistance to oppressors. With their songs, their dances, their living piety, their "underground economy" (their own consumption or production, invisible to the capitalist economy), their communal solidarity, their system of feeding themselves, and so on, they continue to do today what they have done for hundreds of years—bypass the oppressor's "universal culture."

But in the regime of oppression under which the peoples of the peripheral countries suffer, the popular culture must camouflage itself. It does so in its crafts, in its folklore, on the level of a despised, subordinate culture. Only in cases in which a people has managed to organize and is producing a praxis of liberation (8.10) does the popular culture turn creative, as with the popular national cultural revolution of today's Nicaragua. The church of the poor (9.3), the base church communities—along with the prophets and saints who bind themselves to the poor with bonds of identity—have identified with this "culture-creating" process, animating it, vitalizing it, and integrating it into the liturgy, into the celebration of the word and the rite of the eucharistic memorial. Thus a cultural and economic synthesis is effectuated, and "bread" becomes a cultural object, to be experienced in the light of the word (a cultural symbol) and consumed in justice. Now the *community* (1.5) celebrates, in its culture, the fruit of its work in behalf of life.

18.10 CULTURE AND POPULAR PASTORAL PRACTICE

The evangelization of the people is implemented in the culture of that people (*Evangelii Nuntiandi*, 18ff.). "Faith, and consequently the church, are sown and grow in the culturally diversified piety of the people" (Medellín, *Popular Pastoral Ministry*, 5). Indeed, popular culture is the locus of the life, the realization, and the growth of the faith of the people. The Catholic Church, like the Protestant churches, because implanted principally in central countries (which determines the control and exercise of pastoral work), has difficulty in living the Christian life *from within*, living the Christian life as a popular cultural religious life. This is evident in Africa and Asia, where a diversity of races, languages, and even religions and autochthonous cultures, still vigorous and full of life, presents an obstacle to a facile domination by European culture by way of Christianity. But in Latin America this domination passes almost unperceived. In every one of our countries, the churches believe that a Creole culture will of course "understand" the oppressed. But the cultural chasm—dualistic residue of a succession of dominations, beginning with colonial Christendom—is immense. A Creole elite controls the hierarchical structures. But these structures are out of contact with the Christian people. A people can be evangelized only by a people, from within its own popular culture. Where the evangelizing process of liberation is concerned, therefore, it is essential that "the people evangelize the people" from within the popular church *community* itself, in the identity of its own culture. The fate of the church, both in Latin America and in the peripheral world of Africa and Asia, hangs in the balance.

I am not suggesting that our assertions concerning the church have been accepted by the revolutionary movements. However, these movements are making great strides in the reformulation of the question of the culture and religion of the Latin American people as an important aspect of the motivation of the revolutionary changes of which we stand in need today.

CONCLUSIONS

As we have seen, the question of work determines the double relationship "person-earth" (ecology) and "person-bread" (culture). The destruction of nature and the annihilation of the culture of the poor go hand in hand. Both are the fruit of sin—the sin of the domination exercised by the "rich," or sinners, over the "poor," or the dominated Job of the Bible (2.2). We destroy the land we live in. And we destroy the cultures of the dominated, in their dignity, in their beauty, in their splendid multiplicity as so many varieties of "lilies of the field." After all, the Idol is a god of death, and hates life (2.8, 3.5, 12.10).

Thus the poor are dominated and exploited by sin—as workers (chap. 11–12), as impoverished nation (13), as wage-earners of the poor nation (14)—as the tortured and annihilated victims of the arms of empire, sucked dry by debts they have neither contracted nor profited from but that they must pay with their blood (chap. 15), violated from time immemorial and accused of violence whenever, with full right and in all justice, they defend the innocent (chap. 16). When they manage, in rare instances, to defeat this historical regime of injustice, then they must begin the struggle for greater participation in the management of production, for greater freedom and democracy (chap. 17), all over again. When all is said and done, these *peoples*, these poor, these dominated classes—rendered just because they are dominated, dominated by sin—are the agent of the reign of heaven (5.8). The people of God does not surrender. It resists. And knows how to celebrate.

Chapter 19

The Gospel and the Social Teaching of the Church

19.1 STATE OF THE QUESTION

In order to examine the questions posed by the relationship between the gospel and the social teaching of the church, we shall have to distinguish various levels of generality, value, and authority. To this purpose let us examine one of the papal documents of the church's social teaching:

> Confronted with situations this diverse, we find it difficult to pronounce an isolated word, or to propose a situation of universal value. ... It is incumbent on the Christian communities objectively to analyze the actual situation of their country, explain it in the light of the changeless word of the gospel, deduce principles of reflection, norms of judgement, and guidelines for action according to the social teachings of the church such as they have been developed in the course of history. ... It behooves these Christian communites to discern, with the help of the Holy Spirit, and in communion with the responsible bishops, in dialogue with their other Christian brethren and all persons of good will, the options and commitments that it will be suitable to assume in order to realize social, political, and economic transformations it regards as urgent. ... Before all else, Christians shall have to renew their confidence in the power and originality of the demands the gospel. ... The social teaching of the church ... does not intervene to confirm with its authority any given

established structure .... It develops by way of mature reflection ... *under the impulse* of the gospel ... by the disinterested will to service and attention to the very poorest [*Octogesima Adveniens*, 4, 42].

This lengthy citation will guide our reflection. Not surprisingly, it establishes the ethic of the gospel as the supreme norm of the whole of the social teaching of the church. For our own part, then, let us recall the basic illumination, the foundational horizon, of a community ethics of liberation:

When the Son of Man comes in his glory, escorted by all the angels of heaven, he will sit upon his royal throne, and all the nations will be assembled before him. ... The king will say to those on his right: "Come. You have my Father's blessing! Inherit the kingdom prepared for you from the creation of the world. For I was hungry and you gave me food, I was thirsty and you gave me drink, I was a stranger and you welcomed me, naked and you clothed me. I was ill and you comforted me, in prison and you came to visit me. ... As often as you did it for one of my least brothers, you did it for me" [Matt. 25:31–40].

These absolutely primary gospel principles are the *light by which* the social teaching of the church develops the *demands* of "intermediate-level" social moral principles, a level neither concrete (for to make the concrete application is the responsibility of the Christian community) nor absolutely primary (which is the function of the gospel). Further, as we shall see, the social teaching of the church will be situated within an "established, prevailing *morality*" (3.6–7).

19.2 FROM *RERUM NOVARUM* (1891) TO *QUADRAGESIMO ANNO* (1931)

May 15, 1891, the date of the publication of Leo XIII's celebrated encyclical *Rerum Novarum*, marked the end of an era. Never again would Catholicism be inextricably intermeshed with feudalism and monarchy. Inadvertently, however, Catholicism now adopted the principles of capitalism, despite the stirrings of internal criticism against it. "Capital" was now accepted as an independent co-principle with work, endowed with its own rights against the latter (*Rerum Novarum*, 1). The private ownership of capital was approved. As for "those who are without property," the encyclical proclaims that they are to "make up for that with work" (ibid., 6). Socialism was condemned. The reason given was that it denied "private property to be most conformable to human nature" (ibid., 8). Class differences were "natural" (ibid., 13), and the "height of evil" was to pretend that one class was the other's enemy, "as if the difference between rich and poor were not established by nature" (ibid., 14). To be sure, a just wage was demanded: the wealthy were not "to seek their profit in the poverty of others," for this was "permitted neither by divine law nor by human" (ibid.). However, the encyclical promptly retracted this condemnation of profit, this anathematization of the exploitation of surplus value (see 12.3–5), for it was utterly oblivious of the actual *origin* of profit. The encyclical is an enormous step forward in Christian social awareness. But this step is taken entirely within the purview of capitalist *morality* (3.2). Granted, capitalism is also powerfully criticized in the document.

In 1931, socialism was once more condemned in essence, whereas capitalism was criticized from within a basic acceptance of it:

> Inasmuch as the present system rests principally on capital and labor, one must know and put into practice the principles of right reason or Christian social philosophy on capital and labor and their mutual coordination [*Quadragesimo Anno*, 110].

Thus the "true social teaching of the church" (ibid., 20) criticizes capitalism and proposes reforms, but accepts its principal theses. Socialism, for its part, is criticized absolutely.

19.3 FROM *MATER ET MAGISTRA* (1961) TO *OCTOGESIMA ADVENIENS* (1971)

The social teaching of the church has condemned Nazism and Fascism, oblivious of the fact that these distortions of the extreme right are simply capitalism pursued to its ultimate consequences. The church's condemnation of socialism was unqualified at that time. Only after the Second World War, during the years from 1945 onward, while still approving of capital and its right to profit, the church began to insist that a wage, as just recompense for work performed, "permit [the worker] to maintain a genuine human level of life" (*Mater et Magistra*, 71)—not understanding that if the wage were actually to recompense "the effective contribution of each laborer to economic production" (ibid.), there would be no profit or surplus value. However, we now see the church beginning gingerly to distance itself from capitalism in the matter of ownership (ibid., 104–19), especially in the area of North-South relationships:

> Perhaps the *greatest* problem of our day is the one bearing on the relationships that ought to obtain between economically developed nations and nations still economically developing [ibid., 157].
>
> It is likewise necessary that economically advanced nations exercise special care to avoid the temptation to lend assistance to poor countries with the intention of orientating their political situation to their own advantage and thus realizing their plans for world hegemony [ibid., 171].

The spirit of *Pacem in Terris* (1963), the encyclical addressed "to all persons of good will," opened new perspectives. The Second Vatican Council was in session. *Ecclesiam Suam* (1964) now recalled that "the interior liberation produced by the spirit of evangelical poverty makes us more sensitive to and better capable of understanding the human phenomena linked to economic factors" (*Ecclesiam Suam*, 51). John XXIII's "church of the poor" was forging ahead. *Populorum Progressio* (1967) proposed a whole new program for development, and went back to Pius XI's theme of the "international imperialism of money" (ibid., 26)—a theme that was to be resumed at Medellín (*Medellín Document on Peace*, 9e). *Gaudium et Spes* (1965) was a genuine, and genuinely new, theological treatise on the fundamental social question.

Only with *Octogesima Adveniens* (1971), however, did the church distinguish the various types of socialism:

> Among socialism's various forms of expression, as are the

generous aspiration and the quest for a more just society ... distinctions must be drawn to guide concrete options. ... This outlook will enable Christians to consider the degree of commitment possible along these [socialist] paths, preserving the values, in particular, of freedom, responsibility, and openness to the spiritual, which guarantee integral human development [*Octogesima Adveniens*, 31].

A bridge had been built. A new age would dawn in Latin America. The historic initiatives of Medellín (1968) would not have to be in vain.

19.4 *LABOREM EXERCENS* (1981)

Surely a central place in the history of the social teaching of the church must be assigned to *Laborem Exercens*. This encyclical moves to a head-on criticism of capitalism—capitalism in its very essence— and approves of socialism in principle. Now it is socialism that comes in for particular criticisms and a call for internal reform. The orientation conferred on the social teaching of the church in 1891 has been reversed. If the earlier "key" was private property, now "human *work* is a key, probably the essential key, to the entire social question" (*Laborem Exercens*, 3). The basic thesis of the document's criticism of the essence of capitalism is enunciated in terms of "the principle of the priority of *labor* over *capital*" (ibid., 12):

This principle directly concerns the process of production: In this process labor is always a *primary efficient cause*, while capital, the whole collection of means of production, remains a mere instrument or *instrumental cause* [ibid.].

Further consideration of this question should confirm our conviction of the priority of human labor over what in the course of time we have grown accustomed to calling capital [ibid.].

We must emphasize and give prominence to human primacy in the production process, the primacy of humankind over things. Everything contained in the concept of capital in the strict sense is only a collection of things [ibid., 13].

The social teaching of the church no longer held that work can be set in confrontation with capital or detached from it as an independent factor or aspect on the very level of production itself. *Rerum Novarum* had held: "Neither capital can subsist without labor, nor labor without capital" (no. 14). Now we are taught instead:

> This consistent image, in which the principle of the primacy of person over things is strictly preserved, was broken up in human thought .... The break occurred in such a way that labor was separated from capital and set in opposition to it, and capital was set in opposition to labor, as though they were two impersonal forces, two production factors juxtaposed in the same "economistic" perspective [*Laborem Exercens*, 13].

All capital is work. The creative source of wealth, of all wealth or value, is work (11.5, 12.6), not capital. On the other hand, as we have seen (17.6), John Paul II basically accepts socialism: "In consideration of human labor and of common access to the goods meant for humankind, one cannot exclude the *socialization*, in suitable conditions, of certain means of production" (*Laborem Exercens*, 14). But now there is more: socialism is criticized internally. Instead of being criticized from without, as before, it is corrected from within, as I indicated in 17.6–8:

> We can speak of socializing only when the subject character of society is ensured, that is to say, when on the basis of their work all persons are fully entitled to consider themselves part-owners of the great workbench at which they are working with everyone else [*Laborem Exercens*, 14].
>
> If it is to be rational and fruitful, any socialization of the means of production must ... ensure that in this kind of system also persons can preserve their awareness of working "for themselves" [ibid., 15].

As we see, it is no longer a matter of a critique from without. Socialism is now being criticized *from within socialism itself*, which is accepted in its real, specific, actual existence. The critique of socialism is a moral demand for reform. The critique of capitalism is ethical, radical, and total.

19.5 ETHICAL DEMANDS OF THE GOSPEL

The "social teaching" or "social doctrine" of the church is unanimous in its insistence that the norms or directives the hierarchy proposes to the individual "Christian community" are inspired by, and emanate from, the gospel. In other words the social teaching of the church is not the gospel. Its level is one of inferior value, less importance. This at once poses a problem. What need is there of a "social teaching"? After all, we have the gospel, and the demands of that gospel are on a higher level. What is the relationship between the gospel and the social teaching of the church, and again between this pair and the individual "Christian community"?

For the sake of more clarity, the various levels of generality, as well as the various agents involved in this question, in the terminology of *Octogesima Adveniens*, 4 and 42, are sketched in Diagram 13.

The gospel abides as the fundamental horizon, the ultimate ethical reference, of all Christian praxis, that of the social magisterium of the church as well as that of the ethical conscience of the saints and prophets. In reality the only infallible, absolute, really Christian, "once and for all" (*hapax*) "social teaching" is the gospel.

The gospel will always be the Christian utopia (see chaps. 4 and 5):

> The Spirit of the Lord, which animates the person renewed in Christ, continually overturns the horizons where the human intelligence so frequently desires to remain, moved by an overeagerness for security. ... A certain energy totally invades us, thrusting us to *transcend every system*, every ideology [*Octogesima Adveniens*, 37].

This creative impulse is the force of the gospel itself.

19.6 STATUS OF THE SOCIAL TEACHING OF THE CHURCH

We shall have a better sense of the question if we recall some of the texts of the teaching of the popes. By and large this teaching recommends acceptance, albeit critical, of the prevailing order of

212   *Ten Disputed Questions*

Diagram 13

**The Gospel, the Social Teaching of the Church, and
the Christian Community**

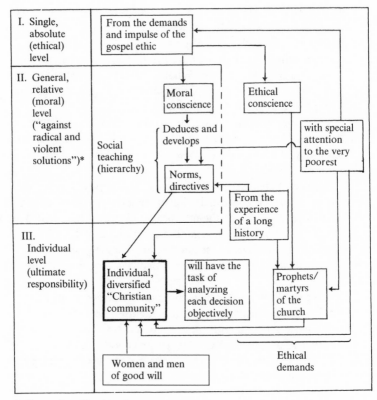

* *Octogesima Adveniens*, 3

things. *Rerum Novarum* advises: "The best thing to do is to see human things *as they are* and at the same time to seek, by other means, as we have said, the opportune alleviation of evils" (no. 13).

Apparently a mere *moral but critical* conscience would apply the gospel demands (19.5) and thus arrive at specific (that is, on a level of lesser abstraction and generality) norms, teachings, and directives for the Christian community: "It is the church that draws from the Gospel those teachings in virtue of which the conflict can be resolved completely, or at least palliated and thereby made more bearable" (ibid., 12).

Thus "let those who ... lack the goods of fortune learn from the church that poverty is no shame in the eyes of God" (ibid., 17). Today this would sound to some ears like a theology of resignation.

It would appear that *Quadragesimo Anno* adopted a "third alternative," inasmuch as it enjoins us from "flying either to liberalism or to socialism for assistance" (ibid., 10). It is true that the encyclical is enunciating general moral principles. But these must never be interpreted as specific socio-economic or political projects. Hence the ambiguity of their status. The social teaching of the church proposes we rise above "the battle between opposing *classes*" (ibid., 81), but we are not told *how* to rise above domination of one class by another. (Indeed, the document fails to show this domination to be a constitutive, structural aspect of the classes themselves.) Finally, we are dealing with "a reform adjusted to the *principles* of reason and *capable* of leading the economy to a right and wholesome order" (ibid., 136). But the means cannot be determined from the social teaching of the church.

We may safely conclude, then, that the social teaching of the church remains on a level of *generality*, and addresses to the Christian community the *advice* of the magisterium. The social teaching of the church is *fallible*, and relative—midway between the absolute level of the gospel and the concrete order of the responsibility of Christian praxis.

19.7 THE PROPHETIC FUNCTION

The social teaching of the church is an element of the ordinary magisterium, transmitting norms and directives for concrete Christian praxis in the fashion of an authoritative "counsel," from a point of departure in the experience of the church's long history and with special attention to the very poorest. It is not the only *ecclesial reference* possible, however, when one is concerned to make a Christian decision in full awareness of one's individual historical responsibilities. The prophets, the martyrs, and the heroes ("persons of good will") are also essential referential features of the taking of a concrete historical decision.

Basing their choices on the demands of the gospel itself—and adopting more radical attitudes in exceptional times—the prophets of Christian history, thanks to their *ethical conscience* (4.2), have performed an exemplary, critical, ethical praxis (3.2). Without renouncing the social teaching of the church, it has served to complement it at certain serious, special times, perhaps such as those in which we are living in Latin America today:

> We stand on the threshold of a *new historical age* on our continent, an age pregnant with a yearning for total emancipation, for liberation from all servitude, for personal maturation and collective integration. We feel the first pangs of the painful birth of a new civilization [Medellín, *Introduction*].

At such crucial moments, when the norms and directives of *normal* eras can no longer alleviate a people's pain or make it more bearable, the prophets call us down new pathways, some of which actually run counter to the social teaching of the church. But as we have observed, that teaching is not infallible: it issues from the ordinary, fallible magisterium of the church.

Latin America is part of the Third World. Its population is sunk in the mire of oppression and poverty. The social teaching of the church, which has been elaborated mainly in a context of developed countries like the European, frequently fails to respond to the *actual situations* of Latin America. "It is difficult ... to pronounce an isolated word" (*Octogesima Adveniens*, 4). Prophets fill the void.

19.8 ULTIMATE RESPONSIBILITY OF THE CHRISTIAN COMMUNITY

The third level (the first being that of the gospel, the second that of the social teaching of the church) is the specific historical, "situated" level. The third level is that of responsibility for practical decisions. This responsibility falls to the *Christian community*. Accordingly, it is incumbent on the Christian community to analyze, objectively, the political and economic reality confronting it. The Christian community, in the light of the gospel, in conformity with the social teaching of the church (when possible), with attention to the counsel of its shepherds, and allowing itself to be guided by its prophets as well—where it must be able to discern true prophets from false—will ultimately have to refer to its own ethical conscience and its own historical community. No one can decide for the Christian community, or supply for any shortcomings that may appear in its political praxis.

By "Christian community" I mean the local church under the authority of the episcopal college (of the nation or continent): a diocese, a parish, a movement, or indeed an ecclesial community. No orthodoxy can supply for *orthopraxis* (20.7). By "orthopraxis" I mean the correct activity engaged in by the *community* as Christian—after compliance with the requirements for an adequate decision—in any given situation. The social teaching of the church could not have indicated what a Christian community ought to have done in Cuba in 1959, in Nicaragua in 1979, or in Brazil in 1988. It is the *community* itself that must *take charge* of (respond in the presence of) its own existence, always keeping in mind its charge of service of the "very poorest." The right to this act of *prudence* (*prudentia, phronesis*) is an inalienable one.

True, the hierarchical church bears the responsibility of a "discernment of spirits"—a judgment as to the appropriateness or timeliness of an action. By no means, however, will the charisms of the creation of the most urgent and innovative (revolutionary) solutions of social problems originate necessarily or even frequently with the ministry of the magisterium. The creation of such solutions is the proper function of the actual *Christian community* and its prophets.

19.9 EVOLUTION OF THE SOCIAL TEACHING OF THE CHURCH

The ethical demands of the gospel cannot "evolve." These demands are valid for all ages and situations. This is an absolute, yet definite, principle (7.7–7.9). However, "the social teaching of the church accompanies us on this quest with all its dynamism. ... It develops through the intermediary of mature reflection, in contact with changing situations in this world" (*Octogesima Adveniens*, 42).

The social teaching of the church, then, does evolve. It is *relative* to changing situations. Thus at certain moments it will be "ahead" of the average critical consciousness in the Christian community. At other moments it will coincide with this awareness, this conscience, and confirm it in its decisions. But it may also happen that, in comparison with the conscience of the prophets of a new age, the social teaching of the church may be somewhat "behind," at least with respect to certain social phenomena in certain parts of the world and among certain sectors of society. The social teaching of the church is itself aware of this:

> To be sure, very many are the various situations in which, willy-nilly, Christians find themselves committed, depending on the region, to socio-political systems and cultures [*Octogesima Adveniens*, 3].

We must face facts. Intraecclesial tensions over divergent socio-political, moral, or ethical commitments are a reality. They are impossible to suppress. But at the same time the existence of such tensions is a sign of the historical vitality of the church.

Rerum Novarum was ahead of contemporaneous Christian praxis by comparison with the *average* level of consciousness in the church community at the end of the nineteenth century, just as *Laborem Exercens* was ahead of the petit bourgeois Christian conscience of Europe or the United States in the early 1980s. This is not to assert that *Laborem Exercens* was on a par with the ethico-prophetic conscience of the many Christians who have had to suffer persecution in order to respond to the "dynamism of the Christian faith, [which] thus triumphs over the petty calculations of selfishness" (*Octogesima Adveniens*, 37).

19.10 THE SOCIAL TEACHING OF THE CHURCH AND COMMUNAL THEOLOGICAL ETHICS

I should like to make one further point concerning the relationship between the social teaching of the church and the communitarian ethical theology of liberation. Some, with very good reason, oppose the existence of a social teaching that would pretend to replace the gospel or the responsibility of the Christian community. But consequently they oppose the existence of the social teaching of the church altogether. Others, as we know, labor precisely under the illusion that this teaching (frequently interpreted according to the criteria of a reformist, petit bourgeois capitalism) gives Christians *all* the criteria, norms, or directives needed for specific action. Christians need only comply with this teaching, we are told. They may then rest assured that their praxis will be without imperfection, error, or deviation. Both positions are erroneous.

We have a gospel, whose force and validity as ultimate reference abides (19.5), and the changing, relative social teaching of the church will never be able to supplant it. On a more concrete level, we have an ecclesial social teaching, but one of such generality that it is simply incapable of replacing a considered, personal, responsible analysis on the part of the Christian community. We also have the example of the behavior of the prophets, the saints, the martyrs, and the heroes. They too are a secure reference for Christian action. But we have a fourth reference, as well: communitarian ethical theology— which, once more, will in no way supply for the Christian community's ongoing, specific examination of conscience.

The reflection that constitutes a communitarian ethical theology will always be "second act" with respect to praxis. That theology *follows upon* Christian praxis, both ecclesial and communitarian or personal. It is this praxis that guarantees and endorses that theology, enabling it to proceed along its course with clarity and lucidity, and thereby reproduce, in community fashion, its own praxis as well. The theological *theory* of praxis opens tactical and strategic perspectives. Community ethical theology is neither the gospel, nor the social teaching of the church, nor the community examination of conscience, nor the community's actual decision. Rather it "rationalizes" the structure of all of these, correctly situating the problematic of the moment. Above all, it will leave the door open for new popular Christian community practices whenever profound, even (in extreme cases) revolutionary, changes are called for.

CONCLUSIONS

Beginning in 1891, the church has gradually developed a "social teaching." This teaching, theorized by the "Roman school" in such a way that its theoretical scope has been limited, has kept account of church tradition. The great social encyclicals have erected the crucial milestones. These documents have proceeded, gradually, from an acceptance of capitalism (together with an internal critique demanding certain reforms) and a total rejection of socialism (on the grounds of an ideological or moral critique initially), to a rejection of capitalism in *Laborem Exercens* (together with the proposal of ways for a Christian nevertheless to live under such a regime) and an acceptance of socialism (along with a demand for full participation in work at all levels of bureaucratized and planned society). On the one hand, this "evolution" teaches us that the gospel, and only the gospel, is Christianity's ethical absolute, and that no social teaching can replace it. It also demonstrates that the social teaching of the church cannot be in force at certain "times of emergency," when radical changes leave the Christian community with full responsibility for its ultimate decisions. In other situations this social teaching indeed plays the role of an authoritative "counsel" on the part of the ordinary, fallible magisterium.

Chapter 20

Liberation Ethics as Fundamental Theology

20.1 STATE OF THE QUESTION

None of the intramural debates of the theology of liberation have contributed much to its *systemization*. Liberation theology is not a chapter of theology. It is a way of doing *all* of theology. And this particular way is visible not only in its point of departure (first praxis, then theory), in its epistemological mediations (the importance of the social sciences), in its original organic links (with the church of the poor, the base ecclesial communities), and in the topics it regards as most important or relevant. This particular way of doing theology is visible also, and by no means least of all, in the *order* in which its questions are situated—in other words, in the systemization of its theological tractates. This is not the place for a comprehensive treatment of the problematic. I shall merely touch on its first point. I shall examine the question of the starting point of all theology— fundamental theology—in a context of the theology of liberation.

Holy scripture teaches us:

> Faith is confident assurance concerning what we hope for, and conviction about things we do not see. Because of faith the men of old were approved by God. ... By faith Abel offered God a sacrifice greater than Cain's. ... By faith Noah, warned about things not yet seen, revered God and built an ark. ... By faith Abraham obeyed when he was called, and went forth to the place he was to receive as a heritage; he went forth,

moreover, not knowing where he was going. ... By faith Isaac invoked for Jacob and Esau blessings that were still to be.

By faith Jacob, when dying, blessed each of the sons of Joseph. ... By faith Moses' parents hid him for three months after his birth. ... By faith [Moses] left Egypt, not fearing the king's wrath. ... Others were tortured and would not receive deliverance. ... Still others endured mockery, scourging, even chains and imprisonment. They were stoned, sawed in two, put to death at sword's point. ... The world was not worthy of them. They wandered about in deserts and on mountains, they dwelt in caves and in holes of the earth. ... All of these were approved because of their faith [Heb. 11:1–39].

Indeed there is neither theology, nor any other Christian praxis, without faith. But faith itself is the subject of a constitutive relationship to praxis, to action, to the effective realization of the reign of God. Here we are at the very source of the Christian experience, the very origin of theology.

20.2 WHAT IS FUNDAMENTAL THEOLOGY?

From the time of the bourgeois industrial revolution, in the eighteenth century, theology has had to defend itself against the critical attack of "reason." Faith, says "reason," is irrational and religion is obscurantism. In response to this attack, a "fundamental theology" (*theologia fundamentalis*) appeared. This theology was conerned with "constituting the rationality of faith" (*rationabilitatem fidei*—S. Iragui, *Manuale Theologiae Dogmaticae*, 1:11). What passed unnoticed was that de facto the "rationality" in question was bourgeois. Too much was unconsciously conceded to what was thought to be *apologetically* convincing. Fundamental theology was apologetics—a defense of faith, or at least of its possibility. Later, liberal European theology confronted a different challenge: how to be a Christian in a secular world. The secularization of society now required that theology initiate a self-justifying discourse for the ears of a world that, though bourgeois, was simply irreligious.

In the poor, peripheral countries today, the theology of liberation initiates its discourse in the face of still other challenges, still other fundamental objections. Liberation theology must deal with a "radical critique of religion" as the "opium of the people," yes, but precisely in a situation of oppression, revolution, and liberation. The criticism is neither rational nor existential, as it has been in Europe. This time it originates with a political praxis. The religious superstructure, we hear, justifies domination. Religion is an ideology of oppression. It produces a false political conscience. It is of its very nature anti-revolutionary.

Theology must now adopt an original demarcation and definition. On the one hand, as a theology of liberation confronted with a theology of oppression it must now work from the relationship between praxis and theory rather than from that between reason and faith. At the same time, it must defend and demonstrate the possibility of a religion of liberation, and thus give an answer to the question: How is it possible to be Christian within a revolutionary process of essential structural change? (see 16.7).

20.3 HOW IS REVELATION POSSIBLE?

The first traditional question of fundamental theology was: How is revelation *possible*? (Sebastian Tromp opens his treatise with a chapter entitled, "De Possibilitate Revelationis," pp. 70ff.). Against illuminism, Schelling, for example, wrote in his *Philosophy of Revelation*: "Revelation is an authentic, special source of cognition" (6:398), which gives us not "an unfounded knowledge, but rather the best founded of all, as it alone contains that before which all transcendence to another term is impossible" (ibid.). Even for Kierkegaard the revealed is "absurd"—absurd to a ludicrously self-centered "reason." The absurd is actually "the real," says the Danish existentialist. In the first fundamental theology, then, the possibility of revelation was posited from a point of departure in (an anti-illuministic) reason or rationality. In the same fashion, the theology of a laissez-faire European thinking had to take account of atheism in order to defeat it and initiate theological discourse. We in the poor periphery of the world, however, confront not atheism (we have no atheists), but fetishists and idolaters (2.3, 12.10, 15.10). Our problem is not atheistic secularization, but the existence of various "idols." We are surrounded with fetishes, and we must know how to distinguish them all from the God of the poor.

The act of revealing is the challenge and call of the other, the call of totality, a challenge irrupting from beyond the world (4.2, 5.2). The voice, the call, the word of the other (in Hebrew *dabar*; in Latin *verbum*) bursts in upon the world and turns it upside down, crying: "I am hungry!"

It is in the act of hearing the voice of the other (*ex auditu*, in Trent) that God's revelation is bestowed. But God can be revealed only *by what is other* than the system of sin, other than the "world" (3.3–3.6). God is revealed essentially *through* and *by way of* the poor. The poor constitute the *place* of the epiphany of God (especially since the moment of the revelation of God in "Jesus *poor*," as Charles de Foucauld loved to call him). To hear the voice of the poor *here and now* (see 5.9, 7.7, 7.10, 10.4) is the *sine qua non* of the actuality of God's revelation. The Bible can be interpreted only in the living tradition of the particular Christian community (*Puebla Final Document*, 373), only when it is read and contemplated from the "place of the poor," from the "perspective of the poor." For the theology of liberation, the crucial question is not the possible irrationality of a positive revelation, but the *impossibility* that God should be revealed to the rich, the impossibility that God should be manifested to those who dominate the poor, or be known by persons who, in the absence of an "ethical awareness" (4.2) on their part, are estranged from that particular, historical position that would have permitted them to hear the Word of God.

20.4 HOW IS FAITH POSSIBLE?

The next question, for traditional fundamental theology, was the possibility of faith: *credibilitas* (Tromp, p. 15), or "the value of the motives for believing" (*credentibilitas*—Garrigou-Lagrange, *De Revelatione*, p. 1). Once more apologetics presented arguments that convinced the already converted and left unbelievers totally indifferent. For us in Latin America the question is very different.

As we know, for Thomas Aquinas the act of faith is "an assent (*assensus*) proceeding not from cognition but originating in the will" (*ex voluntate*; *De Veritate*, q. 14, a. 1). The essential question, then, is the "disposition (*dispositio*) of the believer" (ibid.)—that is, the *practical* conditions (which are of the "order of the will" for Thomas) of the possibility of the act of faith. To put it another way:

the fundamental challenge is to understand the character of one's *praxis* (1.2) with regard to the other, dominator or dominated: Is my praxis sinful or just? In order to *be able to believe*, one must first be an "atheist," an anti-fetishist, with respect to the idol constituted by the prevailing system (2.10, and, e.g., 12.10). Above all, one must be responsible for the poor (4.2)—that is, one must perform orthopraxy (20.7) in which it will be possible to *believe in the voice* of the poor who cry out to me: "I am hungry!"—so that I feel myself called upon, challenged, turned head over heels, converted, like the Samaritan. (In the parable of the good Samaritan, Jesus, as a trained Jewish theologian, gives us to know the hermeneutic *categories* of his theology. In the case of Jesus' theology, and only in the case of that theology, are theology and revelation *identical*.)

20.5 THE STARTING POINT OF THEOLOGY

If what I have said has any meaning, we now understand that the theological discourse upon *praxis*—and not only upon the essence or basic structure of praxis, but most emphatically upon the particular situation in which that praxis transpires—is *first theology*—primary or fundamental theology. The theology of praxis is the *whence* of the theologian's doing or producing of second theology. Theology is theory, yes. But the theologian is a concrete, historical, "situated" subject (situated in a class—8.4; in a sex; in a nation—13.6). All of these determinations contribute to the constitution of the *praxis* out of which *theological theory* arises.

Praxis is the starting point of *all* theology, whether or not the theologian is aware of it. For example, Thomas Aquinas's patriarchal praxis produced an unconsciously sexist theology (indeed it may have been impossible for him to be aware of his sexism). And so Thomas attributed to Adam "being" (*esse*)" and to Eve only the "matter" of the transmission of original sin: "Had Adam not sinned, but Eve had, their offspring would not have contracted original sin." In the same fashion, Thomas's feudal praxis resulted in a feudal theology, which admitted to membership in society only the feudal nobility (and not the serfs, who were under a "seigneurial right"—*jus dominativum*).

The organic nexus between *praxis and theory*, the fact of the "organic intellectual," is inevitable. (Even the conservative theologian, for example, is an organic intellectual—of the bourgeoisie.) The important thing is to be clearly aware of the character of one's praxis, of one's concrete situation, one's organic nexus with theory, and to make of this organic nexus the object of a first *explicit* theological reflection (8.10).

20.6 PRAXIS DETERMINES THEOLOGY

Thus we have a three-term relationship, whose terms are constituted by concrete historical praxis (HP), the theologian as subject (agent) of theology (ST), and the theological discourse itself (TD):

$$HP \longrightarrow ST \longrightarrow TD$$

Theologians performing their praxis only within a system of domination (3.2) would find themselves to be "determined" (always relatively) by that circumstance—in their lives, in society with other women and men, and in the interests they defend. Without their noticing it, their theology (TD), in the subject matter they select, in the manner in which they handle this subject matter, and even in their indifference to subject matter more urgent to the concerns of the oppressed and poor, would be a "theology of domination."

If, on the other hand, a theological praxis were to be communal— for example, as set forth in 4.6—then the action of the theologians would outstrip the exigencies of the prevailing system. This action would be not only praxis, but *diakonia*—service to the other as other, the action of the Samaritan. It would tend to transform the prevailing system. It would be an *ethical* action, and not merely a *moral* one (3.2). In this case the theology (TD) of the theologian (ST) would perform a "prophetic mission" (*Puebla Final Document*, 377, 267–8). It would be a theology of liberation, although this would not exempt it from the specific ideological limitations of any human production.

A praxis situated regionally or continentally, in a matrix determined by autochthonous language, customs, race, or religions, will generate African, Asian, and so on, theologies—which certain congregations of the Roman Curia oppose, but which the Second Vatican Council called for:

It is necessary that in each great socio-cultural territory theological reflection be promoted ... keeping account of the philosophy and wisdom of the peoples [*Ad Gentes*, 22].

In the same way, a praxis situated in the most advanced element of the civilizing task, most especially if it is performed among political groups who feel responsible for the organization of practical systems to serve the poor, will necessarily produce a theology that will avail itself of the tools of the most appropriate sciences and methods, even if this means being called Marxist—a judgment handed down by those who, for their part, support the interests of the dominant classes (the bourgeoisie in capitalist countries):

These difficulties [of harmonizing culture with Christian teaching] do not necessarily harm the life of faith. Indeed they can stimulate the mind to a more accurate and penetrating grasp of the faith. For recent studies and findings of science, history, and philsophy raise new questions that influence life and demand new theological investigations. ...

May the faithful, therefore, live in very close union with their contemporaries. Let them strive to understand perfectly their way of thinking and feeling, as expressed in their culture. Let them blend modern science and its theories and the under-standing of the most recent discoveries with Christian morality and doctrine. Thus their religious practice and morality can keep pace with their scientific knowledge and with an ever advancing technology [*Gaudium et Spes*, 62].

This is precisely what the theology of liberation has done with respect to the social sciences and political movements in Latin America. Those who sit on judgment seats located in other cultural circumstances seem to have forgotten the directives of the council, as they condemn prophetic, missionary endeavors that meet the expectations of contemporary Latin Americans.

20.7 ORTHOPRAXY AND ORTHODOXY

As we see from all that has been said, "true teaching" (in Greek, *orthodoxia*) springs from and is determined by authentic, "true praxis" (*orthopraxia*). Some may regard this proposition rather as a reversal of a proper order of things, or a renunciation of the magisterium, for example. It is nothing of the kind. It is a traditional, ancient position.

Orthopraxia, or true and proper acting, is an attribute of the church in its totality—the church as the universal people of God. If the church were to be mistaken in its action, it would no longer have a concrete point of reference for its teaching, so that its doctrine would now be mistaken as well. It is the *community*—the universal church, the local church, the base community—that holds forth the "orthopraxy" to be followed by the ultimate individual conscience.

The charism of the prophets springs from the "base," from the "grass roots," by the action of the Spirit, in response to the demands of concrete orthopraxy. The ecclesial ministry (including the episcopal) is not the source of this charism. The ecclesial ministry is competent to judge of its authenticity (*Lumen Gentium*, 12), while exercising caution not to "stifle the Spirit, but to test all and abide with the good." In the case of Miguel D'Escoto's fast, one hierarchical authority declared that all activity in the "legitimate religious area" could emanate only from hierarchical authority. This is to forget that it is the Spirit who promotes legitimate prophetic charisms among the people of God. The bishop and the pope are members, or *parts* of that people.

Orthodoxy—sound doctrine—is expressed on at least three levels. First (and this is the most important level because it is the daily one), orthodoxy is expressed in the particular judgments of Christians as members of the base community, where in their examination of conscience they correct their judgment—they draw their orthodoxy from the community orthopraxy. On a second level, orthodoxy is expressed by the magisterium (on many levels and in many qualities: from the advice of a priest to the pastoral practice of an episcopate to the *ex cathedra* infallibility of the pope or the decrees of the councils). This orthodoxy, the orthodoxy of the *people of God*, guides the church through history in response to the orthopraxis of the church *as a totality*. Obviously a pastor may warn his flock if it is wandering from the true way to the pasture. But this warning is an *internal*, ministerial function of the church.

On a third level, theology and theologians engage in a reflection on orthopraxy, in order to "explicitate" the relationship of the latter with orthodoxy. (And I recall that "the unanimity of theologians is *proxima fidei*"—"very near" to being *de fide* or "of faith.") Theology is an expression *of* the church, *in* the church. It has its proper status there by reason of its twofold prophetic service: to orthopraxy to secure it, and to orthodoxy to render it explicit.

20.8 COMMUNITY, PROPHETS, THEOLOGIANS, AND THE MAGISTERIUM

Let me review the matter of the preceding section, in order to have a clearer picture of the various levels and their constitutive relationships (Diagram 14; see *Puebla Final Document*, 372–6).

It is the *community*, the people of God as a totality (*Lumen Gentium*, 9ff.), that receives, in its living *tradition*, the word of God (the Bible). It is this community that constitutes the place of both orthopraxy and orthodoxy. The community consists of "a people who would know God in truth and serve God in a holy manner" (ibid., 9). *Among* that people, and exercising a function of that people in its capacity as a messianic, prophetic community (ibid., 12), prophets are bestowed by the people on the people. The prophets are simply members of the people of God whom the Holy Spirit raises up without *necessarily* passing by way of ministerial functions (priest, bishop, pope, council). Arrow a (Diagram 14) indicates that the prophet arises *among, through*, and *for* the people of God: his or her orthopraxy (novel, creative right action, at times even revolutionary) may be shocking to some. But in the concrete it is only

Diagram 14

The Community and its Ministers

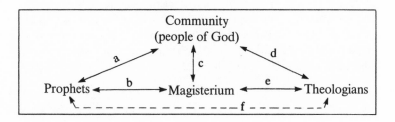

prudential, historical orthodoxy, which everyone will hold one day (including the magisterium). Of course (arrow b) it pertains to the magisterium to pass judgment upon the prophetic charism, but it is not its function to "stifle the Spirit" (ibid.).

The magisterium itself, as a function of the hierarchy, is a ministerial service that the people of God *gives itself* from within (arrow c). The hierarchy is not *outside* or *above* the people of God. Not even a pope or a council is outside or above the people of God. The hierarchy is *within and among* that people. Its function is to "pasture and foster" that people (ibid., 18). The papacy and the council, for their part, are *internal* functions of the hierarchical ministry. Hence, primarily and per se, the infallibility of orthodoxy belongs to the church community as a totality—as "the infallibility that the divine Redeemer willed that the church should have" (ibid., 25).

Likewise, the theologian, and theological discourse (theology), always rest primarily on *church praxis* (arrow d). To call praxis a "first act" and theology a "second act," then, is merely to rehearse the most ancient and traditional teaching in this area. It is the people of God that invests its *theologians* with the charismatic function of explaining or "explicitating" the relationship of orthopraxy (the orthopraxy of the community and the prophets) to orthodoxy (the orthodoxy of sacred scripture, of dogmatic and theological tradition, of customs, doctrines of the extraordinary and ordinary magisterium, and so forth). The community confers this theoretical function upon the theologian from within, and for, itself.

Theologians, for their part, learn from the magisterium, respect it, and submit to its judgments (arrow e). But they find their inspiration very particularly in the orthopraxy of the prophets (arrow f), inasmuch as it is here that they discover the *new* paths along which many members of the community are already working their way, especially if such a path is political or even revolutionary. Theologians of liberation have been very careful to respond to all these demands, not only as individuals, but also and especially as a "theological *community*," inasmuch as, before all else, and as theologians, they are all members of a community of reflection.

20.9 THE POOR AND THE GOD OF THE POOR

The purpose of recalling all of this has been to prepare us to return to our original subject. A communal ethics of liberation is one that reflects upon, describes, clarifies, and explains the every existence of the poor, *here and now*, concretely and historically. Without a clear view of the poor as the launching pad of the whole of theological discourse, theologians will not be able to speak of the God of the poor—for, after all, one cannot know *a priori*, before the fact, who the poor are. This occasions a great many theological ambiguities. Many of those who call themselves theologians of liberation count the landholding oligarchies, or the national bourgeoisies, for example, among the "poor" of a peripheral nation. After all, we are told, a nation includes everyone, does it not? This theological "populism" (13.8, 8.5–7) springs from a confusion over theology's point of departure. Paradoxically, although God is the First, the Origin, the Infinite, the issue today is one of discernment of idols or fetishes that "pass themselves off as God," and the "true God." This true God is the God *of the poor*. The criterion of the discernment of the word of God is the *standpoint of the poor*. We take our place among the poor in order to hear revelation (20.3), in order to be able to create (20.4), in order to know whether a praxis is *ortho*practic (5.7–9). The poor are Christ *here and now*, and constitute the *route* to a discovery of and discourse upon God. Hence community ethics is the *fundamental theology* of the theology of liberation, as it explains the premises, the conditions *sine qua non*, of theological discourse as a totality.

In Latin America today (as in Africa, Asia, and in many respects even in Europe and the United States), the "poor" in the biblical sense (the object of sin, those exploited and murdered by sin) are the dominated (see chap. 2 and 3 in their entirety). Concretely and historically, they are workers (chap. 11), robbed of the work they perform (12.5). This is their most universal and abstract, their most essential, characterization. In Latin America, Africa, and Asia they are precisely the poor nations, sucked dry of their surplus life (13.7) *structurally*. They are the ones impoverished by the transnationals (14.5); those attacked by weapons and the arms race (15.10); those forced to repay loans irresponsibly contracted by others (15.6); those violated in the name of morality (16.8); workers denied their just rights in the name of total planning (17.7–10); the simple citizens of the contemporary world who see their land and culture ecologically destroyed (chap. 18). All these indications, all these reflections on structure, situate for us the various more serious types of impoverishment, of being "the poor," on the community plane (there are many other ways to be poor), and thus situate for us the various types of sin, the *concrete* sins that make so many persons *poor* (2.5, 2.7).

To situate the poor—to describe their origin and the *concrete* modes of their appearance in our age—is the radical *conditio sine qua non* for the initiation of a theological (theoretical), critical, prophetic discourse on liberation. This, then, is *fundamental theology*, for it is the premise, the *a priori*, the prime *conditio sine qua non*, of all the rest of theology.

20.10 FUNDAMENTAL THEOLOGY IN THE THEOLOGY OF LIBERATION

For some years, beginning in 1968, liberation theology was almost exclusively *fundamental theology*. But this theology was fundamental in the sense understood in liberation theology itself, with the result that many on the outside understood nothing at all. Christology and ecclesiology came later, and only gradually. As for the history of the church, we must say (and this was as it should have been) that it not only kept pace with liberation theology, but actually preceded it, preparing the way for it even before entering into its constitution and cementing its very construction. My *Hipótesis para una historia de la Iglesia en América Latina* (1964; English translation, *A History of the Church in Latin America*, Grand Rapids, Eerdmans, 1981), situated church praxis historically, and was itself fundamental theology.

Until 1974 nearly all of the writings of the theologians of liberation were in the area of fundamental theology. But liberation theology's fundamental theology is *community ethics*. This resulted in various confusions among commentators (not in authors). Some concluded that liberation theology was only "social moral theology"—a critical, novel *chapter*, but only a chapter, in moral theology. Others, by contrast, criticized it for sticking to general questions and not moving ahead on concrete topics in christology, ecclesiology, exegesis, and so on—not understanding that an edifice must be begun at its foundations, at its base, and that it must be solid.

This explains why political, economic, and social themes are so important in the theology of liberation. It was the *question of the dependency* of the poor, peripheral, underdeveloped countries that occasioned, around 1968, the explicit and irreversible initiation of the new discourse. But what was not understood (not even by Cardinal Joseph Ratzinger's 1984 "Instruction") is that, above and beyond its social or political treatment, and using the tools of science (as the council required), the theology of liberation was discovering *sin*, and not only sin in the abstract (which would appear to be the only level of religious sin recognized in the Vatican instruction), but sin *in the concrete* really existing sin, which the instruction is at pains to regard as "only" political, social, or economic sin, and *not* as religious, sin—whereas of course sin is always religious sin, as well, whatever else it may be besides).

Inasmuch as the "poor" constituted the hermeneutic point of departure, the locus *whence* the Christian praxis (the orthopraxy) of the community was initiated, the poor were the terminus *a quo* of the new discourse. But to this purpose it had to be known who the poor were, how one comes to be poor, what the structures of sin are that weigh upon the poor. To many these questions were "merely" social, political, or economic (depending on which hermeneutic tools were being used—in compliance with the demand of the council—for the discovery of *the concrete*). They were, however, *strictly theological questions*. Just as Thomas Aquinas had used Aristotelianism (at a time when it had been condemned by the church and the magisterium) as the scientific *instrument* of his elucidation of theological questions, so also the theologians of liberation, in order to build up their theological discourse, made use of the social sciences as practiced in Latin America to clarify, explain, and explicitate *the reality of the poor* as a general biblical category and — thanks precisely to the mediation of these social sciences—as a *concrete* reality.

But today the theology of liberation has to be more than fundamental theology. And over the course of the last decade and longer it has indeed begun to develop its specific theological tractates—although the systemization of these treatises remains to be discussed, and their level (in their criticalness and their consistency with the specific criteria of the theology of liberation) calls for future improvement. The *theological community* itself is the first to recognize and acknowledge their weaknesses.

CONCLUSIONS

On this, my final topic, which in a sense constitutes a compendium of this book, I am reminded that all theoretical reflection, all theology, *presupposes* a praxis that determines it (though not absolutely). Liberation theologians, too, are conditioned, and may never pretend to "absolute knowledge" or lay claim to irrefutable truth. Quite the contrary: in humility, in their militancy with their people, in their organic link with community organizations, in the service of their prophetic *ecclesial* function, they theologize as learners, from within the people of God. (We must not forget that theology is ecclesial, by its origin and by its finality—if by church we understand the people of God *in its totality* and not only the magisterium, which is an internal function of the people of God, and thus ultimately a function of the entire body of that people).

The task of the theology of liberation in this fundamental treatise on community ethics has been more negative than positive. It has charged itself more with the preliminary task of describing the *structures of sin* than with a consideration of the strategy and tactics of the people of God in liberation. First, we have had to discover **the** *poor*.

Appendix

Liberation Ethics: Fundamental Hypotheses

If Paul Tillich found it difficult to explain to North Americans how the church functioned in Europe, how much more difficult it will be for a theologian of Latin America or the peripheral world to explain the critical function of ethics in situations calling for profound social changes.[1]

MORALITY WITHIN SYSTEMS

The years since the 1930s, in the United States and Europe, have witnessed a transition from a criticism of the prevailing system *as a totality* to a mere reformist critique of the social order. By way of a meaningful date we might recall April 13, 1933, when the name of Paul Tillich[2] appeared on the list, drawn up by Hitler's national-capitalist government, of "intellectuals" to be eliminated as "critical" of the system.[3] Tillich himself would later write:

> So many creative events of the 1920s were destroyed by persecution or exile. But there is one thing that they have not managed to undo in the church and culture. I mean the horizon of Germany and Europe.[4]

In 1932 Reinhold Niebuhr published *Moral and Immoral Society*,[5] and Emil Brunner *Das Gebot und die Ordnungen*.[6]

The crisis of 1929—a capitalistic crisis resulting in increased repression of the working class of the countries of the "center"—the triumph of the Russian revolution, and the rise of Stalin produced an upheaval in theology. The "early Tillich" and the "early Niebuhr" (and somewhat earlier, the "early Barth") wielded a Christian critique that began to move back from a criticism of the system as such to propound a reformist, prodent morality. "Illusion is dangerous. It fosters terrible fanaticisms," wrote Niebuhr in the conclusion of his *Moral and Immoral Society*.[7] With Tillich, who had written *Die sozialistische Entscheidung*,[8] "Christian realism" moved on to develop a theology of culture.

In those same years another movement of great importance finally expired: the "social gospel."[9] It is a wondrous experience today to read the work of a Richard Ely, *French and German Socialism* (New York, 1883), or, in Washington Gladden's *Tools and the Man: Property and Industry under the Christian Law*, chapter 10, "Christian Socialism":[10]

> In the most recent works on socialism we always find a chapter entitled, "Christian Socialism." Does the expression have any meaning? Is Christianity socialistic in some sense? Or might socialism be Christian?[11]

Explanations are no longer important. Neither is Gladden's criticism of Marx (which is remarkable, for Gladden knew him).[12] The important thing today is that, once upon a time, there was a Christian criticism of the capitalist system as a totality. W. Rauschenbusch excoriated "our semi-Christian social order" and said that it was governed by the "law of profit."[13] Those Christians of yesterday, so intimately involved with social struggles from the turn of the century to 1929, were soon to be buried by the violence of European/North American capitalism, and by the hegemony of that capitalism, and during the two world wars, from which the United States emerged triumphant (and the Commonwealth defeated, no less than Germany and Japan).

Postwar moral theologies failed to shake off the reformist mold. The system was to be accepted *as is* and reformed *in part*. This is the only conclusion we can draw from an honest examination of the major moral treatises.[14]

Emil Brunner's early *Das Gebot und die Ordnungen* is especially interesting. Beginning with chapter 34, "Essence and Function of the Economy "[15]—far superior in its treatment of the Catholic moral theologies of the time—Brunner launches out on a forthright criticism of capitalism itself ("Capitalism is an economic anarchy, hence the Christian is obligated to struggle against it in favor of a true social order").[16] But then he criticizes *de facto* socialism.[17] In the same fashion Helmut Theilicke, in his *Theologische Ethik*,[18] clearly betrays his reformism ("Revolution as *Ultima Ratio*").[19] Of course neither here nor in any of the other works cited in my consideration of this series of writers do we find the oppression of peripheral countries referred to. And yet Bartolomé de Las Casas had posed the question, theologically and forthrightly, four hundred years before.

We may observe that this shift from a criticism of capitalism to its critical acceptance has now culminated, in the current crisis, in its downright moral justification. The entire North American neocon-servative (and European conservative) movement[20] would be quite comfortable with Robert Benne's conclusions in his *The Ethic of Democratic Capitalism: A Moral Reassessment*,[21] in chapter 7, "The Virtues of Democratic Capitalism." Benne showed us these "virtues," and concluded:

> Democratic capitalism has been a misjudged social system, especially by the liberal intellectual community, religious as well as secular.,.... For our part, we return to democratic capitalism, and give it full credit for its historical potential, viewing it from the standpoint of its practical and moral values.[22]

For these intrasystemic moralities, utopia, or any radical critique of the system is anarchy and fantacism. It is the irrational side of "historicism," seemingly refuted by Karl Popper and translated into economic terms by Milton Friedman in the neo-capitalism of the "self-regulated competition of the free market." And behold, conservative moral theologies are expected to treat of the question of the "norm" (or law), the question of values, virtues, good and evil, the problem of language, of technology, and even of peace, without ever questioning the "system" as such. Analytic conservative thinking is radically opposed to dialectical proposition.

LIBERATION ETHICS

By contrast, the capitalism of the *peripheral* capitalist countries, and the oppressed classes of these countries, owing to the capitalistic hegemony that had emerged between the two wars, entered into an irreversible state of crisis after the Second World War. A decade after the war's end the expansion of North American capitalism wiped out the projects of peripheral national capitalism. (In 1954 Vargas committed suicide in Brazil. In 1955 Perón fell in Argentina. In 1957 Rohas Pinilla in Colombia, Nasser in Egypt, Sukarno in Indonesia, others in Africa and Asia.) The "populisms" in the periphery had represented the last attempt of an autonomous, non-dependent, *national capitalism*, under the hegemony of a *national* bourgeoisie, as with the Congress Party in India, to resist the North American onslaught. The crisis of the "dependent capitalism" model (1955–65) in Latin America (from Kubitschek to Goulard in Brazil, or in Argentina from Frondizi to Ilía to the Onganía coup of 1966) showed the non-viability of peripheral capitalism. The so-called assistance of "capital and technology" (which worked *against* the capital and the technology of the poor and backward national capitalism of the periphery) did not produce "development," but only implanted the "transnational corporations," thus accelerating the extraction of wealth (in economic terms, "profit"; in theological terms, "life" and "blood"—the life and blood of the poor peoples, the life and blood of the workers) from the periphery.[23]

The ethics of liberation began historically as a theoretical attempt (in the form of theology and philosophy) to explain a praxis occasioned by the failure of "developmentalism."[24] Hence, if Karl Barth said of theology in general that "the relation of *this* God with *this* human being and of *this* human being with *this* God are for me the theme of the Bible and of theology"[25]—his way of indicating the concrete, existential element in the relationship—then for liberation ethics (and thus for fundamental theology, as we shall see) we should have to say that the relationship of the *living* God with this *poor* human being, and of this *poor* human being with the *living* God, is the theme of the Bible and theology. Thus we make contact with, and develop from new foundations (no longer European/North American, but *world*)—the great themes of the "early" Barth, Tillich, Niebuhr, and so many others. But this *theoretical* interface is possible only because of a historical connection—a connection in praxis. Those Christian pioneers opposed a capitalism in crisis (and were buried by Fascist capitalism in Europe and the United States); we too oppose capitalism, but a capitalism in *structural*, and far more profound, *crisis*; an autonomous, national capitalism is now *impossible* in the periphery.

It is impossible for capitalism to produce wealth in peripheral and underdeveloped countries, or to ensure its distribution to the immense impoverished majorities. To be sure, this is denied by theologians who have identified Christianity's lot with that of capitalism.[26] In recent times, in a philosophical approach, John Rawls[27] has once more proposed individualistic liberal positions, and Ronald Dworkin is right:

> Rawls does argue that this fundamental right to equality
> requires a liberal constitution, and supports an idealized form
> of present economic and social structures.[28]

Nevertheless, Dworkin himself is a prisoner of liberalism. Nor does Alisdair McIntyre's *After Virtue* overcome the impossibility of propounding a social ethics, this work remaining stuck on an abstract level.[29] Hence neither does the theological attempt of a Stanley Hauerwas[30] manage to so much as surmise the remote legitimacy of criticizing the capitalistic system, being enveloped by it and presupposing it as a totality. If a Stephen Charles Mott reaches a better solution than do others in the question of violence in situations of social change,[31] nevertheless neither does he suspect the emergence of a prophetic criticism, in biblical categories, of the system as a totality. All these authors remain caught in an ineluctable reformism.

Liberation ethics arises as a theory preceded by and demanded by a praxis opposed to the system *as a totality*. Reformist "developmentalism" in Latin America proposes—fruitlessly—substitute models ("developmentalisms" under the aegis of CEPAL [Ecumenical Council for Latin America], "national security," "neo-populism," "Christian Democracies," and the like), but accepts the system as a whole. It is just another morality. For a liberation ethics, by contrast, the first task is to penetrate and overthrow the *basis* of the system and replace it with *another* basis, one beyond, transcending, the present system. Analytic thinking leaves room for dialectic, and negative dialectic permits an "analectic" (or the affirmation as origin of negation, as we shall see).

The "Flesh" (in its Totality)

The reformist moralities ask how to be good *in* Egypt. They debate about norms, virtues, and so on—but accept Egypt as the prevailing system. But Moses asks how to escape *from* Egypt. In order to be able to "emerge" or "escape,"[32] however, I must be aware of a whole that *envelops* me, and an *outside* through which I can pass. Indeed, liberation *ethics* (as contradistinguished from "intrasystemic" *moralities*)[33] begins with a description of the system *always already* "enveloping" the subject: the practical subject (as oppressor/ oppressed), and the theoretical subject (the theologian). In the Bible the system as a whole is thought of as "this *world*,"[34] or the "flesh" (*basar* in Hebrew, *sarx* in Greek—not to be confused with *soma* in Greek, "body," although the two are indeed sometimes confused in the Septuagint and Paul). The "sin of the flesh" or the "sin of Adam" is precisely idolatry, fetishism: the affirmation of the prevailing totality as the absolute, ultimate totality, and the denial, in that assertion, of the existence of the other (Abel) and hence of God (the absolute Other). The absolutization of the prevailing totality is the sin of the flesh, inasmuch as the other has *already* been negated *practically*; "Cain fell upon his brother Abel and killed him" (Gen. 4:8).

In Latin America today, the "system" is Anglo-Saxon capitalism on the social plane, machismo on the erotic, ideological domination on the pedagogical—and idolatry on *all* levels. The theme has the unfathomable depth of reality, and manifests the human being's infinite capacity to create systems—systems that can be literally "idolized," set up over and against God.

The "Other" (Analectic Exteriority)

Before entering upon an ontic treatment of a multitude of moral problems, ethics must explain the fact and reality that *beyond* the whole there is still the other. Levinas's *Totalité et Infini* has shown this is a phenomenological approach,[35] but not from the standpoint of political economics.[36] Despite its critics, liberation ethics is no "Marxism for the people" (to recall Nietzsche). It has a deep implantation in metaphysics (Xavier Zubiri correctly asserts in his *On Essence* that reality transcends being), in an ethics as first philosophy (as Levinas repeats so frequently—hence, as we shall see, a theological ethics, in its most essential aspect, is fundamental theology).

"Beyond," transcending (ontologically transcendent to), the horizon of the system (beyond the horizon of the flesh, beyond totality), "the other" is presented or appears (is an "epiphany" and not a mere "phenomenon") as one who "provokes" (Lat., *pro-*, "from ahead," and *vocare*, "to call") and demands justice. "Others" (the "widow, orphan, and alien" of the prophets' mighty cries, under their universal name of "poor") vis-à-vis the system are the metaphysical *reality* beyond the *being* of the system. They are the outside, then.[37] They are those most foreign to the totalized system. Franz Hinkelammert dubs them "inner transcendence."[38] They are the locus or "place" of the epiphany of God: *the poor. In* the system, the only possible *place* for the epiphany of God is constituted by those who *are not* the system—those distinct from the system: the poor. Jesus' identification with the poor in Matthew 25 is not a metaphor; *it is a logic.* God, the Absolute Other, is revealed *in the flesh* (the system) by the other: the poor. The metaphysical (and eschatological) exteriority of the poor (simultaneously theological and economic, if we understand what is meant by a theological or divine economy),[39] situates them as (historical) reality and posits their concept as the *key* (epistemological) category of all liberation ethics (that is, of fundamental theology as such).

Alienation, Sin, Oppression

In the system (first methodic aspect and first concept), the other (second aspect, but the "key" aspect, and a more radical one than the first) is *alienated* (third aspect and category). The "alterification" (rendering them "other," different from what they are) of the "others" is, metaphysically, to make them "the same": a mere functional, internal part of the system. The human being, the living and free subject (agent) of creative work, sells his or her work and becomes a "wage-earner"—in an intrinsic, ontic, aspect founded in the *being* of capital, founded in capitalism. The (free) "other" now becomes "other" in the sense of being divorced from himself, a thing. Just as Christ "emptied himself and took the form of a slave,"[40] so the "other" is converted into an oppressed individual, the "poor" one as complex category (as exteriority, and as interiority dominated in the *flesh*). The "poor," those who do not enjoy the fruit of their labor, *in the system* are the manifestation of sin. Sin, which is only domination of the other, is revealed when someone is poor. The poor are the *others*, despoiled of their exteriority, their dignity, their rights, their freedom, and transformed into an *instrument* for the ends of the dominator, the lord—the "good" of the idol, the fetish.

All of this is readily applicable, of course, to the social reality of the exploited classes, the dominated countries, the violated sex, and so on. But this "application" destroys in its very cementing the organic interface of the prevailing European–North American theologies and poses problems that cannot "conveniently" be relegated to an appendix of a theology of social ethics, but which (as the matter at hand is that of the very constitution, the very *a priori*, of theologizing *subjectivity*—as theory—and of Christian subjectivity—practically) are the *first* questions of any theology (as fundamental theology). The question, "Is it possible to believe?" is preceded by the question, "What are the conditions of historical praxis for this very question?" To pose this latter, antecedent question from the locus of the "pharaonic class" in Egpyt is not the same thing as to pose it from the locus of the "slaves." *Whence* do I pose my very first question in fundamental theology? That *whence*, that "*from* where" of my historical social situation, is itself the first chapter of *all theology*, and not an adventitious question under "almsgiving": "aid to underdeveloped countries." We know that our colleagues of the "center" are not in agreement in this matter. The next decades will tell who is right.

Liberation, Salvation, Emergence ("Going Out")

Only in this "fourth" (methodic and real) sense can the question of redemption (christology) be understood as (eschatological) salvation and liberation. Each of these concepts denotes *the same thing*, but in relation to distinct terms. "Liberation" connotes a relationship to an antecedent term (*ex quo*), to a "whence": one emerges *from* a prison. "Prison" is at one and the same time (because it is *the same thing*) the system of oppression and sin. The concept (and reality) of liberation includes two terms and one reality (inasmuch as it is a concept of motion): *whence* the motion begins, *whither* it is heading, and the *motion* itself. Theologically, metaphorically, and historically: *from* Egypt, *to* the promised land, *through* the wilderness.

The concept of "freedom"—as in Häring's moral theology—lacks the dialectical density, the historical complexity, and the practical clarity of the category (and praxis) of liberation. The fact that Abraham, Moses, and so many others "leave" the "land" of Chaldea or Egypt for another "land" that "I shall show you"[41] posits a dialectic between *two* terms. Prevailing theological moralities (those cited above), in failing to call radically into question the former "land" (the "old man"—in Latin America, the *current* system of oppression, dependent capitalism), in failing to posit as the *necessary* horizon of *all* of its discourse the utopia of the future "land" (the "new man"), can propound only a reformist morality: a reform of the system under which one lives *in* the land of Chaldea, in Egypt. Never will they "go out" or "emerge" to the wilderness, nor therefore will they ever receive, in the wilderness, the "new" law (the "new" ethical normativity).

The question of norms, laws, virtues, values, and even ends must *be posed within* the problematic of *both* lands (totality versus exteriority, prevailing system versus utopia, dependent capitalism versus alternatives, and so on). Hence the question of an ethics *of liberation* (the propositional phrase is "objective," corresponding to the Latin or Greek "objective genitive") is that of how to be "good" (just, saved) not in Egypt, nor in the monarchy under David, but in the sojourn in the wilderness—in the passage or transition from an "old" order to the "new," not *yet* prevailing, order. The heroes and saints refused to allow their behavior to be governed by prevailing norms. Otherwise Washington would have remained a loyal subject of the British monarchs, Father Hidalgo would have obeyed the laws of the Spanish Indies, the heroes of the *Résistance française* would have complied submissively with Hitler's orders in France, and Fidel Castro would have permitted Cuba to go on being a United States weekend colony. What is the foundation of the ethicity of the praxis of the heroes when they rise up against laws, norms, so-called virtues or values, and even the ends of an *unjust* system? This question may constitute an appendix to the moral theology of Europeans and North Americans. But for Christians of the periphery, it is chapter 1 of all fundamental theology—inasmuch as it constitutes the answer to the question, "*What* is theology, as a whole, for?" Barth, Tillich, Niebuhr, before the crisis of 1929, had glimpsed these questions. But they were very far from being able to approach them from the complex world situation that faces us today, or even to handle them on a world level.

Liberation ethics is a rethinking of the totality of moral problems from the perspective and exigencies of "responsibility"[42] for the poor, responsibility for a historical alternative that would *permit a struggle* in Egypt, a journey in the wilderness in a *time of transition*, and the *construction* of a promised land—the historical land of promise that is always to be judged in the light of that eschatological land "beyond all hope of historical material production," the reign of heaven, which will never be *completely* built in history (but which is ever a-building in the construction of the transitory, perishable "lands" of history).

SOMETHING ABOUT METHOD

To argue that any alternative to the prevailing system must be "utopian," by which is meant a reference to the origin of all evils— as Popper does in his *The Open Society and Its Enemies* (which argues for an anti-utopian Christianity)—means to limit methodology in moral theology to either analytical (in the tradition of Ayer, Wittgenstein, et al.),[43] or more or less eclectic (taking something from sociology, something from medicine, something from politics, and so on, according to the branch of morality that happens to be under consideration). Such methods are valid, but only so long as they are understood as constituting means to a merely partial theological moral discourse. When they pretend to be the only valid methods, and when they criticize holistic methods as "imprecise" and "unscientific," then they are transforming themselves into ideological methods—methods for covering up reality.

After all, to call the system *as a whole* into question is the task of the dialectical method, from Plato to Aristotle[44] to Thomas Aquinas to Kant, Hegel, or Sartre. In reality—as Heidegger, whose concept of "world" is strictly dialectical, would say—the dialectical method is an ontological situating of every object or thing that appears to me ontically. *To know how to refer* the means, the instrument "at hand," *the object, to its foundation (being)* is the property of the dialectical method. Here Marx merely asks questions about merchandise, money, production, and so on, in the light and on the foundation of the *being of capital* (the essence of capitalism).

The ontological method (in this case an economic ontology)[45] has nevertheless emphasized the "negation of the negation" or the "negative dialectic" (Adorno, for example, or the Frankfurt School, including even Ernst Bloch). The revolutionary process, or the process of negating the prevailing totality (Lukács), is a praxis arising out of the negation of a negation. It springs from the negation of the oppression produced in the oppressed by the system. One might even say that the negation of the negation has the system as its horizon, and that the system is transcended only from a point of departure in a utopia that, as artistic fantasy (Marcuse, *Eros and Civilization*) or as projected alternative, is really possible only from within "the very" system. The origin of the negation is the system itself. In other words, the negation is an empty horizon (pure possibility, or transcendent horizon: the reign of freedom as an age of absolute "free time").

Liberation ethics, on the other hand, takes its point of departure in an affirmation of the real, existent, historical *other*. I have designated this "transontological" (metaphysical) *positive moment* of departure, this active point of the initiation of the negation of the negation, *the "analectical."*[46] By the prefix, the Greek *ana-*, I wish to denote a point "beyond" the ontological horizon (of the system, of the "flesh"), a point "beyond" or transcending being. It is this *logos* (*ana-logos*), this discourse originating in transcendence of the system, that reflects the originality of the Hebreo-Christian experience. If "in the beginning God created" (Gen 1:1), this can be only because the *other* is antecedent to the very principle of the cosmos, of the system, of the "flesh." The metaphysical "anteriority" of the *other* (who creates, who gives self-revelation) has its historical, political, and erotic aspects as well.

The poor, the oppressed class, the peripheral nation, the female sex object, all have their *reality* "beyond" the horizon of the system that alienates them, represses them, dehumanizes them. The *reality* residing in the Nicaraguan people, the "beyond" within them, the transcendence within them of the horizon of Somozism, of dependent capitalism, has provided them with a fulcrum for their negation of their oppression and a motivation for their liberation praxis. The oppressed contain (in the structure of their subjectivity, their culture, their underground economy, and so forth), the trans-systemic (eschatological) wellspring permitting them to discover themselves as oppressed *in the system*. They discover themselves oppressed when they experience themselves eschatologically as distinct from the system in their exteriority to it. The analectic affirmation of their "dignity," of their freedom (negated in the system), of their culture, of their work ("unproductive work" for capital, but *real for them*) *outside* the system (and "outside" the system not because the poor have overcome that system, but often enough because the system considers them "nothing," non-being, and it is from that *nothing*— which is real—that *new* systems are built) is what originates the very mobility of the positive dialectic.

This method and historical reality do not commence with the negation of oppression. Rather, the negation of oppression commences with the *analectic affirmation* of the (eschatological and historical) exteriority of the other, from out of whose project of liberation the *negation of the negation* is effectuated and *new* systems are constructed. These systems are not mere *univocal* realizations or actualizations of something already existing *in potentia* in the old, unjust system. The new system is an *analogous* realization, so that it includes something of the old system (*similitudo*), but something absolutely new (*distinctio*) as well. The new system was impossible for the old. Thus the former has been *creation*, through the irruption of the analectic otherness of the poor in their self-liberation.[47]

The method of liberation ethics—as an aspect of the creative act of God's unconditioned freedom and of the redemptive act of Christ's subsumption (*subsumptio*) of flesh (the system) by the analectic irruption of the Word (brought about in the negation of sin and the construction of the reign of God)—is analectical. It is more than a negative dialectic: it is a positive dialectic, in which the exteriority of the other (of the Creator, of Christ, of the poor) is the positive practic condition of the methodic movement itself. The poor, and their actual, concrete liberating praxis, in the analectical anteriority of this reality, constitute the fundamental and first stage of the dialectic. Ethics is *subsequent* to this moment—but ethics itself begins by asserting the absolute priority *of the poor: this* poor person in whom "Christ *poor*," God, is revealed as absolute challenge and responsibility.

In Latin America, liberation ethics is the justification of the goodness, heroism, and holiness of an oppressed people's liberation praxis in El Salvador, Guatemala, Argentina, or Brazil (in "Egypt")—the goodness, heroism, and holiness of a people already sojourning in the desert (as the Nicaraguan people), where the "priest Aaron"—longing to return to Egypt—offers worship to the golden calf (the idol), while the prophet Moses (liberation ethics?) must not only destroy the fetish, but offer the people being freed a "new" law. The "new" law, however, emerges in dialectical antithesis to the law of Egypt. One cannot begin as the moralities begin—by positing the morality of the act in its non-transcendent relationship to the norm or law. On the contrary, the absolute ethicity of the act connotes a transcendent relationship to the building of the reign of God in the historical processes of liberation that constitute the praxis of the real, material poor, the "hungry." Only from this horizon, and *only subsequently*, can all of the problems of abstract moral subjectivity (with which all moral theologies begin) be posed.

The encyclical *Laborem Exercens* furnishes us with a fine starting point for founding an ethics of liberation in the exploited fleshliness of the poor in their work. Such a eucharistic or economic radicality merits further reflection.[48]

NOTES TO APPENDIX

1. See Paul Tillich, *Die Bedeutung der Kirche für die Gesellschaftsordnung in Europa und Amerika* [The meaning of the church for the social order in Europe and America], in *Gesammelte Werke*, vol. 3 (Stuttgart, 1962), pp. 107ff. Tillich writes: "The social function of the Church cannot really be understood without a clarification of its social and economic structure, and without relating it to the social order" (p. 119).

2. How could I fail to recall another date—March 30, 1975? My name then appeared on similar lists in Mendoza, Argentina, and I was expelled from Cuyo National University, for similar reasons—a phenomenon that was occurring in so many other parts of Latin America as well.

3. Hitler's Nazism was a government of laws and statutes that provided for the "viability" of German *national* capitalism (Krupp, Thiessen, Siemens, and so forth), with an eye to a world hegemony over the capitalist market. The Latin American military governments (since 1964) provide for

the "viability" of a capitalism *dependent* on the United States, which is far worse.

4. Paul Tillich, *Christentum und Sozialgestaltung* (1919–33), vol. 2 of *Gesammelte Werke*, p. 11.

5. New York: Scribner's, 1932.

6. Tübingen: Mohr, 1932.

7. Niebuhr, *Moral and Immoral Society*, p. 277. Niebuhr refers to his book as "a social analysis written at least partially from the persective of a disillusioned generation" (p. xxv). "In Germany E. Bernstein ... transformed expectations of catastrophe into hope for evolutionary progress toward equal justice" (p. 181),

8. Vol. 2 of *Gesammelte Werke*.

9. See Charles Howard Hopkins, *The Rise of the Social Gospel in American Protestantism (1865–1915)*, Yale Studies (New Haven: Yale University Press, 1940); Robert Handy, *The Social Gospel in America, 1870–1920* (Oxford University Press, 1966); Aaron Abell, *American Catholicism and Social Action, 1865–1950* (Garden City, N.Y.: Doubleday, 1960).

10. Boston: Houghton-Mifflin, 1893, pp. 275ff.

11. Ibid., p. 275.

12. On pages 257ff. there is a discussion on the meaning of value in Marx (fifty years before the publication of the *Manuscripts of 1844* and hence with naive distortions). At one moment the author wonders, "We go part way with Marx and Robertus; then we part company with them. How far can we wisely go with them? How many of their projects may we safely adopt?" (p. 280). But then, suddenly: "Socialism, as we have seen, is simply a proposition to extend the functions of the state so that it shall include and control nearly all the interests *of life*. Now, I take it, we are agreed that, as Christians, we have a right to make use of the power of the state, both in protecting life and property, and in promoting, to the same extent, the general welfare" (p. 281)—written in the United States in 1893! What happened? What happened was that the labor movement was brutally repressed. (see James Weinstein, *The Decline of Socialism in America, 1912–1925* [Boston: MR Press, 1967].)

13. W. Rauschenbusch, *Christianizing the Social Order* (New York, 1919), pp. 222ff.

14. See, for example, Bernard Häring, *Free and Faithful in Christ: Moral Theology for Priests and Laity*, 3 vols. (Slough, Berks., 1978–81). Although far superior to other Catholic moral theologies, this work relegates questions like economic and political ethics to an appendix (vol. 3, chap. 7), or else relates "life" only with medical questions or abortion (3:21–130). It fails to relate life to work or social life (repression of the poor, and so on).

Similarly in *Handbuch der christlichen Ethik*, edited by A. Hertz, W. Korff, T. Rendtorff, and H. Ringeling (Freiburg: Herder, 1978–82), the great problems are "modernity" (the first moral topic ["The Norm," 1:108ff.]); "life," related only with medicine; politics, examined in virtue of a *Verfassungsprinzip* or "principle of composition" (2:215ff.). There is something on economics, but under the title (for peripheral countries), "Developmental Assistance" (2:417ff.). The "new international order" is given neither a biblical nor an ontological nor an anthropological basis, but is studied from an exclusively sociological viewoint (3:337ff.). And so on, with the articles of this collection generally.

15. Emil Brunner, *Das Gebot und die Ordnungen*, pp. 380ff.

16. Ibid., p. 411.

17. Ibid., pp. 412ff. The Christian position is a kind of social-democratic "third way" for the author (pp. 417ff.).

18. Tübingen, Mohr. See esp. vol. 2/2 (1958), pp. 224ff. Thielicke relegates the problem of property to a special appendix (vol. 3 [1964], pp. 224ff.), where he manifests what might be called a certain "economic blindness." His analyses are almost exclusively juridical or socio-political.

19. Ibid., 2:423ff.

20. See Jürgen Habermas, "Die Kulturkritik der Neokonservativen in den USA und in der Bundesrepublik," *Praxis* (Haverford), vol. 2/4 (1983), pp. 339ff. See Habermas, *Theorie des Kommunikativen Handelns* (Frankfurt, 1981).

21. Philadelphia: Fortress, 1981. The odyssey of a Michael Novak is a case in point. Having launched his career as a liberal Catholic theologian, with works like *The Open Church* (1964) and *The Men Who Make the Council* (1964), a scant two decades later Novak is writing *The Spirit of Democratic Capitalism* (1982) and *Toward a Theology of the* [transnational] *Corporation* (1981), published by the American Enterprise Institute. These neoconservative theologies are *not* "economically blind": "The official documents of the popes and the Protestant ecumenical bodies are notably strong on moral vision, much less so in describing economic principles and realities. The coming generation will inherit as a task the need to create and to set forth systematically a theology of economics" (*Theology of the Corporation*, p. 21).

22. Robert Benne, *The Ethic of Democratic Capitalism: A Moral Reassessment*, p. 174.

23. See my "The Bread of the Eucharistic Celebration as a Sign of Justice in the Community," *Concilium*, no. 152 (1982), where I show the relationship obtaining among life, blood, work, and product. A "theology of money" and economics must begin with these metaphysical and biblical

premises. (See Rudolf Bultmann's article on *zao* [the verb, "to live"], in Kittel, *Theologisches Wörterbuch des Neuen Testaments*, vol. 2 [1935], pp. 833–77.)

24. The pejorative suffix ("developmental-ism") is used to suggest the ideological, false character of the European and North American doctrine of "development" (and "developmental assistance") prevailing in some Christian circles (and in CEPAL). Developmentalism seeks to remedy *effects* without attacking the (principal) *causes* of the crisis, which are structural and pervasive. Thereby it aggravates the evil.

25. Karl Barth, *Der Römerbrief* (Zurich, 1954), p. xiii.

26. See Michael Novak, *Will it Liberate? Questions about Liberation Theology* (Mahwah, N.J.: Paulist Press, 1987).

27. John Rawls, *A Theory of Justice* (Cambridge University Press [Mass.], 1971). See O. Oeff, *Über Rawls Theorie der Gerechtigkeit* (Frankfurt, 1977).

28. Ronald Dworkin, *Taking Rights Seriously* (Cambridge: Harvard University Press, 1977), p. 182.

29. A. McIntyre, *After Virtue* (University of Notre Dame Press, 1981). McIntyre's keen critique of earlier moralists is tarnished by his return to Aristotle, and his taking a position between Aristotle and Nietzsche. Neither of the two, obviously, can be ethicians of liberation.

30. Stanley Hauerwas, *A Community of Character* (University of Notre Dame Press, 1981); idem, *The Peaceable Kingdom* (University of Notre Dame Press, 1983).

31. Stephen Charles Mott, *Biblical Ethics and Social Change* (New York: Oxford University Press, 1982), pp. 188–9. One's attention is arrested by the remark of John Coleman: "As a social sicentist I have often been puzzled, if not irritated, by the almost religious importance many Latin American theologians of liberation give to the writings and analysis of Karl Marx" (John Coleman, *An American Strategic Theology* [Paulist Press, 1982], p. 125).

32. The concept of emerging, of being "led to the outside"—"*Leave* your land" (Gen. 12;1); "Lead him *out of Egypt*" (Exod. 13:16); etc.—is a fundamental theological metaphor.

33. See my explanation of the difference between "morality" and "ethics" at the end of the present article as it appears in *Para una ética de la liberación latinoamericana* (Buenos Aires: Siglo XXI, 1973), vol. 2, section 21, and in "One Ethic and Many Moralities," *Concilium*, 150 (1980).

34. See my *Para una ética de la liberación*, vol. 2, section 21. For the category of "flesh" or "totality," see ibid., 1:33ff. See also my *Philosophy of Liberation* (Maryknoll, N.Y.: Orbis, 1985), pp. 21–9.

35. Emmanuel Levinas, *Totalité et Infini: Essai sur l'extériorité* (The Hague, 1961).

36. See my view of Emmanuel Levinas in *Emmanuel Levinas y la liberación*

latinoamericana (Buenos Aires, 1975).

37. See my *Philosophy of Liberation*, pp. 39–49.

38. *The Ideological Weapons of Death: A Theological Critique of Capitalism* (Maryknoll, N.Y.: Orbis, 1986), p. 61.

39. See "The Bread" (n. 23, above).

40. As we know, Luther translated the *ekenosen* of Phil. 2:7 *entäusserte sich* ("emptied himself, poured himself out")–the essential note of a "kenotic" theology—whence it passed to Hegel by way of his professors of christology in Tübingen. It is a basic Christian concept.

41. The category "land" (*'eres*) has a strict eschatological meaning in the Bible. See the article *Ge* ("land") in Kittel, *Theologisches Wörterbuch*, 1:676. This meaning appears in Ps. 37:11, Matt. 5:3, Heb. 11:9. What I am emphasizing here is the dialectic of the *two* lands: "From the land (*me' areska*) ... to the land (*'el-ha 'ares*) that I will show you" (Gen. 12:1); "From this *land* to the beautiful, rich *land* flowing with milk and honey" (Exod. 3:8). We are "leaving Egypt (*mi-misraym*)" (Exod. 3:10).

42. "Irresponsibility" *for others*, for the oppressed, *in the face of* the concrete economic system of oppression. Hans Jonas, *Das Prinzip Verantwortung* (Frankfurt, 1982) fails to establish the concrete meaning of "responsibility." Jonas keeps to an abstract level. He deals with "technology," but never as an aspect "of capital" (*als Kapital*). He fails to understand this "subsumption" (*Subsumption*).

43. See F. Böckle, "Der sprachanalytische Ansatz" in Hertz et al., eds., *Handbuch der christliche Ethik*, 1:68ff.

44. See my *Método para una filosofía de la liberación* (Salamanca, 1974).

45. Karl Marx, *Grundrisse der Kritik der politischen Ökonomie (1857–1858)* (Berlin, 1974), and more recently, the *Manuscripts of 1861–3 (Zur Kritik der politischen Oekonomie [Manuskript 1861–1863], MEGA*, 3.2, vols. 1–6 [1977–82]), authorize my reinterpretation of Marx from a point of departure in an ontology in the strict sense. (*So wird das Kapital ein sehr mysteriöses Wesen*—"Thus capital becomes a very mysterious being," ibid., p. 2163, line 11).

46. See my "Pensée analectique en philosophie de la libération" in *Analogie et Dialectique* (Geneva, 1982), pp. 93–120; my *Philosophy of Liberation*, pp. 158–60. See also Roberto Goizueta, "Domination and Liberation: An Analysis of the Analectical Method of E. Dussel," dissertation, Graduate School, Marquette University (Milwaukee), May 1984, 298 pp.; Anton Peter, "Der Befreiungstheologische und der Transzendentaltheologische Denkansatz. Ein Beitrag zum Gerspräch zwishen E. Dussel und K. Rahner," dissertation, Theologische Fakultät Luzern (Switzerland), Feb. 1987, 625 pp.

47. *Para una ética de la liberación*, section 25 (2:58ff.); section 47 (3:109ff.); section 66 (4:109ff.); section 73 (5:91ff.).

48. The Polish thinker Josef Tischner (*La svolta storica*, Italian trans. [Bologna, 1981]; *Etica del lavoro* [Bologna, 1982], especially "Il lavoro privo di senso," pp. 76ff.) has rightly taken "work" as a proper center of theological reflection. For Poland the problem is the worker's *control* of the product. For Latin America the problem is *consumption* of the product of work (for there is hunger, the result of oppression and structural theft). In Poland workers (the *nation*) seek to know *what* they produce bread *for*, and try to control its production. In Latin America workers (the people) seek to *possess* the fruit of their work, the eucharistic bread. See John Desrochers, *The Social Teaching of the Church* (private publication, Bangalore, 1982, esp. pp. 637ff.). Clearly, *Laborem Exercens* permits liberation ethics a material radicalization of its discourse.

Bibliography

The aim here is to provide a short bibliography for those who wish to pursue this line of investigation further. This book does not set out to be a complete treatise on the subject, but to indicate the questions that liberation theology brings to it. The following works contain ample bibliographies for a more exhaustive examination of the subject:

Häring, B. *La ley de Cristo*. Vol. 3. Barcelona: Herder, 1968.
_____. *Responsabilidad del hombre ante la vida*, vol. 3 of *Libertad y fidelidad en Cristo*. Barcelona: Herder, 1983.
Messner, J. *Etica social, política y económica*. Madrid: Rialp, 1967, pp. 1481–1525.
Utz, A. *Etica social*. Barcelona: Herder, vol. 1 (1961): pp. 459–536; vol. 2 (1965): 279–414.
Vidal, M. *Moral de actitudes*. Vol. 3. Madrid: PS Editorial, 1980, pp. 137–50.

Reference Works: besides the more general Kittel (ThWNT), LThK and *Dictionnaire de Théologie Catholique*, the following are more specifically concerned with the subject:

Hastings, J. *Encyclopaedia of Religion and Ethics*. 13 vols. New York: C. Scribner's Sons; Edinburgh: T & T Clark, 1908–26.
Hertz, A., W. Korff, T. Rendtorff, and H. Ringeling. *Handbuch der Christlichen Ethik*. 3 vols. Freiburg: Herder, 1978–82.
Karrenberg, Fr. *Evangelisches Soziallexikon*. Berlin: Kreuz Verlag, 1980.
Klose, A. *Katholisches Soziallexikon*. Innsbruck: Tyrolia, 1964.
Kunst, H., and S. Grundmann. *Evangelisches Staatslexikon*. Stuttgart; Kreuz Verlag, 1975.
Roberti, F. *Diccionario de teología moral*. Barcelona: Litúrgica, 1960.
Various. *Diccionario enciclopédico de teología moral*. 5th ed. Madrid: Paulinas, 1986.
_____. *Nuevo diccionario de espiritualidad*. 2nd ed. Madrid: Paulinas, 1985.
Viller, M. *Dictionnaire de spiritualité*. 11 vols. Paris: Beauchesne, 1937–82.

Individual works dealing with the subject in general, from a wide variety of viewpoints:

Aubert, J. M. *Moral social para nuestro tiempo*. Barcelona: Herder, 1973.

Barth, K. *Community, State and Church*. New York: Anchor Books, 1960.

———. *The Doctrine of God*, vol. II/2 of *Church Dogmatics*. Edinburgh: T & T Clark, 1957.

Benne, R. *The Ethic of Democratic Capitalism: A Moral Reassessment*. Philadelphia: Fortress, 1981.

Bennet, J. C. *The Radical Imperative*. Philadelphia: Westminster, 1975.

Bigo, P. *Doctrina social de la Iglesia*. Barcelona: Herder, 1967.

Brunner, E. *Das Gebot und die Ordnungen*. Tübingen: Mohr, 1932.

Cobb, John B., Jr. *Process Theology as Political Theology*. Philadelphia: Westminster, 1982.

Cosbe, R. "Las comunidades políticas." In *El misterio cristiano*. Barcelona: Herder, 1971.

Cotham, P. C. *Christian Social Ethics*. Grand Rapids: Baker Books, 1979.

Deats, P., ed. *Toward a Discipline of Social Ethics*. Boston: University Press, 1972.

De Laubier, P. *Das Soziale Denken der Katholischen Kirche*. Freiburg: Universitätsverlag, 1982.

Desrochers, J. *The Social Teaching of the Church*. Madras: Sidma Press, 1982.

Dussel, E. *Ethics and the Theology of Liberation*. Maryknoll, N.Y.: Orbis, 1978.

Forell, G. *Christian Social Teaching*. Minneapolis: Augsburg, 1971.

Gustafson, J. *Ethics from a Theocentric Perspective*. Vol. 1. University of Chicago Press, 1981.

———. *Theology and Christian Ethics*. Philadelphia: United Church Press, 1974.

Henry, C. *Aspects of Christian Social Ethics*. Grand Rapids: Eerdmans, 1964.

Hillerdal, G. *Kirche und Sozialethik*. Gütersloh: Gütersloher Verlag, 1963.

Höffner, J. *Christliche Gesellschaftslehre*. Kevelaer: Butzon-Bercker, 1962.

Künneth, W. *Politik zwischen Dämon und Gott: Eine Christliche Ethik des Politischen*. Berlin: Lutherisches Verlagshaus, 1954.

Lehmann, P. *Ethics in a Christian Context*. New York: Harper and Row, 1963.

Manaranche, A. *Y-a-t-il une éthique sociale chrétienne?* Paris: Seuil, 1969.

Novak, M. *The Spirit of Democratic Capitalism*. New York: American Enterprise Institute/Simon & Schuster, 1982.

Ramsey, P. *Basic Christian Ethics*. New York: Scribner's, 1954.

Schulze, H., *Theologische Sozialethik*. Gütersloh: Gütersloher Verlag, 1979.

Thielicke, H. *Theologische Ethik*. 3 vols. Tübingen: Mohr, 1951–64.

Tiberghien, C. P. *Sens chrétien et vie sociale*. Paris: Ed. Ouvrières, 1954.

Tillich, P. *Love, Power and Justice*. New York and London: Oxford, 1954.

_____. *Christentum und sociale Gestaltung*, vol. 2 of *Gesammelte Werke*. Stuttgart, 1919–33.

Troeltsch, E. *The Social Teaching of the Christian Churches*. 2 vols. London: George Allen, 1931.

Utz, A. *Die Katholische Sozialdoktrin in ihrer geschichtlichen Entfaltung*. 2 vols. Aachen: Scientia Humana Institut, 1976.

Villain, J. *L'enseignement social de l'Eglise*. 2 vols. Paris: Spes, 1953–4.

Welty, E. *Herders Sozial Katechismus*. Freiburg: Herder, 1951–8.

The following works may also be found useful:

Assmann, H., ed. *El banco mundial: Un caso de "progresismo conservador."* San José: DEI, 1980.

Avila, R. *Implicaciones socio-políticas de la eucaristía*. Bogotá: Policrom, 1977.

Chenu, M. D. *La doctrine sociale de l'Eglise comme idéologie*. Paris: Ed. Ouvrières, 1979.

Coleman, J. *An American Strategic Theology*. New York: Paulist, 1982.

Comblin, J. *Teología de la revolución*. Bilbao: Desclée de Brouwer, 1973.

Curran, C., and R. McCormick. *Moral Theology*, 2 vols. New York: Paulist, 1980.

Dos Santos, T. *Imperialismo y dependencia*. 2nd ed. Mexico City: Era, 1980.

Dussel, E. *Caminhos de libertação latino-americana*. 4 vols. São Paulo: Paulinas, 1985.

_____. *Filosofía de la producción*. Bogotá: Nueva América, 1984.

_____. *Herrschaft und Befreiung*. Freiburg: Exodus Verlag, 1985.

_____. *History of the Church in Latin America*. Grand Rapids: Eerdmans, 1981.

_____. *El humanismo helénico*. Buenos Aires: EUDEBA, 1976.

_____. *El humanismo semita*. Buenos Aires: EUDEBA, 1969.

_____. *Para una destrucción de la historia de la ética*. Mendoza: Ser y Tiempo, 1970.

_____. *Para una ética de la liberación latinoamericana*. Vols. 1-2: Buenos Aires: Siglo XXI, 1973; vol. 3: Mexico City: Edicol, 1977; vols. 4-5: Bogotá: USTA, 1979–80.

_____. *Para un método de la filosofía de la liberación*. Salamanca: Sígueme, 1974.

_____. *Philosophy of Liberation*. Maryknoll, N.Y.: Orbis, 1985.

————. *Praxis latinoamericana y filosofía de la liberación*. Bogotá: Nueva América, 1983.

————. *La producción teórica de Marx. Un comentario a los "Grundrisse."* Mexico City: Siglo XXI, 1985.

Eppler, E. *Die tödliche Utopie der Sicherheit*. Hamburg: Rowohlt, 1983.

Evans, S. *The Social Hope of the Christian Church*. London: Hodder, 1965.

Garaudy, R., and E. Balducci. *El cristianismo es liberación*. Salamanca: Sígueme, 1976.

Garrigou-Lagrange, R. *De Revelatione. Theologia fundamentalis*. Rome: Desclée, 1950.

Gauthier, P. *Les pauvres, Jésus et l'Eglise*. Paris: Editions Universitaires, 1962.

Gustafson, J. M. *Protestant and Roman Catholic Ethics: Prospects for Rapprochement*. London: SCM, 1979.

Hebblethwaite, B. *Christian Ethics in the Modern Age*. Philadelphia: Westminster, 1982.

Hinkelammert, F. *Crítica a la razón utópica*. San José: DEI, 1984.

————. *Ideología del desarrollo y dialéctica de la historia*. Santiago; Ediciones Universidad Católica, 1970.

————. *The Ideological Weapons of Death*. Maryknoll, N.Y.: Orbis, 1986.

Honecker, M. *Konzept einer socialetischen Theorie*. Tübingen: Mohr, 1971.

Jaguaribe, H., et al. *La dependencia político-económica de América Latina*. Mexico City: Siglo XXI, 1970.

Jones. M. J. *Christian Ethics for Black Theology*. Nashville: Abingdon, 1974.

Kudo, T., and C. Tovar. *La crítica de la religión. Ensayo sobre la conciencia social según Marx*. Lima: CEP, 1980.

Levinas, E. *Totalité et infini: Essai sur l'extériorité*. The Hague, 1961.

McDonag, E. *Social Ethics and the Christian*. Manchester University Press, 1979.

MacIntyre, A. *After Virtue*. South Bend, Ind.: University of Notre Dame, 1981.

Markovic, M. *Dialética de la praxis*. Buenos Aires: Amorrortu, 1972.

Mott, S. *Biblical Ethics and Social Change*. New York and London: Oxford University Press, 1982.

Muelder, W. *Moral Law in Christian Social Ethics*. Richmond: John Knox Press, 1966.

Munby D. L. *Christianity and Economic Problems*. London: Macmillan, 1956.

National Conference of Catholic Bishops. *Economic Justice for All: Pastoral Letter on Catholic Social Teaching and the U.S. Economy*. Washington, D.C.: U.S. Catholic Conference, 1986.

———. *The Challenge of Peace: God's Promise and Our Response.* Washington, D.C.: U.S. Catholic Conference, 1983.

Nelson, B. *The Idea of Usury from Tribal Brotherhood to Universal Otherhood.* University of Chicago Press, 1969.

Niebuhr, R. *Moral Man and Immoral Society.* New York: Charles Scribner's Sons, 1960.

Ogden, M. S. *Faith and Freedom: Toward a Theology of Liberation.* Nashville: Abingdon, 1979.

Pannenberg, W. *Wissenschaftstheorie und Theologie.* Frankfurt: Suhrkamp, 1973.

———. *Ethics.* Philadelphia and London: Westminster, 1981.

Richard, P., and D. Irarrázaval. *Religión y política en América Central. Hacia una neuva interpretación de la religiosidad popular.* San José: DEI, 1981.

Senhaas, D. *Armamento & militarismo.* Mexico City: Siglo XXI, 1974.

Solari, A. E., R. Franco, and J. Jutkowitz. *Teoría, acción social y desarrollo en América Latina.* Mexico City: Siglo XXI, 1976.

Sunkel, O., and P. Paz. *El subdesarrollo latinoamericano y la teoría del desarrollo.* 2nd ed. Mexico City: Siglo XXI, 1971.

Tamez, E., and S. Trinidad, eds. *Capitalismo: Violencia y anti-vida. La opresión de las mayorías y la domesticación de los dioses.* 2 vols. San José: EDUCA, 1978.

Tawney, R. H. *Religion and the Rise of Capitalism.* London: John Murray, 1948.

Tillich, P. *The Socialist Decision.* New York: Harper & Row, 1977.

Tischner, J. *Etica della solidarietà.* Bologna: CSEO, 1981.

———. *Etica del lavoro.* Bologna: CSEO, 1982.

———. "Per capire il lavoro." In *CSEO* 15, 163 (1981).

———. *La svolta storica. Cristiani e marxisti in Polinia.* Bologna: CSEO, 1981.

Torres, C. *Camilo Torres por el padre Camilo Torres Restrepo (1956–1966).* CIDOC, Sondeos Nr. 5. Cuernavaca, 1966.

Tromp, S. *De Revelatione Christiana.* Rome: Gregorian University, 1950.

Varios. "Militarismo y sociedad." In *Iztapalapa* 10–11 (December-January 1984) (Mexico: UAM, 1984).

———. *Las relaciones entre cristianismo y revolución.* Madrid: IEPALA-IDOC, 1982.

———. *Praxis cristiana.* Vol. 3. Madrid: Paulinas, 1986.

Vidal, M., and P. Santidrián. *Etica comunitaria.* Vol. 2. 6th ed. Madrid: Paulinas, 1985.

———. *Etica social y política.* 4th ed. Madrid: Paulinas, 1983.

Subject Index

References are to chapters and numbered sections